IFIP Advances in Information and Communication Technology

609

Editor-in-Chief

IFIP – The International Federation for Information Processing

IFIP was founded in 1960 under the auspices of UNESCO, following the first World Computer Congress held in Paris the previous year. A federation for societies working in information processing, IFIP's aim is two-fold: to support information processing in the countries of its members and to encourage technology transfer to developing nations. As its mission statement clearly states:

> *IFIP is the global non-profit federation of societies of ICT professionals that aims at achieving a worldwide professional and socially responsible development and application of information and communication technologies.*

IFIP is a non-profit-making organization, run almost solely by 2500 volunteers. It operates through a number of technical committees and working groups, which organize events and publications. IFIP's events range from large international open conferences to working conferences and local seminars.

The flagship event is the IFIP World Computer Congress, at which both invited and contributed papers are presented. Contributed papers are rigorously refereed and the rejection rate is high.

As with the Congress, participation in the open conferences is open to all and papers may be invited or submitted. Again, submitted papers are stringently refereed.

The working conferences are structured differently. They are usually run by a working group and attendance is generally smaller and occasionally by invitation only. Their purpose is to create an atmosphere conducive to innovation and development. Refereeing is also rigorous and papers are subjected to extensive group discussion.

Publications arising from IFIP events vary. The papers presented at the IFIP World Computer Congress and at open conferences are published as conference proceedings, while the results of the working conferences are often published as collections of selected and edited papers.

IFIP distinguishes three types of institutional membership: Country Representative Members, Members at Large, and Associate Members. The type of organization that can apply for membership is a wide variety and includes national or international societies of individual computer scientists/ICT professionals, associations or federations of such societies, government institutions/government related organizations, national or international research institutes or consortia, universities, academies of sciences, companies, national or international associations or federations of companies.

More information about this series at https://link.springer.com/bookseries/6102

Ganesh Bhutkar · Barbara R. Barricelli ·
Qin Xiangang · Torkil Clemmensen ·
Frederica Gonçalves · José Abdelnour-Nocera ·
Arminda Lopes · Fei Lyu · Ronggang Zhou ·
Wenjun Hou (Eds.)

Human Work Interaction Design

Artificial Intelligence and Designing for a Positive Work Experience in a Low Desire Society

6th IFIP WG 13.6 Working Conference, HWID 2021
Beijing, China, May 15–16, 2021
Revised Selected Papers

Editors
Ganesh Bhutkar (iD)
Vishwakarma Institute of Technology
Pune, India

Qin Xiangang (iD)
Beijing University of Posts
and Telecommunications
Beijing, China

Frederica Gonçalves (iD)
Universidade da Madeira
Funchal, Portugal

Arminda Lopes (iD)
Polytechnic Institute of Castelo Branco
Castelo Branco, Portugal

Ronggang Zhou
Beihang University
Beijing, China

Barbara R. Barricelli (iD)
University of Brescia
Brescia, Italy

Torkil Clemmensen (iD)
Copenhagen Business School
Frederiksberg, Denmark

José Abdelnour-Nocera (iD)
University of West London
London, UK

Fei Lyu (iD)
Beijing University of Posts
and Telecommunications
Beijing, China

Wenjun Hou
Beijing University of Posts
and Telecommunications
Beijing, China

ISSN 1868-4238   ISSN 1868-422X (electronic)
IFIP Advances in Information and Communication Technology
ISBN 978-3-031-03102-1   ISBN 978-3-031-02904-2 (eBook)
https://doi.org/10.1007/978-3-031-02904-2

This Springer imprint is published by the registered company Springer Nature Switzerland AG
The registered company address is: Gewerbestrasse 11, 6330 Cham, Switzerland

Preface

Human Work Interaction Design (HWID) was established in September 2005 as the sixth working group (WG 13.6) of the IFIP Technical Committee 13 on Human-Computer Interaction (HCI). The scope of this group is the analysis and interaction design of a variety of complex work and life contexts found in different business and application domains. For this purpose, it is important to establish relationships between extensive empirical work domain studies and HCI design. WG 13.6 aims to provide the basis for an improved cross-disciplinary cooperation and mutual inspiration among researchers from many disciplines that by nature are involved in the deep analysis of a work domain. Complexity is hence the key notion in the activities of this working group, but it is not a priori defined or limited to any particular domain. WG 13.6 initiates and fosters new research initiatives and developments, as well as an increased awareness of HWID in the HCI curriculum.

This volume includes chapters extending the papers presented at the 6th HWID Working Conference (HWID 2021) that was held virtually from the Beijing University of Posts and Telecommunications (BUPT), Beijing, China, during May 15–16, 2021. In continuation of the Human Work Interaction Design Working Conference series, the sixth edition was aimed at investigating the theme "Artificial Intelligence and Designing for a Positive Work Experience in a Low Desire Society".

Initially, a 'Call for Papers' was announced on the website of the HWID 2021 conference and authors were invited to submit papers through Springer's Online Conference Service (OCS). In total, 14 research papers were submitted for the conference, out of which nine papers were accepted as extended versions for the proceedings, along with one additional paper. All papers were reviewed by the Program Committee, along with external reviewers, with two reviewers allocated to each paper. Accepted papers were virtually and/or physically presented at the conference. All presenters were encouraged to submit a revised version based on the input from the audience at the conference to the conference organizers (paper chairs and general chairs). In addition, a 'Call for New/Extended Papers' was announced to the authors and through the IFIP 13.6 - HWID email list after the conference. From the group of organizers of the conference, an editor team was put together. The lead editor, Ganesh Bhutkar, then configured a cloud / google drive to which potential authors could submit their extended / new papers. The review process was further extended with three reviews per paper. The pool of reviewers was the same as for the main conference with a few additional reviewers added. The review round was followed by two additional rounds of editorial reviews. Papers with at least two positive single blind reviews and also consensus-acceptance among the editors were then accepted for the LNCS book.

HWID has been endeavoring to enhance the positive work experiences at workplaces by providing employees pleasurable and meaningful user experiences via the tools used at work. HWID 2021 directed attention to the 'low desire' phenomenon, where people have lower desire for success, no ambitions, needs, or expectations.

These people push back against working around the clock, avoid conflicts, yearn to be free of strong feelings, and do not take anyone or anything too seriously. HWID 2021 attempted to look into the relationship between happiness and IT-enabled overworking, the resulting work experiences, and how to provide solutions from the perspective of Human Work Interaction Design.

Artificial intelligence (AI) is making a difference to the workplace and complicating the situation further. On one hand, AI replaces human workers by working faster with fewer errors than humans, which enables AI to do many of the boring and redundant jobs. On the other hand, many organizations are already beginning to use AI as a design element to enhance human intelligence, and design positive experiences in the workplace. As a result, there are growing concerns that AI will take away jobs from humans or in other ways become dominating. The theme of HWID 2021 emphasized the insights into the relationship between low desire and work experience, and how AI will moderate this relationship because parts of the work might be taken away by AI.

The chapters in this book focus on answering these questions to support professionals, academics, national labs, and industry engaged in human work analysis and interaction design for the workplace. The first section of the book has a collection of chapters focusing on 'Trends in Human Work Interaction Design'. The second section has chapters related to 'Workplace and Work Experience Analysis for Interaction Design'. The third and last section has chapters presenting case studies about 'Artificial Intelligence (AI) for Human Work'.

February 2022

Ganesh Bhutkar
Barbara Rita Barricelli
Xiangang Qin
Torkil Clemmensen
Frederica Gonçalves
Jose Abdelnour-Nocera
Arminda Guerra Lopes
Fei Lyu
Ronggang Zhou
Wenjun Hou

The original version of the book was revised: The institutional affiliation of a volume editor was corrected. The correction to the book is available at https://doi.org/10.1007/978-3-031-02904-2_11

Organization

General Chairs

Barbara Rita Barricelli   Università degli Studi di Brescia, Italy
Xiangang Qin   Beijing University of Posts and Telecommunications, China

Program Chairs

Ganesh Bhutkar   Vishwakarma Institute of Technology, India
Arminda Guerra Lopes   ITI/LARSyS, Polytechnic Institute of Castelo Branco, Portugal
Fei Lyu   Beijing University of Posts and Telecommunications, China
Frederica Gonçalves   ITI/LARSyS, University of Madeira, Portugal
Jose Abdelnour-Nocera   University of West London, UK

Poster Chairs

Shrikant Salve   MIT Academy of Engineering, India
Stefano Valtolina   Università degli Studi di Milano, Italy

HWID Legacy Chairs

Philippe Palanque   ICS-IRIT, Université Paul Sabatier, France
Torkil Clemmensen   Copenhagen Business School, Denmark

HWID Membership Chairs

Judith Molka-Danielsen   Molde University College, Norway
Pedro Campos   University of Madeira, Portugal

Local Organizing Chairs

Ronggang Zhou   Beihang University, China
Wenjun Hou   Beijing University of Posts and Telecommunications, China

Student Volunteer Chair

Yang Ma   Beijing University of Posts and Telecommunications, China

Publicity Chair

Xi Cheng   Beijing University of Posts and Telecommunications, China

Program Committee

Elodie Bouzekri	University of Toulouse, France
Virpi Roto	Aalto University, Finland
Yohannes Kurniawan	Bina Nusantara University, Indonesia
Anmol Srivastava	UPES University, India
Chhaya Gosavi	Cummins College of Engineering for Women, India
Xiu Miao	Beijing University of Posts and Telecommunications, China

Contents

Trends in Human Work Interaction Design

Drifting Towards a New HCI Field: A Review of 10 Years of HWID Research

Frederica Gonçalves[1](✉) [iD], Torkil Clemmensen[2] [iD], Judith Molka-Danielsen[3] [iD], and Pedro Campos[4] [iD]

[1] ITI/LARSyS, Universidade da Madeira - Escola Superior de Tecnologias e Gestão, Funchal, Portugal
frederica.goncalves@iti.larsys.pt
[2] Department of Informatics, Copenhagen Business School, Frederiksberg, Denmark
tc.digi@cbs.dk
[3] Molde University College, Molde, Norway
j.molka-danielsen@himolde.no
[4] ITI/LARSyS, Universidade da Madeira, Funchal, Portugal
pedro.campos@iti.larsys.pt

Abstract. Over the last decade, empirical relationships between work domain analysis and HCI design have been identified by much research in the field of Human Work Interaction Design (HWID) across five continents. In this paper, we review 142 papers about HWID from workshops, conferences, journals and Springer books from 2005 up to and including 2015. Using bibliometric techniques, text-mining and co-word analysis, we discover patterns and articulate information that drifts towards a new HCI field, formed around research on the relationships between work analysis and interaction design. Our findings reveal two major opportunities for design research in the work domain: a) human-centered design approaches for specific work domains (workplaces, smart workplaces); b) visions of new roles for workplaces that enhance both work practice and interaction design. Drifting towards new HCI fields opens up new possibilities.

Keywords: Human Work Interaction Design · HCI field · User experience · Literature review · Co-word analysis · Text-mining · Bibliometric study

1 Introduction

Today, it is a true challenge to design applications that support users of technology in complex and emergent organizational and work contexts. To meet this challenge, the Working Group 13.6 (WG13.6) on Human Work Interaction Design (HWID) was established in September 2005 as the sixth working group under the International Federation for Information Processing specifically the Technical Committee 13 on Human Computer Interaction (HCI). A main objective of the WG13.6 as defined in 2012 is the analysis of this complexity and its relationships between extensive empirical work domains studies and HCI designs [1].

© IFIP International Federation for Information Processing 2022
Published by Springer Nature Switzerland AG 2022
G. Bhutkar et al. (Eds.): HWID 2021, IFIP AICT 609, pp. 3–33, 2022.
https://doi.org/10.1007/978-3-031-02904-2_1

This paper introduces the research done under the name of HWID, identifying patterns and its relations to the HWID field and related fields. The challenge that HWID attempt to overcome is that today's technology changes the way we work with pervasive technologies and smart places, shifting often our physical boundaries and our operational modes. From health care, to traffic control, interaction with new technologies, researchers have raised challenging issues for HCI researchers and experts.

In line with recent suggestions that HCI should "turn to practice" [2] and do practice based research [3], the utility and merit of defining a field from its published works stems from providing a conceptual frame to organize a variety of issues emerging in recent HCI research. In this paper we take a practice oriented, bottom-up approach to a group of HCI researchers' publication practice by analyzing and synthesizing published works under the HWID heading during 10 years.

Stephanidis [4] states that interactive technologies are entering all aspects of everyday life, in communication, work and collaboration, health and well-being, home control and automation, public services, learning and education, culture, travel, tourism and leisure, and many others. An extensive variety of technologies are already available, and new ones tend to appear frequently, and on a regular basis. Because of this we have to be attentive towards the development of studies that will help the growth of new technologies itself.

The scope of WG13.6 is to provide the basis for an improved cross-disciplinary co-operation and mutual inspiration among researchers from the many disciplines that by nature are involved in a deep analysis of and design for a work domain [5]. To support this scope, the HWID framework was developed. In 2008, Ørngreen et al. [6] presented a framework that aims at establishing relationships between the characteristics of humans and work domain contents and the interaction during their tasks and decisions activities, individually or in collaboration.

Clemmensen [7] developed a revised HWID framework (Fig. 1) to provide an easy understandable version of the framework that is applicable across domains. The HWID framework has four parts and a set of lines connecting the parts. The top box illustrates the theories used, the left is the analysis of users' work and life, in the middle column the artefacts, and to the right the design of interactive information technologies. The box at the bottom indicates that environmental contexts, such as national, cultural, social, and organizational factors, impact the way in which users interact with computers in their work and life. The lines connecting the left-right boxes illustrate the various relations between empirical work analysis and interaction design activities and products, which are the focus of HWID research.

Gonçalves et al. [8] reviewed 54 papers in the emerging practice and research of HWID. The review reflected diverse topics and problems that the authors of the 54 papers perceived to be the major concerns and challenges. We believe that the papers presented in this review illustrates that researchers have developed the understanding of the HWID notion by experiencing and texting the contextualization of the concepts and framework, either empirical or theoretically [8]. So, it was decided to deepen the analysis of all articles published since the beginning of the working group.

We have reviewed the 142 papers about HWID from workshops, conferences, journals and Springer book from 2005 until and including 2015. HWID research has until now largely been published at workshops and conferences, in line with the format and

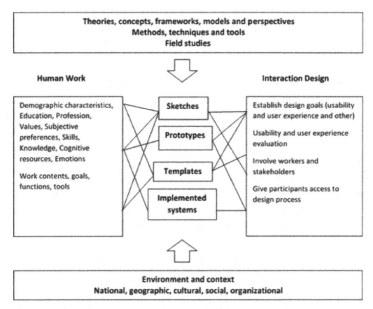

Fig. 1. Human work interaction design framework [7].

aim of HWID being an IFIP working group. Furthermore, the 142 studies that are taking up the challenge are still relatively few as compared with other subfields of HCI [9, 10]. With this paper we would like to give some insights from the 142 publications that have been created in the WG TC 13.6 in the last decade. Researchers across five continents have studied what empirical relationships in work domain and HCI design also providing a cross-disciplinary cooperation studies, can enhance the HCI curriculum.

The remainder of this paper is organized as follows: in the next section, we present the methods employed to discover patterns or articulate information. We then present a section describing the results using bibliometric techniques, text mining techniques and co-word analysis. We sum up with a discussion that includes reflections on the entire literature review and gives a new design framework. The paper ends with the overall conclusions.

2   Method

The goal of this study is to analyze systematically the occurrence and characteristics of the studies in HWID. To contribute towards understanding the big picture of HWID evolution this study applies various methods for analyzing information that is being produced. Yet most of the information in this study is in its raw form: data, so we tried to perform a quantitative analysis collecting the data in a rigorous way for that. For that reason, we used tools and techniques for machine learning that are used in data mining to underlie the data.

We collected the data from the established sources that would represent the most prominent part of HWID research such as: conferences, workshops, journals and

Springer books. Then we analyzed using three different techniques. We used these techniques to discover patterns or articulate information that can be potentially important and useful to this field.

a) **Bibliometric techniques** – bibliometric technique is used as an approach to explore evidence of transitions in different fields. For example, to demonstrate the centrality of various authors to the field of HCI [11] to determinate statistic like the most first authors or most cited papers [12], or to clustering publications into thematic categories [13]. Others, such as Newman [14] used and combining with other techniques to categorized products of HCI research. Guha [15] expose relationships between sub-disciplines in computer science and showed evidence of transitions in the field.

b) **Text-mining** – Text-mining it is the process of analyzing text to extract information that is useful for particular purposes [16]. In other words, it is looking for patterns in text. Godbole et al. [17] presents their study focusing on dictionary-based text mining and its role in enabling practitioners in understating and analyzing large text datasets. They showed how to adapt one or more dictionaries across domains and tasks to reuse in industrial practice. In other fields, Valencia [18] highlights the text mining techniques to characterization of the human mitotic spindle apparatus showing results that were quite good in the categories of publication raking, detection of experimental methods. Furthermore, his working with his group in fostering the creation of text mining systems that can be integrated in Genome analysis pipelines and contribute effectively to the understanding of complex Biological Systems. Romero et al. [19] used text mining techniques to define a glossary of terms related to Empirical Software Engineering.

c) **Co-word analysis** - It's possible with co-word analysis to map the strength of association between keywords in textual data. Coutler et al., [20] used to map the evolution of the research literature to characterize software engineering and distinguish it from other disciplines. In their work this methodology identified associations among publication descriptors (indexing terms) from the Computing Classification System and produced networks of terms that had reveal patterns of associations. Other researchers such as Liu et al. [10] conducted an analysis to compare the underlying trends in CHI community between 1994 and 2013. Their study identifies the evolution of major themes in the discipline and highlights individual topics as popular, core or backbone research topics within HCI.

3   Findings

3.1   The HWID Papers

The 142 papers involving 251 co-authors included in this study about Human Work Interaction Design were identified from 14 different scientific meetings between 2005 to 2015 (Table 1). For each paper, we collected the following information: year of publication, title, subtitle, list of keywords attributed by the authors, abstract, first and last name of the authors and their country. Considering the relevance of each article presented in HWID, and since most of them are only published in the website of HWID specific group, we had to manually extract all information from them. Data was then output to different type of files that were analyzed in Microsoft Excel, Weka [21], and with an R algorithm [10].

Table 1. Description of the sample considering in this study.

Type	Local	Theme	Year	Total of papers
Workshop INTERACT	Rome, Italy	Describing Users in Context - Perspectives on Human Work Interaction Design	**2005**	**9**
Conference - 1st HWID	Madeira, Portugal	Human Work Interaction Design, Designing for Human Work	**2006**	**14**
Workshop - INTERACT	Rio, Brazil	Social, Organisational and Cultural Aspects of Human Work Interaction Design	**2007**	**5**
Workshop - NordiCHI	Sweden	Cultural Usability and Human Work Interaction Design - techniques that connects	**2008**	**8**
Symposium - HCI - IFIP	Symposium	Themes in Human Work Interaction Design	**2008**	**1**
Conference - 2nd HWID	Pune, India	Usability in social, cultural and organizational contexts	**2009**	**22**
Workshop NordiCHI-	Iceland	Crisis Management Training Design and Use of Online Worlds	**2010**	**12**
Workshop - INTERACT	Lisbon, Portugal	Human Work Interaction Design for e-Government and Public Information Systems	**2011**	**9**
Conference - 3rd HWID	Copenhagen, Denmark	Work Analysis and HCI	**2012**	**16**

(*continued*)

Table 1. (*continued*)

Type	Local	Theme	Year	Total of papers
Workshop - INTERACT	Cape Town, South Africa	Past History and Future Challenges of Human Work Interaction Design (HWID): Generating Cross-Domain Knowledge about connecting work analysis and Interaction Design	**2013**	**8**
SIG - CHI	Paris, France	HWID SIG: Past History and Future Challenges	**2013**	**1**
Workshop - NordiCHI	Helsinki, Finland	Human Work Interaction Design for Pervasive and Smart Workplaces	**2014**	**10**
Conference - 4th HWID	London, England	Human Work Interaction Design	**2015**	**18**
Workshop - INTERACT	Bamberg, Germany	Human Work Interaction Design (HWID): Design for Challenging Work Environments	**2015**	**9**

3.2 Timeline and Trends

Beside the prominence, we considered comparability as an important factor, but we had to make different analyzes in the sample. The major reason for this was because all the papers for our sample are not published in digital libraries (Fig. 2). Also, some papers had no keywords and for the year 2007 we only have information such as: first and last name of the authors, country and the title of the papers. The solid bars indicate the coverage of publications data.

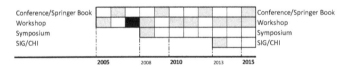

Fig. 2. Timeline of the 10 years of HWID.

We employed a bibliometric study to find out the total of wise contributions, the authorship pattern, and to determine the geographical distributions of contributions in the field. From analysis (Table 2) we can see that HWID has been unstable in terms of publications per year.

Table 2. Paper frequency distribution per year.

	Frequency per year	Frequency distribution
2005	9	6,34%
2006	14	9,86%
2007	5	3,52%
2008	9	6,34%
2009	22	15,49%
2010	12	8,45%
2011	9	6,34%
2012	16	11,27%
2013	9	6,34%
2014	10	7,04%
2015	27	19,01%

3.3 Authorship

Table 3 shows that the multiple authorship has the largest proportion of publications 110 papers (77.47%) while the single authorship pattern has 32 papers (22.54%).

Table 3. Authorship pattern.

Authorship	Number of	Frequency distribution
Single	32	22,54%
Two	47	33,10%
Three	33	23,24%
More than three	30	21,13%

The average number of authors per paper is 1.76 ($M = 1.76$), i.e., 251 authors written 142 papers the last 10 years.

3.4 Collaboration

To determine the amount of collaboration in quantitative terms, we used the formula given by Subramanyam [22] $C = Nm/Nm + Ns$ *Where* (C represents the degree of collaboration; *Nm* represents the number of multi authored contributions; *Ns* represents the number of single authored contributions), also knowns as a correlation coefficient in Social Network Analysis [23].

Table 4. Degree of collaboration of authors.

Year	Degree of collaboration
2005	1,000
2006	0,786
2007	0,600
2008	0,444
2009	0,682
2010	0,667
2011	0,556
2012	1,000
2013	0,889
2014	1,000
2015	0,481

In this study (ten years) de degree of collaboration is $C = 0.71$. Table 4 shows that years 2005, 2012 and 2014 had the highest degree of collaboration and the year 2008 and the year 2015 the lowest.

3.5 Geography

The figure below (Fig. 3) depicts pattern of the geographical distribution of contributions in the HWID field under study.

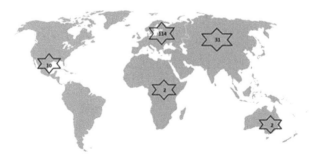

Fig. 3. Geographical distribution of contributions.

As would be expected, the largest contribution comes from Europe (Austria, Belgium, Denmark, Finland, France, Germany, Greece, Iceland, Ireland, Italy, Norway,

Portugal, Spain, The Netherlands, United Kingdom), followed by Asia (China, Japan, India, Russia) and America (Brazil, Canada, USA), and finally by Africa (South Africa, Namibia) and Oceania (New Zealand).

3.6 Themes, Topics, Subjects

To identify patterns of themes associations and their relations to the field, we employed a machine learning technique such as text mining. We used the add-in eTable Utilities [24] and XLMiner Plataform [25] for that.

In this analysis we used only the titles of each paper since from our sample this was the variable that we had in common for all 142 papers. As previously mentioned from the year 2007 we only have the title and their authors, and we didn't want to discard this data. To present an at-a-glance overview of the HWID research in the last decade, we have created a word cloud over the years and ending with an encompassing up every year at once (Fig. 4, Table 5). We used IBM'S Word Cloud Generator [26].

Fig. 4. Word cloud for the titles of each paper over the last decade.

Table 5. Frequency of terms of titles of each paper over the last decade.

	Frequency
Challenges	5
Framework	8
Experience	8
Environments	10
Users	13
Human	17
Usability	19

(continued)

Table 5. (*continued*)

	Frequency
Interaction	26
Work	42
Design, designing	62

Figure 5 and Table 5 displays the total count for each theme (subject) in the papers. We can see that users, usability, human, interaction, work and design were the most research themes (subjects).

We decided at this stage to pragmatically assume that we could have a tendency about the most prolific subjects of research. So, we decided to find out what the most discussed topics and their relationships. Using eTable Utilities [24], we could have results about the most prolific terms in the titles in our sample. Table 6 shows the number of papers per most frequent subjects.

Table 6. Group the papers per most frequent subjects.

ID	Terms	N° papers	References
Cluster T1	Designing for, design of, design sketching, design framework, collaborative design, system design, design requirements, experience design	38	[27– 64]
Cluster T2	Human work interaction, work interaction, human work interaction design, interaction design	15	[5, 6, 8, 65–76]
Cluster T3	Case study	12	[77– 88]
Cluster T4	Work analysis, workplaces, workers, workcentered, telework, smartplaces	21	[89–109]
Cluster T5	Scenarios, personas, cultural, cultural usability	21	[110– 130]
Cluster T6	Users, user experiences, user-centered	20	[131– 150]
Cluster T7	Information systems, mobile computing, specific contexts	15	[151–164]

We manually grouped all the papers through resemblance of words (e.g. "design as", "design", "design for", and so on) and by reading them, we could make a more accurate topic cluster analysis. From clusters T1 and T4 in Table 6 and making a more extensive analysis we can see in Table 7 and Table 8 that the authors make the transitions in research from interaction design to work analysis or reversely.

Relating cluster T1 (designing for, design of, etc.) represented here in Table 7, whit cluster T4 (work analysis, workplaces, etc.) we can see that in cluster T1, research has focused more precisely on the holding and supporting technologies and its transitions to interaction design, while cluster T4 (*see* Table 8) has been the opposite.

The most common concerns for work and exposed in the papers from cluster T4 (*see* Table 8) has been the challenging and preeminent differences with cultural contexts, new interfaces and new work environments that can influence and improve HCI design.

The findings from the 142 conference, workshop, symposium and SIG papers, indicate that a) many of the papers are not easily accessible because early work are not included in digital libraries, b) frequency of papers per year is growing, c) nearly three fourths of papers are multiple authored, d) most papers are from European events, followed by Asian and Americans, and e) users, usability, human, interaction, work and design were the most research themes.

Table 7. Extract words from cluster T1

Terms	Years	N. Papers	Extract words
Designing for, design of, design sketching, design framework, design as, collaborative design, system design, design requirements, experience design,	2005	6	**Emerging** from an understanding nature of tasks; influence user's information behaviour; **requirements elicitation** process for the design; **focus** on who we are as humans in the perspective of the designers of the technologies; **potential improvement** of how can information technology better support the coordination of co-operative work; patterns may be **leveraged to enhance** the work people perform in socio-technical and other complex systems
	2006	9	**Designed to support a person** making resource allocation decisions; **design** of information visualisation software **to support work**; how design sketching can be used as a technique for exploring and creating common understanding between users; **design sketching** process from rough drawings of conceptualisations and detailed storyboards of functionalities; **guidelines** for a different perspective on design; interface design when developing **new tools to support** creative activity; **explore the role of design** sketches in interaction design and work analysis; **approach to designing** a visual application; **to design** tailored fitness **that allow** performing simultaneously home routine tasks and physical exercise
	2009	2	**Explores** the concept of design as a multimodal conversation; **identify** the cognitive needs of museum visitors and the content selection parameters for designing the interactive kiosk software
	2010	1	The paper contains **design ideas, analysis and evaluation of current work** with mobile equipment and augmented reality features, utilizing experiences from Human Work Interaction Design

(continued)

Table 7. (*continued*)

Terms	Years	N. Papers	Extract words
	2011	3	We argue that human work interaction design can be a solid, **useful approach to better support** diverse users of public information systems; **focused on** the design of the future centre unique online booking; **challenges** to applying user centered design in the public sector
	2012	5	Discusses two **cognitive science paradigms** and then present third **approach related to** interaction with the world as known as embodied cognition; an **exploration** of how children adapt their interactions with different graphical user interfaces (GUIs) in varied task situations; describe the use of an interactive online questionnaire **to facilitate** a photovoltaic; specifically **investigate the problems and issues related** to throw-away prototypes in sensor-intensive systems; pinpoint the **limitations** of the design target formulation in current HCI approaches
	2013	1	Through our participatory design and user-centred design evaluation processes to date, we have established that this **approach is promising** for improving overall care for the residents in long-term care
	2014	1	**Focus on a new tool** for mobile video journalism, and how it fits into the existing work practices and the ecology of tools that the journalists use to support their pervasive workplace

(*continued*)

Table 7. (*continued*)

Terms	Years	N. Papers	Extract words
	2015	10	**Identified the need** to consolidate information originating from various interfaces and ubiquitous systems deployed throughout the factory in order to improve their workflow. On the other hand, **design needs to facilitate awareness** for broken and serviced equipment; currently undergoing work is **focused on the co-design** of a cloud of services able at integrating all the tools into a bigger frame-work to support the archaeological practice in a more pervasive way; **explores the systems design requirements** through the design a demonstrator that is tested by a small pilot group; **a design** of intelligent food carrier **helps** in providing information about food item quantity; the **influence** of this type of tools to assess if a creative writing user interface can positively influence the productivity and mental well-being of users; following **experience design and positive design** we investigated the **feasibility of increased** positive experiences for users in such environments; the paper **discusses the reasons** to keep in mind the user base that will use product (for all). The **need of universal design** is today's requirement; were interested **to find evidence** concerning how students' creativity supported the design process and the interactions that occur in creative activities mediated by technology; an **integrative review** with a personal ethnographic narrative that draws on literature on Design-Based Research, and **identifies and discusses** elements from Interaction Design and Action Research that the Design-Based Research approach could consider, situating the research in online educational projects; describe the results of a survey where we studied **experience design practitioners' views** of experience goal setting and approaches to communicate about these goals with stakeholders

From this analysis we identified two major opportunities for design research on the work domain: there is a great need for human-centered design research on the work domains (workplaces, smart workplaces) and also there is a great need for research that envisions new roles for workplaces that enhance both work practice and interaction design.

3.7 Key HWID Concepts

Finally, our analysis relies on techniques from hierarchical cluster and graph theory, using co-word analysis. In this case we use the variable keywords. We could manually assign keywords to papers, but we chose to work with "pure" sample, so we discard all the data that had not keywords. Our sample to analysis in with 92 papers referring only to 2008 year until 2015 (Table 9).

Table 8. Total of papers and total of keywords per year 2008–2015.

Year	Total papers	Total keywords
2008	9	71
2009	21	193
2010	12	111
2011	9	82
2012	14	141
2013	8	95
2014	9	79
2015	10	102

Table 9. Extracts words in cluster T4.

Terms	Years	N. papers	Extract words
Work analysis, workplaces, workers, workcentered, telework, smartplaces,	2005	1	Argue that **work style models can be very useful** as a Human-Work design methodology, since it forces the designer to think about solutions supporting the important contexts of work as well as changes in those contexts

(continued)

Table 9. (*continued*)

Terms	Years	N. papers	Extract words
	2006	1	Describe a **set of principles that were proven successful** during this design process, illustrate sketches of the tools, and highlight the relevant design aspects that worked and those that didn't work
	2007	1	**Improving existing driver interfaces** with tools from the framework of cognitive work analysis
	2012	4	**Data** from observed bathing assistance, night shift operations, and handover tasks at a private elderly care home; we describe and elaborate around the usage of different **work analysis methods** in a complex, real world work domain: collaborative review of large-scale 3D engineering models; aims to **understand the importance** of early work analysis in a real context during the design of such a simulator; the intention is to present some **recommendations for companies that work** with this type of products to improve their productivity and profit;
	2013	3	**There is a gap between** the technological artefact produced and the social requirements that govern how well the system will fit in the organisation; **an application model for supporting** human collaborative works is proposed; In order to **prevent possible negative work environment** consequences, a checklist has been developed for analysis of the proposed new work situation;

(*continued*)

Table 9. (*continued*)

Terms	Years	N. papers	Extract words
	2014	4	**Sociotechnical gaps,** which are of central interest to researchers and designers of ICTs supporting telework. **Visualising these gaps is even more challenging due to the different cultural contexts** where telecommuting is taking place nowadays; we call for extensive discussion on **using the well-being data for designing work** and a working environment that supports well-being and productivity; **pervasive workplace based on designing simple interactions** for a complex domain: creative writing; **aim is to design and develop a platform that supports** older employees to remain longer active and satisfied in the workplace;
	2015	7	This attempt may **contribute to improve the interaction among** the whole partners and to address organizations' agility and innovation; we discuss **challenges when conducting** action research and formulating research projects in a fairly volatile organisational setting; Working as an HCI researcher in the **domain of healthcare can be challenging;** we discuss our initial plans for conducting such data-collection and **the problems and challenges** presented by the forestry environment; describes in case of **mobile news** making the synthesized **findings on context of use categorized** to five components and nineteen subcomponents based on twelve cases studies; present and discuss **a modified version of personas** called contextual personas **to address the new working life; presents our experience of this solution** in the context of our Paris office **and discusses** its potential for building smart and sustainable workplaces

The 874 keywords for the 2008–2015 led to 12 clusters (labeled as K1–K14, in Table 10). Each cluster represents a research theme or subfield. For each one we have: a) Size: the number of keywords; b) Co-word frequency: on average a keyword appears in our dataset; c) Centrality: degree of interaction of a theme with other parts of the network [165, 166]; d) Density: making up the research theme by measuring the internal cohesion, or the strength of the links that tie together the cluster keyword [166, 165]; e) Keywords: set of keywords that constitute the cluster.

To visualize the cohesion and maturity of each research themes in HWID, we constructed a strategic diagram (based on Fig. 5) to visualize it [20, 165, 10]. Figure 6 shows the strategic diagram degree of density and centrality for HWID. The x-axis shows the strength of interaction between a specific research theme with others – Centrality. The y-axis reflects the density of the research theme, or the internal cohesion of a specific research theme [10].

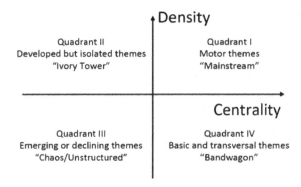

Fig. 5. Strategic diagram's degree of density and centrality [165, 166].

We can see in Fig. 6 the results from the average centrality and density across all the clusters for the designated sample.

Table 10. Major research themes in HWID during 2008–2015

ID	Keywords	Size	Total frequency	Total CW frequency	Centrality	Density
K1	Approach, behaviour, content, contextual, experience, interactive, interviews, kiosk, museums, needs, parameters, questionnaire, selection, social, software, survey, visitor, visitor-centred	18	27	407	0,284	1,000
K2	Control, ergonomics, fine, illiterate, motor, phone, productivity, racial, semi-literate, stylus, thumb, tools, touchscreen	13	13	247	0,050	1,000
K3	And, cultural, factors, interface, smart	5	24	211	0,585	1,200
K4	Augmented, computing, creative, creativity, crowdsourcing, glass, glassware, google, reality, support, tablets, tools, wearable, writing	14	16	240	0,043	1,000
K5	Children, computers, context, education, eLearning, environments, Indian, instructional, socio-cultural, usability, website	11	20	203	0,220	1,000
K6	Data, designs, empirical, for, gathering, ict., learning, methods, mobile, probes,	10	19	186	0,169	1,022
K7	Analysis, care, evaluation, intensive, medical, model, system, unit, usability, ventilator, video	11	46	295	0,340	1,418

(*continued*)

Table 10. (*continued*)

ID	Keywords	Size	Total frequency	Total CW frequency	Centrality	Density
K8	Ambient, experience, intelligence, methods, older, study	6	15	65	0,137	0,800
K9	Action, analysis, case, centred, cognitive, communication, computer, computing, context, context, culture, design, design, development, embodied, evaluation, future, graphical, guidelines, human-computer, human-work, hwid, information, interaction, interaction, interdisciplinary, interface, interfaces,, knowledge, organizational, participatory, personas, pervasive, recognition, service, services, technologies, technology, theory, touch, usability, user, voice, work,	44	198	876	0,852	0,221
K10	Analysis, based, design, human, interaction, work	6	74	436	0,630	3,733
K11	Co-operative, crisis, management, online, situation	5	23	137	0,272	2,300
K12	Analysis, emergency, environment, management, realism, simulations, training, virtual	9	38	215	0,329	0,917

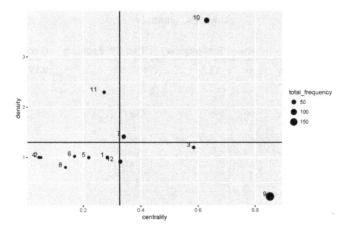

Fig. 6. Strategic diagram for HWID for the period 2008–2015

Analyzing our results, we can assert from the 92 papers most of them are in quadrant III, i.e. these themes have low density and low centrality, mainly representing either emerging or disappearing themes (Clusters: K 1, 2, 4, 5, 6, 8, 12).

Results also show that data from cluster K9 it presents significant data of themes that are under-developed yet transversal, with potential to be of considerable significance to the entire research network. Finally known as the motor-themes we have data from cluster K10 with strong centrality and high density.

The combination of these analyses is a great way to study patterns or articulate information in a particular field, and in this case for the field of Human Work Interaction Design.

Based on results from analysis and almost parallel to it, new research has emerged which will be addressed in the future as a consequence of a new HCI field called HWID. Figure 7 frames the vision of this new field. This vision places artefacts at the core that are outcomes of interactive systems designs, theories, methods, approaches in the context of human work within complex contexts. The vision allows for future design of a flexible yet integrating framework that can take into consideration the ever-blurring boundaries of what is work and the workplace. In addition, it anticipates that HWID systems must be research, designed and developed within complex contexts of multi-organizations, cultures and perspectives of understanding.

The framework is defined as a hexagon. The inner-core represents "practical" constructs of HWID systems based on higher level "theoretical" constructs that include theories and concepts, frameworks and models, methods, technologies and tools, information on HW and information on ID. There is a need to develop this visionary meta-framework for HWID. Such a meta-framework will help bridge the gap between theoretical constructs and future practical implementations of HWID systems.. These elements form a set of sub aspects of Human Work and Interaction Design that identify what can be considered of great relevance for future search in the field of Human Computer Interaction.

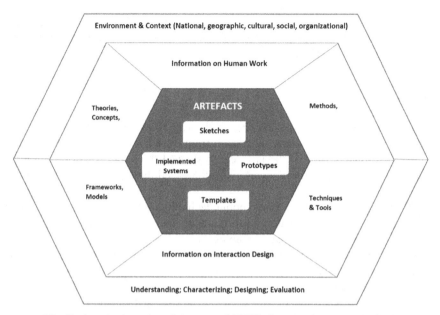

Fig. 7. A revised version of the general HWID framework a new HCI field.

4 Discussion

While previous work [8] has outlined a research gap in the HWID framework and the need to better theories, concepts, frameworks models and perspectives in HWID, our work provides a new perspective to better understand the HWID and the way forward for research. Clemmensen [68] suggest that the development of a HWID framework may make it a better tool for mapping the combinations of multiple other theories onto the relations between Human Work and Interaction Design. We also argue that we should approach HWID with a flexible yet integrating framework, that is useful to guide the application of other theories to study the relation between work analysis and interaction design.

Our analysis in this paper have several implications. First, the distribution of key words as highlighted in Table 10 and Fig. 7 indicate that there is a large body of work that centers on the theme of HWID. This would be an expected finding within this data set. However, there are numerous clusters of themes (K 1, 2, 4, 5, 6, 8, 12) that can represent a wide variety of practical application areas. This further emphasizes the importance of those themes within the context of HWID.

Second, this analysis highlighted the frequency of terms as represented in Fig. 4, and Tables 5, 6, 7 and 9. The implications in these Figures and Tables are to draw attention not only to the terms that are frequent, but to those that are infrequent (e.g., framework, methods, modelling, etc.). The former research has emphasized an interest in the practical outcomes (e.g., smart places, workplaces, systems design). This highlights that the concepts of HCI are finding relevancy in the field of human work and workplace design. In addition, the appearance of the less frequent terms, demonstrate a need to relate to the theoretical constructs to practical solutions. This research indicates that there is a refocus, or drifting, of the traditional field of HCI towards one that centers on themes of importance to HWID.

5 Conclusion

Over the last decade great studies have been made in the Human Work Interaction Design. Interestingly, as these studies have moved out from work domains to interaction design and vice versa. Our review of the last decade showed the importance of the number of researchers analyzing of user's work and life as well the design of computer-based information systems.

In 2005 we were concerned about mobile technologies that were used to drift contexts, today we have to be aware and to maintain focus on users and complex user situations with pervasive and smart technologies.

Through 142 studies, 251 researchers involved from five continents, have studied what empirical relationships in work domain and HCI design can provide a cross-disciplinary cooperation enhancing the HCI field. These can function as a starting emerging field for design practitioners who wants to improve and expand the scope of new technologies.

There is a great need for human-computer interaction research to understand the boundaries of human work, its relations, contexts, as well as several opportunities for design research to impact this existing area to better situate different technologies. In addition, there is a great need for research that envisions new roles for technologies to play that both enhances the work performance of workers and that enhance the relationships between design and their interaction. On the reflection on the state of the research, we identified several opportunities for HCI research to impact pervasive technologies, work domain and smart places.

References

1. Campos, P., Clemmensen, T., Nocera, J.A., Katre, D., Lopes, A., Ørngreen, R. (eds.): HWID 2012. IAICT, vol. 407. Springer, Heidelberg (2013). https://doi.org/10.1007/978-3-642-411 45-8
2. Kuutti, K., Bannon, L.J.: The turn to practice in HCI: towards a research agenda. In: Proceedings of the 32nd Annual ACM Conference on Human Factors in Computing Systems (2014)
3. Wulf, V., Müller, C., Pipek, V., Randall, D., Rohde, M., Stevens, G.: Practice-based computing: empirically grounded conceptualizations derived from design case studies. In: Wulf, Volker, Schmidt, Kjeld, Randall, David (eds.) Designing Socially Embedded Technologies in the Real-World. CSCW, pp. 111–150. Springer, London (2015). https://doi.org/10.1007/ 978-1-4471-6720-4_7
4. Stephanidis, C.: Design for all. In: The Encyclopedia of Human Computer Interaction 2nd Edition, Interaction Design Foundation, pp. 2453–2550 (2015)
5. Abdelnour Nocera, J., Barricelli, B.R., Lopes, A., Campos, Pedro, Clemmensen, Torkil (eds.): HWID 2015. IAICT, vol. 468. Springer, Cham (2015). https://doi.org/10.1007/978-3-319-27048-7

6. Ørngreen, R., Pejtersen, A.M., Clemmensen, T.: Themes in human work interaction design. In: Forbrig, P., Paternò, F., Pejtersen, A.M. (eds.) HCIS 2008. IIFIP, vol. 272, pp. 33–46. Springer, Boston, MA (2008). https://doi.org/10.1007/978-0-387-09678-0_4

7. Clemmensen, T.: A human work interaction design (HWID) case study in E-government and public information systems. In: IFIP INTERACT 2011 Workshop on Human Work Interaction Design for e-Government and Public Information Systems, Lisbon, Portugal (2011)

8. Gonçalves, F., Campos, P., Clemmensen, T.: Human work interaction design: an overview. In: Abdelnour Nocera, J., Barricelli, B.R., Lopes, A., Campos, P., Clemmensen, T. (eds.) HWID 2015. IAICT, vol. 468, pp. 3–19. Springer, Cham (2015). https://doi.org/10.1007/978-3-319-27048-7_1

9. Kostakos, V.: The big hole in HCI research. Interactions 22(2), 48–51 (2015)

10. Liu, Y., Goncalves, J., Ferreira, D., Xiao, B., Hosio, S., Kostakos, V.: CHI 1994–2013: mapping two decades of intellectual progress through co-word analysis. In: CHI 2014, 26 April–1 May, Toronto, Ontario, Canada (2014)

11. Wania, C., Atwood, M., Mccain, K.: How to design and evaluation interrelate in HCI research? In: Proceedings DIS, pp. 90–98 (2006)

12. Oulasverta, A.: A bibliometric exercise for SIGCHI conference on human factors in computing systems (2006). https://www.hiit.fi/node/290

13. Kaye, J.: Some statistical analyses of CHI. In: Proceedings of CHI EA 2009, pp. 2585–2594 (2009)

14. Newman, W.: A preliminary analysis of the products of HCI research, using pro forma abstracts. In: Proceedings of CHI 1994, pp. 278–284 (1994)

15. Guha, S., Steinharddt, S., Lagoze, C.: Following bibliometric footprints: the ACM digital library and the evolution of computer science. In: JCDL 2013, Indianapolis, USA (2013)

16. Witten, I.H., Frank, E., Hall, M.A.: Data Mining - Practical Machine Learning Tools and Techniques. Elsevier Inc. (2011)

17. Godbole, S., Bhattacharya, I., Gupta, A.: Building re-usable dictionary repositories for real-world text mining. In: CIKM 2010, Toronto, Ontario, Canada (2010)

18. Valencia, A.: Text mining in genomics and systems biology. In: Proceedings of the 2nd International Workshop on Data and Text Mining in Bioinformatics, pp. 3–4 (2008)

19. Romero, F., Olivas, J., Genero, M., Piattini, M.: Automatic extraction of the main terminology used in empirical software engineering through text mining techniques. In: Proceedings of the Second ACM-IEEE International Symposium on Empirical Software Engineering and Measurement (2008)

20. Coulter, N., Monarch, I., Konda, S., Carr, M.: An evolutionary perspective of software engineering research through co-word analysis. Carnegie Mellon University (1996)

21. WEKA: Waikato Environment for Knowledge Analysis (WEKA) (2003). http://www.cs.waikato.ac.nz/weka/index_related.html

22. Subramanyam, K.: Bibliometric studies of researh collaboration: A review. J. Inf. Sci. 6, 33–38 (1983)

23. Wasserman, S., Faust, K.: Social Network Analysis: Methods and Applications. Cambridge University Press, Cambridge (1994)

24. eTable: The essentials data tools add-in for excel (2016). http://www.etableutilities.com/

25. XLMiner (2016). http://www.solver.com/xlminer-platform

26. IBM: Word Cloud Generator (2016). http://www.ibm.com/us-en/

27. Bondarenko, O., Janssen, R.: Diagram method: bringing users' context into the system design. In: Workshop HWID: Describing Users in Context - Perpectives on Human Work Interaction Design, INTERACT, Rome, Italy (2005)

28. Buchner, R., Fuchsberger, V., Weiss, A., Tscheligi, M.: Designing for the factory: UX prototyping for the cleanroom. In: Workshop HWID at INTERACT - Human Work Interaction Design (HWID): Design for Challenging Work Environments, Bamberg, Germany (2015)

29. Burmester, M., Zeiner, K., Laib, M., Perrino, C., Quebeleit, M.: Experience design and positive design as an alternative to classical human factors approaches. In: Workshop HWID at INTERACT - Human Work Interaction Design (HWID): Design for Challenging Work Environments, Bamber, Germany (2015)

30. Campos, P.: The challenges of designing for diverse users: an interactive tourism office. In: Workshop HWID at INTERACT - Human Work Interaction Design for e-Government and Public Information Systems, Lisbon, Portugal (2011)

31. Gaspar, M.C., Ventura, F., Pereira, C., Santos, C.M.: Continuous fitness at home: designing exercise equipment for the daily routine. In: Clemmensen, T., Campos, P., Orngreen, R., Pejtersen, A.M., Wong, W. (eds.) HWID 2006. IIFIP, vol. 221, pp. 147–160. Springer, Boston, MA (2006). https://doi.org/10.1007/978-0-387-36792-7_9

32. Clemmensen, T.: A simple design for a complex work domain - the role of sketches in the design of a Bachelor study's new folder structure for use by teachers, students and administrators. In: Clemmensen, T., Campos, P., Orngreen, R., Pejtersen, A. M., Wong, W. (eds.) HWID 2006. IIFIP, vol. 221, pp. 221–240. Springer, Boston, MA (2006). https://doi.org/10.1007/978-0-387-36792-7_13

33. Craft, B., Cairns, P.: Using sketching to aid the collaborative design of information visualisation software - a case study. In: Clemmensen, T., Campos, P., Orngreen, R., Pejtersen, A.M., Wong, W. (eds.) HWID 2006. IIFIP, vol. 221, pp. 103–122. Springer, Boston, MA (2006). https://doi.org/10.1007/978-0-387-36792-7_6

34. Dai, Z., Paasch, K.: A game-like interactive questionnaire for PV application research by participatory design. In: Campos, P., Clemmensen, T., Nocera, J. A., Katre, D., Lopes, A., Ørngreen, Rikke (eds.) HWID 2012. IAICT, vol. 407, pp. 65–72. Springer, Heidelberg (2013). https://doi.org/10.1007/978-3-642-41145-8_6

35. Deshpande, Y., Yammiyavar, P., Bhattacharya, S.: 'Adaptation' in children – a GUI interaction based task-performance study. In: Campos, P., Clemmensen, T., Nocera, J. A., Katre, D., Lopes, A., Ørngreen, R. (eds.) HWID 2012. IAICT, vol. 407, pp. 22–34. Springer, Heidelberg (2013). https://doi.org/10.1007/978-3-642-41145-8_3

36. Duignan, M., Noble, J., Biddle, R.: Activity theory for design from checklist to interview. In: Clemmensen, T., Campos, P., Orngreen, R., Pejtersen, A.M., Wong, W. (eds.) HWID 2006. IIFIP, vol. 221, pp. 1–25. Springer, Boston, MA (2006). https://doi.org/10.1007/978-0-387-36792-7_1

37. Franssila, H., Okkonen, J.: Adjusting the design target of life-cycle aware HCI in knowledge work: focus on computing practices. In: Campos, P., Clemmensen, T., Nocera, J. A., Katre, D., Lopes, A., Ørngreen, R. (eds.) HWID 2012. IAICT, vol. 407, pp. 150–160. Springer, Heidelberg (2013). https://doi.org/10.1007/978-3-642-41145-8_13

38. Garg, A.B.: Universal design requirements for pervasive workplaces using HWID framework. In: Workshop HWID at INTERACT - Human Work Interaction Design for e-Government and Public Information Systems, Lisbon, Portugal (2011)

39. Garg, A., Govil, K.K.: Empirical evaluation of complex system interfaces for power plant control room using human work interaction design framework. In: Campos, P., Clemmensen, T., Nocera, J. A., Katre, D., Lopes, A., Ørngreen, R. (eds.) HWID 2012. IAICT, vol. 407, pp. 90–97. Springer, Heidelberg (2013). https://doi.org/10.1007/978-3-642-41145-8_8

40. Gonçalves, F., Campos, P., Garg, A.: Understanding UI design for creative writing: a pilot evaluation. In: Workshop HWID at INTERACT - Human Work Interaction Design (HWID): Design for Challenging Work Environments, Bamberg, Germany (2015)

41. Guribye, F., Nyre, L., Torvund, E.: Viz reporter in vivo - design implications for mobile journalism beyond the professional newsroom. In: Workshop HWID at NordiCHI - Human Work Interaction Design for Prevasive and Smart Workplaces, Helsinki, Finland (2014)

42. Hamilton, F., Pavan, P., McHale, K.: Designing usable e-Government services for the citizen: success within user centred design. In: Workshop HWID at INTERACT - Human Work Interaction Design for e-Government and Public Information Systems, Lisbon, Portugal (2011)

43. Kale, P., Bhutkar, G., Pawar, V., Jathar, N.: Contextual design of intelligent food carrier in refrigerator: an indian perspective. In: Abdelnour Nocera, J., Barricelli, B. R., Lopes, A., Campos, P., Clemmensen, T. (eds.) HWID 2015. IAICT, vol. 468, pp. 212–225. Springer, Cham (2015). https://doi.org/10.1007/978-3-319-27048-7_15

44. Katre, D., Sarnaik, M.: Identifying the cognitive needs of visitors and content selection parameters for designing the interactive kiosk software for museums. In: Katre, D., Orngreen, R., Yammiyavar, P., Clemmensen, T. (eds.) HWID 2009. IAICT, vol. 316, pp. 168–179. Springer, Heidelberg (2010). https://doi.org/10.1007/978-3-642-11762-6_14

45. Kimani, S., Gabrielli, S., Catarci, T.: Designing for primary tasks in mobile computing. In: Workshop HWID: Describing Users in Context - Perpectives on Human Work Interaction Design, INTERACT, Rome, Italy (2005)

46. Lopes, A.: Design as dialogue - a new design framework. In: HWID 1st Conference - Human Work Interaction Design, Designing for Human Work, Madeira, Portugal (2006)

47. Lopes, A.: Design as a multimodal conversation. In: HWID 2th Conference - Usability in Social, Cultural and Organizational Contexts, Pune, India (2009)

48. Lopes, A.G.: Creative artifacts mediated by technology. In: HWID 4th Conference - Human Work Interaction Design, London, England (2015)

49. Molka-Danielsen, J., Fominykh, M., Swapp, D., Steed, A.: Systems design of a virtual learning environment to teach space syntax: seeing from the user's perspective. In: HWID 4th Conference - Human Work Interaction Design, London, England (2015)

50. Morrow, C., Amaldi, P., Boiardi, A.: Approaches to designing for highly collaborative, distributed and safety-critical environments: the case of ACAS/TCAS. In: Workshop HWID: Describing Users in Context - Perpectives on Human Work Interaction Design, INTERACT, Rome, Italy (2005)

51. O'Hargan, K., Guerlain, S.: Design of a resource allocation planning system. In: Clemmensen, T., Campos, P., Orngreen, R., Pejtersen, A.M., Wong, W. (eds.) HWID 2006. IIFIP, vol. 221, pp. 67–92. Springer, Boston, MA (2006). https://doi.org/10.1007/978-0-387-367 92-7_4

52. Orngreen, R.: The design sketching process. In: HWID 1Th Conference - Human Work Interaction Design, Designing for Human Work, Madeira, Portugal (2006)

53. Orngreen, R.: Interaction and educational design of mobile equipment for crisis management training. In: Workshop HWID at NordiCHI - Crisis Management Training Design and Use of Online Worlds, Iceland (2010)

54. Ørngreen, R.: Reflections on design-based research. In: Abdelnour Nocera, J., Barricelli, B. R., Lopes, A., Campos, P., Clemmensen, T. (eds.) HWID 2015. IAICT, vol. 468, pp. 20–38. Springer, Cham (2015). https://doi.org/10.1007/978-3-319-27048-7_2

55. Orngreen, R., et al.: The human being in the 21st century - design perspectives on the representation of users in IS development. In: Workshop HWID: Describing Users in Context - Perpectives on Human Work Interaction Design, INTERACT (2005)

56. Pedersen, R., Clemmensen, T.: A design science approach to interactive greenhouse climate control using lego mindstorms for sensor-intensive prototyping. In: Campos, P., Clemmensen, T., Nocera, J. A., Katre, D., Lopes, A., Ørngreen, R. (eds.) HWID 2012. IAICT, vol. 407, pp. 73–89. Springer, Heidelberg (2013). https://doi.org/10.1007/978-3-642-41145-8_7

57. Pejtersen, A., Field, R.: A multi-dimensional approach to describing digital library users in context. In: Workshop HWID: Describing Users in Context - Perpectives on Human Work Interaction Design, INTERACT, Rome, Italy (2005)

58. Rozzi, S., Wong, W., Amaldi, P., Woodward, P., Fields, B.: Design sketching for space and time. In: Clemmensen, T., Campos, P., Orngreen, R., Pejtersen, A.M., Wong, W. (eds.) HWID 2006. IIFIP, vol. 221, pp. 161–183. Springer, Boston, MA (2006). https://doi.org/10.1007/978-0-387-36792-7_10

59. Sanna, F.G.: E-Government and e-Health. The design of digital services to citizens in health care: the project CUP online of Sassari. In: Workshop HWID at INTERACT - Human Work Interaction Design for e-Government and Public Information Systems, Lisbon, Portugal (2011)

60. Silvestre, R., Anacleto, J., Fels, S.: Designing a health-care WorkerCentred system for a chronic mental care hospital. In: Workshop HWID at INTERACT - Past History and Future Challenges of Human Work Interaction Design (HWID): Generating Cross-Domain Knowledge About Connecting Work Analysis and Interaction Design, Cape Town, South Africa (2013)

61. Stanard, T., Wampler, J.: Work-centered HCI design patterns. In: Workshop HWID: Describing Users in Context - Perpectives on Human Work Interaction Design, INTERACT, Rome, Italy (2005)

62. Upton, C., Doherty, G.: Visual representation of complex information structures in high volume manufacturing. In: Clemmensen, T., Campos, P., Orngreen, R., Pejtersen, A.M., Wong, W. (eds.) HWID 2006. IIFIP, vol. 221, pp. 27–45. Springer, Boston, MA (2006). https://doi.org/10.1007/978-0-387-36792-7_2

63. Valtolina, S., Barricelli, B., Gadia, D., Marzullo, M., Piazzi, C., Garzulino, A.: Co-design of a cloud of services for archaeological practice. In: HWID 4th Conference - Human Work Interaction Design, London, England (2015)

64. Varsaluoma, J., Vaataja, H., Karvonen, H., Lu, Y.: The fuzzy front end of experience design: eliciting and communicating experience goals. In: HWID 4th Conference - Human Work Interaction Design, London, England (2015)

65. Abdelnour-Nocera, J.B.B., Clemmensen, T.: ICT design and evaluation for transmediated workplaces: towards a common framework in human work interaction design (2013)

66. Abdelnour-Nocera, J., Hall, P., Dunckley, L.: Reconfiguring producers and users through human-work interaction. In: Workshop HWID: Describing Users in Context - Perpectives on Human Work Interaction Design, INTERACT, Madeira, Portugal (2005)

67. Barricelli, B., Valtolina, S.: Interaction Design for Stratigraphic Analysis in Archaeology (2015)

68. Clemmensen, T.: The form of HWID theory. In: Workshop INTERACT - Human Work Interaction Design (HWID): Design for Challenging Work Environments, Bamberg, Germany (2015)

69. Clemmensen, T., Pedersen, R.: A human work interaction design (HWID) perpective on internet - and sensor based ICT systems for climate management (2010)

70. Clemmensen, T., Campos, P., Katre, D.: CHI 2013 Human Work Interaction Design (HWID) SIG -Past History and Future Challenges (2013)

71. Espana, S., Pederiva, I., Panach, J., Abrahao, S., Pastor, O.: Linking requirements specification with interaction design and implementation (2006)

72. Ham, D., Wong, W., Amaldi, P.: Comparison of three methods for analyzing human work - in terms of design approaches. In: Workshop HWID: Describing Users in Context - Perpectives on Human Work Interaction Design, INTERACT, Madeira, Portugal (2005)

73. Kotzé, P.: Towards integrative human work analysis in national health information systems: an enterprise engineering approach (2011)

74. Minocha, S., Reeves, A.: Interaction design and usability of learning spaces in 3D multi-user virtual worlds. In: Katre, D., Orngreen, R., Yammiyavar, P., Clemmensen, T. (eds.) HWID 2009. IAICT, vol. 316, pp. 157–167. Springer, Heidelberg (2010). https://doi.org/10.1007/978-3-642-11762-6_13

75. Murer, M., Fuchsberger, V., Tscheligi, M.: Staged inquiries: studying contextual interaction through industrial showcasing (2014)

76. Wurhofer, D., Fuchsberger, V., Meneweger, T., Moser, C., Tscheligi, M.: Insights from user experience research in the factory: what to consider in interaction design. In: Abdelnour Nocera, J., Barricelli, B. R., Lopes, A., Campos, P., Clemmensen, T. (eds.) HWID 2015. IAICT, vol. 468, pp. 39–56. Springer, Cham (2015). https://doi.org/10.1007/978-3-319-270 48-7_3

77. Katre, D., Bhutkar, G., Karmarkar, S.: Usability heuristics and qualitative indicators for the usability evaluation of touch screen ventilator systems. In: Katre, D., Orngreen, R., Yammiyavar, P., Clemmensen, T. (eds.) HWID 2009. IAICT, vol. 316, pp. 83–97. Springer, Heidelberg (2010). https://doi.org/10.1007/978-3-642-11762-6_8

78. Clemmensen, T.: A human work interaction design (HWID) case study in e-government and public information systems: the Danish one-for-all authentication system "NemID" (2011)

79. Eriksson, E., Swatling, A.: UCD guerrilla tactics: a strategy for implementation of UCD in the Swedish defence (2012)

80. Erlandsson, J.: Collegial verbalisation - a case study on a new method on information acquisition (2007)

81. Gattol, V., Bobeth, J., Röderer, K., Egger, S., Tscheligi, M.: From bottom-up insights to feature ideas: a case study into the office environments of older computer workers (2015)

82. Gupta, M., Saini, N.: Micro loan & micro credit: a usability case study in financial inclusion initiatives in India (2011)

83. Katre, D., Gupta, M.: Usefulness and usability evaluation of 28 state government web portals of India (2011)

84. Liu, H., Liu, Y.: Evaluation of Chinese finger writing recognition on touch-sensitive keypad of mobile phones (2008)

85. Pereira, C., Mal, J., Caspar, F., Ventura, F.: Human motion analysis in treadle pump devices (2006)

86. Rasmussen, T.: Internet use in eastern europe a case study (2007)

87. Regal, G., Lehner, U., Gattol, V., Bobeth, J., Tscheligi, M.: Pen and display: a multimodal interaction approach for older office employees (2015)

88. Yammiyavar, P., Kate, P.: Developing a mobile phone based GUI for users in the construction industry: a case study. In: Katre, D., Orngreen, R., Yammiyavar, P., Clemmensen, T. (eds.) HWID 2009. IAICT, vol. 316, pp. 211–223. Springer, Heidelberg (2010). https://doi.org/10.1007/978-3-642-11762-6_17

89. Abdelnour-Nocera, J., Law, E.: Towards a sociotechnical understanding of smart and pervasive technologies used by high-managed and low-managed teleworkers (2014)

90. Bobeth, J., et al.: Platform for ergonomic and motivating ICT-based age-friendly workplaces (2014)

91. Bowen, J., Hinze, A., Cunningham, S.: Into the Woods (2015)

92. Cajander, A., Nauwerck, G., Lind, T., Larusdottir, M.: Challenges for action research on HWID in activity based workplaces (2015)

93. Cajander, A., Larusdottir, M., Eriksson, E., Nauwerck, G.: Providing a holistic view and bringing life into the conversation: eliciting it-based administrative work with contextual personas (2015)

94. Campos, P., Noronha, H.: On the usage of different work analysis methods for collaborative review of large scale 3D CAD models. In: Campos, P., Clemmensen, T., Nocera, J. A., Katre, D., Lopes, A., Ørngreen, R. (eds.) HWID 2012. IAICT, vol. 407, pp. 12–21. Springer, Heidelberg (2013). https://doi.org/10.1007/978-3-642-41145-8_2

95. Campos, P., Nunes, N.: A human-work interaction design approach by modeling the user's work styles (2005)

96. Campos, P., Nunes, N.: Principles and practice of work style modeling: sketching design tools (2006)

97. Chino, T., Torii, K., Uchihira, N., Hirabayashi, Y.: Work and speech interactions among staff at an elderly care facility (2012)

98. Chino, T., Torii, K., Uchihira, N., Hirabayashi, Y.: Supporting human collaborative works by monitoring everyday conversations (2013)

99. Druzhinina, O.R., Hvannberg, E.: Feedback in a training simulator for crisis management: information from a real life exercise (2012)

100. Gonçalves, F., Campos, P.: Towards pervasive and inspiring workplaces for creative writers: simple interactions for a complex domain (2014)

101. Ianeva, M., et al.: Pervasive technologies for smart workplaces: a workplace efficiency solution for office design and building management from an occupier's perspective. In: Abdelnour Nocera, J., Barricelli, B. R., Lopes, A., Campos, P., Clemmensen, T. (eds.) HWID 2015. IAICT, vol. 468, pp. 73–82. Springer, Cham (2015). https://doi.org/10.1007/978-3-319-27048-7_5

102. Jansson, A., Olsson, E., Erlandsson, M.: Bridging the gap between analysis and design: improving existing driver interfaces with tools from the framework of cognitive work analysis (2007)

103. Lind, T., Cajander, A.: Mind the gap - towards a framework for analysing the deployment of IT systems from a sociotechnical perspective (2013)

104. Lopes, A.: The work and workplace analysis in social solidarity institutions to address organization agility and innovation (2015)

105. Sandblad, B.: Using a vision seminar process to evaluate the work environment of future work (2013)

106. Väätäjä, H.: Characterizing the context of use in mobile work. In: Abdelnour Nocera, J., Barricelli, B. R., Lopes, A., Campos, P., Clemmensen, T. (eds.) HWID 2015. IAICT, vol. 468, pp. 97–113. Springer, Cham (2015). https://doi.org/10.1007/978-3-319-27048-7_7

107. Valtonen, T., Kalakoski, V., Paajanen, T.: Using well-being data to support work design (2014)

108. Vandenberghe, B., Geerts, D.: Out in the cold, the loneliness of working with doctors and patients (2015)

109. Velhinho, L., Lopes, A.: IT frameworks: are they useful or not? (2012)

110. Cabrero, D., Winschiers-Theophilus, H., Mendonca, H.: User-created personas - a micro-cultural magnifier revealing smart workplaces in thriving Katutura (2015)

111. Camara, S., Oyugi, C., Abdelnour-Nocera, J., Smith, A.: Augmenting usability: cultural elicitation in HCI. In: Katre, D., Orngreen, R., Yammiyavar, P., Clemmensen, T. (eds.) HWID 2009. IAICT, vol. 316, pp. 46–56. Springer, Heidelberg (2010). https://doi.org/10.1007/978-3-642-11762-6_4

112. Clemmensen, T.: The Cultural Usability (CULTUSAB) (2007)

113. Clemmensen, T.: A comparison of what is part of usability testing in three countries. In: Katre, D., Orngreen, R., Yammiyavar, P., Clemmensen, T. (eds.) Human Work Interaction Design: Usability in Social, Cultural and Organizational Contexts. HWID 2009. IFIP Advances in Information and Communication Technology, vol. 316. Springer, Heidelberg. (2009). https://doi.org/10.1007/978-3-642-11762-6_3

114. Coutinho, A., Ferreira, P.: Promoting culture sensitive education through a common sense based games (2007)
115. Dalvi, G.: Development of an intuitive user-centric font selection menu. In: Katre, D., Orngreen, R., Yammiyavar, P., Clemmensen, T. (eds.) HWID 2009. IAICT, vol. 316, pp. 144–153. Springer, Heidelberg (2010). https://doi.org/10.1007/978-3-642-11762-6_12
116. Deshpande, S., Mayank, K.: Cultural factors influencing elements of interface design for indian youth: study and guidelines (2009)
117. Duvaa, U., Ørngreen, R., Mathiasen, Anne-Gitte Weinkouff., Blomhøj, U.: Mobile probing and probes. In: Campos, P., Clemmensen, T., Nocera, J. A., Katre, D., Lopes, A., Ørngreen, R. (eds.) HWID 2012. IAICT, vol. 407, pp. 161–174. Springer, Heidelberg (2013). https://doi.org/10.1007/978-3-642-41145-8_14
118. Gruneberg, M., Yamaoka, Y., Huang, H.: Creating a standardized corpus of multimodal interactions for enculturating conversational interfaces (2008)
119. Khambete, P., Tripathi, S., Athvankar, U.: Sustained service provider–customer relationships in the indian context: factors influencing the choice of touch points (2009)
120. Kheterpal, S., Baral, B.: Culture-cognition connection and its relevance for designing web-based educational products in Indian context (2009)
121. Kurosu, M.: Usability and culture as two of the value criteria for evaluating the Artifact Development Analysis (ADA). In: Katre, D., Orngreen, R., Yammiyavar, P., Clemmensen, T. (eds.) HWID 2009. IAICT, vol. 316, pp. 67–75. Springer, Heidelberg (2010). https://doi.org/10.1007/978-3-642-11762-6_6
122. Madsen, S., Nielsen, L.: Exploring persona-scenarios - using storytelling to create design ideas. In: Katre, D., Orngreen, R., Yammiyavar, P., Clemmensen, T. (eds.) HWID 2009. IAICT, vol. 316, pp. 57–66. Springer, Heidelberg (2010). https://doi.org/10.1007/978-3-642-11762-6_5
123. Nielsen, L.: Different Cultures' Perception of Personas Descriptions (2008)
124. Nielsen, L.: Personas in Cross-Cultural Projects. In: Katre, D., Orngreen, R., Yammiyavar, P., Clemmensen, T. (eds.) HWID 2009. IAICT, vol. 316, pp. 76–82. Springer, Heidelberg (2010). https://doi.org/10.1007/978-3-642-11762-6_7
125. Nielsen, J., Yssing, C., Levinsen, K., Clemmensen, T., Ørngreen, R., Nielsen, L.: Embedding complementarity in HCI methods and techniques — designing for the "cultural other." In: Clemmensen, T., Campos, P., Orngreen, R., Pejtersen, A. M., Wong, W. (eds.) HWID 2006. IIFIP, vol. 221, pp. 93–102. Springer, Boston, MA (2006). https://doi.org/10.1007/978-0-387-36792-7_5
126. Clemmensen, T., Roese, K.: An Overview of 1998–2008 journal publications about culture and human-computer interaction (HCI). In: Katre, D., Orngreen, R., Yammiyavar, P., Clemmensen, T. (eds.) HWID 2009. IAICT, vol. 316, pp. 98–112. Springer, Heidelberg (2010). https://doi.org/10.1007/978-3-642-11762-6_9
127. Sahasrabudhe, S., Bhatt, P.: Moment of Truth (MoT) – a deeper insight into user's culture (2009)
128. Shi, Q.: A study of usability problem finding in cross-cultural thinking aloud usability tests (2008)
129. Vatrapu, R.: Cultural usability in computer supported collaboration (2008)
130. Yammiyavar, P., Clemmensen, T.: Extracting users' data: towards development of a cultural and semantically sensitive combinatorial methodology (2008)
131. Abramov, V., Roto, V.: Accounting for intermediate parties in experience-driven product design for business-to-business environment (2012)
132. Bhutkar, G., Katre, D., Ray, G. G., Deshmukh, S.: Usability model for medical user interface of ventilator system in intensive care unit. In: Campos, P., Clemmensen, T., Nocera, J. A., Katre, D., Lopes, A., Ørngreen, R. (eds.) HWID 2012. IAICT, vol. 407, pp. 46–64. Springer, Heidelberg (2013). https://doi.org/10.1007/978-3-642-41145-8_5

133. Björndal, P., Eriksson, E., Artman, H.: From transactions to relationships: making sense of user-centered perspectives in large technology-intensive companies. In: Abdelnour Nocera, J., Barricelli, B. R., Lopes, A., Campos, P., Clemmensen, T. (eds.) HWID 2015. IAICT, vol. 468, pp. 114–124. Springer, Cham (2015). https://doi.org/10.1007/978-3-319-27048-7_8

134. Clemmensen, T., Barlow, S.: Identifying user experience goals for interactive climate management business systems (2013)

135. Clemmensen, T., Yadav, M.: Multiple data stream measurement of UX in a work context (2014)

136. Figueiredo, F., Martins, C., Pocinho, T.: Promoting usability in large enterprises (2009)

137. Fuchsberger, V., Murer, M., Meneweger, T., Tscheligi, M.: Capturing the in-between of interactive artifacts and users: a materiality-centered approach (2014)

138. Iyengar, J., Belvalkar, M.: Case study of online banking in india: user behaviors and design guidelines. In: Katre, D., Orngreen, R., Yammiyavar, P., Clemmensen, T. (eds.) HWID 2009. IAICT, vol. 316, pp. 180–188. Springer, Heidelberg (2010). https://doi.org/10.1007/978-3-642-11762-6_15

139. Jaafarnia, M., Yammiyavar, P.: Graphic interfaces for sales interaction : a case of a consumer choosing colour for a product (2009)

140. Jain, P., Yammiyavar, P.: Usability issues in developing an intra office communication system (2009)

141. Jenvald, J., Morin, M., Eriksson, H.: Challenges for user interfaces in VR-supported command team training (2010)

142. Johansson, N., Sandblad, B.: VIHO - efficient IT support in home care services (2006)

143. Katre, D.: One-handed thumb use on smart phones by semi-literate and illiterate users in India: a usability report with design improvements for precision and ease (2008)

144. Meerbeek, B., Van Loenen, E.: Understanding user experience of smart workplaces: mixed methods (2014)

145. Quercioli, S., Amaldi, P.: A grounded theory study of perspectives on automation amongst aviation industry stakeholders (2015)

146. Raman, A.: SMART user experience framework 1.0 making information technology products & services better for users (2009)

147. Scandurra, I., Ahfeldt, R.-M., Persson, A., Hagglund, M.: Challenges in applying a participatory approach in a nation-wide project -the case of 'usability of Swedish eHealth systems (2013)

148. Vasal, I., Gangopadhyay, D., Yammiyavar, P.: A comparative study of handwriting based solutions using keypad for Hindi text entry (2009)

149. Wiles, A., Roberts, S., Abdelnour-Nocera, J.: Library usability in higher education: how user experience can form library policy. In: Campos, P., Clemmensen, T., Nocera, J. A., Katre, D., Lopes, A., Ørngreen, R. (eds.) HWID 2012. IAICT, vol. 407, pp. 139–149. Springer, Heidelberg (2013). https://doi.org/10.1007/978-3-642-41145-8_12

150. Yammiyavar, P.: Status of HCI and usability research in indian educational institutions. In: Katre, D., Orngreen, R., Yammiyavar, P., Clemmensen, T. (eds.) HWID 2009. IAICT, vol. 316, pp. 21–27. Springer, Heidelberg (2010). https://doi.org/10.1007/978-3-642-11762-6_2

151. Adderley, S.: Assessing stress in immersive training environments (2010)

152. Barnett, J., Wong, B.W., Coulson, M.: Situation awareness and sensemaking in crisis management: similarities between real world and online co-operative environments (2010)

153. Hansen, K.B., Boe, K.: Behavior based training improves safety through online simulation environments (2010)

154. Jansson, A., Erlandsson, M., Fröjd, C., Arvidsson, M.: Collegial collaboration for safety: assessing situation awareness by exploring cognitive strategies (2013)

155. Pinchuk, R.: Semantically enabled after action review (2010)

156. Proença, R., Guerra, A.: Natural interactions: an application for gestural hands recognition. In: Campos, P., Clemmensen, T., Nocera, J. A., Katre, D., Lopes, A., Ørngreen, R. (eds.) HWID 2012. IAICT, vol. 407, pp. 98–111. Springer, Heidelberg (2013). https://doi.org/10.1007/978-3-642-41145-8_9

157. Rankin, A., Kovordanyi, R., Eriksson, H.: Episode analysis for evaluating response operations and identifying training needs (2010)

158. Rankin, A., Kovordanyi, R., Eriksson, H.: Foresight training as part of virtual-reality-based exercises for the emergency services (2010)

159. Righi, V., Sayago, S., Ferreira, S., Malón, G., Blat, J.: Fostering an active participation of older people in local communities: preliminary results of an ethnographical study (2011)

160. Rooney, C., Passmore, P., Wong, W.: CRISIS research priorities for a state-of-the-art training (2010)

161. Rudinsky, J., Hvannberg, E.T.: Voice communication in online virtual environments for crisis management training (2010)

162. Schreder, G., Siebenhandl, K., Mayr, E., Smuc, M., Nagl, M.: Narrative interaction as means for intuitive public information systems (2011)

163. Serra, J., Leitão, J., Alves, P., Lopes, A.: How to improve the interaction quality of psychologists and patients: a mediated interface (2014)

164. Shepherd, I.D.H.: Get real - the many faces of realism in virtual training environments (2010)

165. Callon, M., Courtial, J., Laville, F.: Co-word analysis as a tool for describing the network of interactions between basic and technological research: the case of polymer chemistry. Scientometrics, 155–205 (1991)

166. He, Q.: Knowledge discovery trhough co-word analyis. Libr. Trends **48**(1), 133–159 (1999)

"Organized UX Professionalism" – An Empirical Study and Conceptual Tool for Scrutinizing UX Work of the Future

Torkil Clemmensen[1]([⊠]) [iD], Netta Iivari[2] [iD], Dorina Rajanen[2] [iD], and Ashok Sivaji[3]

[1] Copenhagen Business School, Copenhagen, Denmark
Tc.digi@cbs.dk
[2] University of Oulu, Oulu, Finland
{netta.iivari,dorina.rajanen}@oulu.fi
[3] MIMOS Technology Solutions, Kuala Lumpur, Malaysia
ashok.sivaji@mimos.my

Abstract. This paper proposes the notion of 'Organized User Experience (UX) Professionalism' to describe the nature of the UX work in organizations and support the development of the UX profession. The conceptual model of Organized UX Professionalism is observed in practice and evaluated using data from a survey of 422 UX professionals in five countries. The model recognizes that the UX profession and work are guided not only by the principles of user experience and usability, but also by organization and management issues. The empirical evidence shows that indeed Organized UX Professionalism consists of a management-minded work orientation, innovative tool use, highly social best practices, organizational user centeredness, community participation, and the maturity of the UX and usability concepts in the local society. The study also shows that UX professionals largely adopt system-oriented definitions of usability and UX, rather than changing their conceptions towards organizational and human-oriented definitions. We discuss implications of the findings and possible actions of returning to 'certified usability professionalism' versus 'going beyond the idea of the UX professionalism' towards organization specific UX only. From the human work interaction design perspective, we believe that the notion of Organized UX Professionalism helps conceptualize, measure, develop, and manage the work of UX professionals in different social contexts as well as understand the outcomes and role of this work in the organization. Further, we propose a few concrete research directions to continue this research.

Keywords: Organized UX Professionalism · User experience practice · Usability practice · HCI community · UX tools · HCI theory

1 Introduction

The notion of user experience (UX) has been central in the information systems (IS) and human-computer interaction (HCI) research communities for studying usability and the hedonic qualities of user interaction with computers [121, 122]. The notion of UX has spawned an entire profession of people who research, design, and evaluate the UX of products and services. This paper focuses on characterizing the nature of work of the UX professionals who generally can find support in their professional development from the User Experience Professional Association (UXPA) International (https://uxpa.org). UX professionals provide professional services within the information technology (IT) field in the same way as doctors, nurses, lawyers, accountants, and teachers provide services in the fields of health care, law, accounting, and education, respectively. They are a significant professional group contributing to positive work experiences at workplaces as their work aims at ensuring pleasurable user experiences for digital tools employees use at work. Recently, intelligent technologies have transformed work in significant ways; for instance, Artificial Intelligence (AI), robotics and IoT (Internet of Things) based tools have entered the workplaces with significant implications on both work and work well-being (e.g., [14]). UX professionals are ever more needed for ensuring positive work experiences for people, which has already been acknowledged by the HCI research community (e.g., [43, 123]).

In this paper, we conceptualize the nature of the UX profession and provide evidence towards understanding the integration of UX professionals and their work into organizations. We propose the notion of 'Organized UX Professionalism' to describe the nature of UX work and the further development of the UX work in terms of the integration of UX work into organization. Studies concerning the UX professional practice have shown that this is an emerging profession displaying the features of traditional professionalism [5, 32, 35, 54, 76], while with unique and different attitudes, knowledge, experience, and perspectives compared to other IT professionals [35, 91]. Academic controversies about what UX profession is and how it can be fit into the development processes of an organization have a long history in HCI and IS research (e.g., [6, 29, 83, 116]). This paper draws on the literature in both IS and HCI fields and organizational science to achieve a rich understanding of the phenomenon of UX professionals and associated professionalism within organizations.

Professionalism itself, however, has become controversial in recent years due to the complexity of problems facing organizations in the age of globalism and digitalization with the new requirements of delivering services everywhere and constant development of digital means [86]. The UX profession in specific and the IT profession in general are no exceptions [71]. Compared to non-IT professions, the IT profession may even be at higher risk of obsolescence due to the fast developments in IT-specific knowledge and skills required by organizations [71].

From an organizational point of view, it is not clear that it is important to employ UX professionals with a traditional, strong sense of professionalism. An organization's strategy for development and innovation may mediate UX work practices, and even the competence [44] and qualifications [32] of individual UX professionals. A good example is the current trend of 'Agile UX', where UX professionals are often not allowed to have face-to-face contact with customers and end-users for user testing (the hallmark of the UX profession), and instead are encouraged to work as expert advisers and consultants [26]. More broadly, the next step in organizational development strategies may be to apply advanced participatory design practices that appeal to paying customers, by delivering techniques to IT professionals to safeguard user interests through achieving consensus with users about design decisions [74].

Examining professionalism in the IT workforce and how it impacts UX professionals' integration into organizations further reveals the importance of professionalism. A high degree of IT professionalism contributes to traditional workforce parameters in organizations, such as turnover/retention, job performance, job satisfaction, and motivation [40]. Hence, UX Professionalism is something that an employer should strive to identify, retain, and cultivate, as the right combinations of required skills, knowledge, and mindset may not be visible in the entry level professional, emerging only with years of work experience [31].

A balanced view of the relationship between professionalism and an organization can be achieved by recognizing and developing additional competences to ensure integration of the emerging UX profession - as a profession in its own right - into organizations. A UX professional needs both technical and business competence with the latter referring to both organization-specific and general interpersonal and management skills [12]. Furthermore, the integration of UX professionals into organizations may also be approached as a matter of team performance within major organizational endeavors [6]; for example, encouraging UX professionals to become good team members of an agile development team.

On a societal level, factors influencing UX professionals' integration into organizations may also need clarification. Professionals' identification with their national professional community may have ambiguous effects on their integration into the organization in which they are employed; for example, if someone develops a strong professional identity rather than a strong bond with their organization, they may be relatively more prone to search for another job outside this organization [40]. Furthermore, the relationship between academic researchers and educators on one hand and practicing professionals on the other may be diminutive when measured by several face-to-face meetings at professional events and in terms of the membership of the same professional communities [46]. Finally, national differences in the cultural background of UX professionals can moderate the factors shaping UX professionals' integration into organizations [60].

As in the case of professionalism in general [86], the current knowledge about UX Professionalism is characterized by controversy, with some researchers arguing for a 'return to the professional' original values and knowledge, while others calling for a move toward 'beyond professionalism' to prioritize the goals, methods, and procedures of organizations that employ professionals [86]. Both stances are unsatisfactory, and a better solution may be to further develop the idea of both technical and business competences [12]. We argue that relevant stakeholders should aim to establish new forms of 'organized professionalism' with "professional practices that embody organizational logics" [86]. In concrete terms, this means that organizational roles and processes are adopted by professionals in order to provide organizational capacities and resources to perform work-related tasks and comply with requirements. This notion of organized professionalism can be transferred into the HCI domain through a discussion of issues related to team managing roles and lead design roles, and how to adopt theories, methods, techniques and tools to help UX professionals be effective and efficient when performing organizational and work-related tasks, as well as engaging in communication with different stakeholders, including users, colleagues, and upper management. Furthermore, higher-level societal issues such as professional associations and government policies should be considered as they potentially affect the matter. The impact of clarifying the notion of 'Organized UX Professionalism' may potentially be substantial for not only professionals and organizations but also governments. Thus, in this study, our aim was to help clarify what should and should not be done to improve UX professional services. For this purpose, we asked the question, "What is Organized UX Professionalism?".

The paper is structured as follows. Section 1.1 elaborates further the motivation of the study and its relevance to the human-work interaction design (HWID) research area. Section 2 presents related work concerned with studying the UX profession and its integration in organizations. Section 3 defines the concept of 'Organized UX professionalism' and the research model. Section 4 and 5 describe the research method and the empirical evidence for studying and illustrating the model in practice. Section 6 and 7 discuss the findings, implications and propose research directions.

1.1 The Relevance of Organized UX Professionalism to Human Work Interaction Design

This paper addresses what kind of UX professionalism is needed to carry out Human Work Interaction Design (HWID)[1] [11, 36]. HWID is a socio-technical HCI approach that aims to link empirical studies of human work and organizations with IT interaction designs in local contexts. The HWID social analysis may cover organizational and work analysis of workers' experience of and actions towards task, procedures, workspace/place, and work domains, including society level analysis. The HWID technical analysis concerns interaction designs activities (persona, scenario, sketching, prototyping, think aloud usability evaluation, etc.) can be in focus. The relations between the social and the technical, e.g., 'facilitating between users and designers', are created in HWID by designing 'relation artefacts' that are local interventions into work and IT. An important type of these relation artefacts are the alignments of the technical designs with organizational strategies [34]. In particular, the integration of usability work 'culture' into the culture of the organization [63] calls for Organized UX Professionals.

We point out that for HWID in practice, UX professionals are to be considered central actors: they possess valuable type of expertise for HWID. UX professionals doing HWID should be able and willing to engage in work and organizational analysis. Moreover, we underline that evaluations and interventions with prototypes in organizational settings require UX professionals to engage with management in organizational strategy alignments. The new HWID prototypes should fit with the organization's long-term strategy if those are to be used. Thus, a factor for successful organizations is the close linkage of IT and business strategy [7]. This is also true for HWID and business strategy. Following the idea of strategy as practice [68], that is, how management practices are used to put strategy into practice, practices of interaction design for human work may

---

[1] http://ifip-tc13.org/working-groups/working-group-13-6/.

at some point be morphed into organizational strategies by aligning the organizational UX culture with the business and organizational goals.

What activities do UX professionals engage in to ensure they are in the room when important business decisions about product direction and business strategy are made have been raised by UX leaders from industry and by researchers [45, 75]. This is a significant consideration for HWID, too. The answer appears to be that UX leaders are concerned with not only aligning UX strategy with the organizational strategy but also with broader questions of developing and managing a UX culture in the organization. They see UX strategy at the corporate level as being about the UX team being aligned with the overall goals and objectives of the business. They aim to shape the strategic plans, operational needs, and interdependencies between their own organization and the rest of the company, to and to increase UX team's effectiveness and synergies with other business functions. They see UX strategy at the level of a business unit as being about plans for delivering products, systems, or services that offers a high value to customers, and differentiates the company's brand. However, this requires multiple parts of the organizations to be involved [75]. Thus, UX strategy alignment has to be done within a UX organizational culture that can support the strategy and make it realistic and ensure it has an impact on company outcomes [45].

Thus, organizing and managing are increasingly considered as issues for UX professionals to deal with, and the culture of UX is changing towards this. Studying 'Organized UX Professionalism' may help reveal the unique UX culture dimensions important to all aspects of HWID. Both from academic research and industrial practice perspectives, aligning interaction design practices with organizational and work strategies is an important type of intervention.

2   Related Work

Practices and organization related to the UX profession have been explored by HCI researchers from their particular disciplinary perspectives in multiple studies. This section discusses these studies through the insights provided by general research on professionalism.

2.1 Organizations and UX

Organization and management aspects have been addressed in relation to UX professionals for a long time. The interest in this area has further increased in recent years. HCI researchers reconsider key notions of HCI, such as usability and user experience in terms of their use in organizational departments and by management [75]. The management of local and global UX teams is higher on the agenda at key HCI conferences and publications than ever before [67, 73, 97, 106, 113]. New organizational topics, such as procurement and usability, have emerged [77], and new perspectives; for example, entrepreneurial UX mindsets have been proposed [110]. Within the HCI education research, attention has been directed toward questions such as whether the objectives and achievements of the HCI curriculum prepare students to address the new gaps in the job market and how to meet the increasing demand for a diversity of UX professionals [4, 49, 109].

Despite much research on UX professional services, it is still not clear what UX Professionalism is. According to research on professionalism in general, the issues of the type of work, organizational context, and external changes reinforce unfruitful conceptual and practical dualisms in professions [86]. Traditional distinctions, such as 'occupations versus organizations' and 'managers versus professionals' keep coming back to the discussion in attempts to understand the phenomenon [86]. Such dualisms are also observed in HCI research on UX professionals. In the next two sub-sections, we will further address the distinctions between 'occupations versus organizations' and 'managers versus professionals' within the HCI field.

2.2 UX Occupation and UX Organizations

HCI research on UX occupation has contributed to deepening our knowledge about how UX professional work can be institutionalized in a country and the education and development of UX professionals. A 'living' HCI curriculum takes into account local conditions across the world [1, 109]. The importance warranted to HCI in the curriculum perhaps reflects the priority given by practice; for example, Sari and Wadhwa [102] reported that the development of the UX profession was not seen as a priority in developing countries. Similarly, Ogunyemi, Lamas, Adagunodo, and da Rosa [88], referring to the situation in Nigeria, stated that the country had evolved quickly into the information age, but the level of HCI practices was not yet known. The authors conducted a survey and found that the industry knowledge about the existence of the UX profession was limited, with none of the companies in the study employing a UX professional and that the Nigerian market environment seemed to be driving Nigerian software companies toward adopting HCI practices [88].

For decades, HCI research has proposed frameworks and theories for institutionalizing UX professional work practices in various parts of the world [27, 53, 58, 108]. For example, frameworks have been proposed to adapt UX practices developed in the US or EU to the local culture in India or China, embed these practices in local national organizations, and roll-out the new localized UX practices locally [108]. Today, the UX occupation (though not necessarily the profession) may be more widely institutionalized than ever before; a recent global survey with 758 practitioners and researchers found that the respondents believed that UX was not a new concept and that it covered existing engineering approaches based on user-centered design and usability [76]. For instance, frameworks widely adopted by HCI research and practitioners such as System Usability Scale (SUS) [9, 22] have been widely used and found to be reliable and technology independent for almost any engineering/IT solutions.

HCI research on UX organization; that is, an organization that has clear and explicit policies about UX in its development, has taught us about organizational structures and dynamics of an UX organization and how UX professional services are coordinated and standardized. Organizations have for long had a wish for standardized UX concepts and services [85], which appear to be easy and simple to procure. The notion of a "certified usability professional"; i.e., a UX practitioner who has gone through a specific process to prove her/his knowledge of usability, keeps popping as a hot topic [85, 120]. In this regard, it is unfortunate that although there is widespread consensus about the ISO definitions of usability [92], there is less so about the newer concept of UX [76, 92]. Furthermore, historically, the standard notion of usability as an individual's effectiveness and efficiency has been challenged by attempts to define usability as organizational usability [72], and more recently, a diversity of concepts of usability have appeared [37, 59, 75] despite its international standardization [65].

With regard to organizational structures and dynamics of a UX organization, a tutorial that ran for years at HCI conferences taught the effective implementation of 'Corporate User Experience Teams' in the areas of conflict between top management, marketing, sales, IT, customer service, and product development, considering these teams as "the users' lawyers" in technology design [58]. However, at the time, most organizations were still far from setting up UX teams in everyday organizational life [58].

2.3 UX Professionals and UX Managers

There is plenty of HCI research on UX professionals and UX managers. HCI research on UX professionals revealed the nuances between various kinds of UX professionals that were emerging and how UX professionals differed from other IT professionals. It is a repeated finding from surveys that there are sub-groups of UX professionals, ranging on a continuum from the UX researcher, who aims to understand users, to UX designer, who aims to improve their experience [4, 30]. This gap in the views and practices of UX professionals and software developers appear to be a constant interest of research [20, 69]. In some developing countries, UX professional job titles are hardly used at all, with professionals in this job area referring to themselves as 'software engineers', 'graphic designers', or 'executives of multimedia and infrastructure' [62]. Lárusdóttir, Cajander and Gulliksen [78] found differences between various roles of IT professionals (scrum managers, team members, usability specialists, and business specialists) when conducting user-centered evaluations and noted that business specialists tended to depend more on asking users for their opinions compared to other professionals.

HCI research on UX management has also provided insights into the rise of the category of UX managers, how they work, and what their educational backgrounds and competences may be. Issues that have emerged are related to questions such as "Where does UX stand in the organization?", "How do you define and explain UX to the team in a new product development?", "How do customers understand and react to their invoice including a fee for UX?", "In which stages or phases in the product life cycles/development are UX people involved?", "What is the perfect UX development team in terms of skills and size?", and "How to manage the perfect UX team?" These and other related issues have been repeatedly investigated in the HCI field [67, 113] both in case studies of specific UX management practices in large UX tech companies [113] and in panel debates about 'managing global UX teams' [67]. A recent survey by Lallemand et al. [76] did not address the job title or job content, but reported the role and business domain of 758 self-selected UX professional respondents as falling into five subgroups: researcher 17%, consultant 26%, manager 11%, practitioner 37%, and student 10%. Hence, among UX professionals, a considerable subgroup works in management positions. Furthermore, the word 'senior' in the job title may explicitly be used to specify the authority position in organizational hierarchy related to the design or development processes [62]. Hussein, Mahmud, Tap, and Jack [61] found indications that having senior developers with little UX knowledge inhibited the impact of UX professionals, that is, they identified a need for more UX professionals to take up positions as managers. Austin [4] examined the cognitive profiles of UX professionals from small- to medium-sized enterprises and found that they tended to be somewhat more intuitive than analytical in their thinking style compared to management professionals, which Austin linked to the nature of the UX professionals' work (design) tasks.

2.4 Integration of UX Professionals and their Work in Organizations

The distinction between business/organizational UX and professional/specialist UX is becoming blurred and unclear in practice as UX professionals take up organizing and management roles. However, HCI research may implicitly maintain a fundamental opposition between UX professional work and organizational contexts through separate research communities: AIS HCI (Association for Information Systems) that focusses on HCI in business contexts and ACM HCI (Association for Computing Machinery) that focusses on general human-technology interaction [41]; while another important international HCI community with a perhaps broader profile is the IFIP HCI (International Federation for Information Processing). In business-oriented AIS HCI, 80% of the research focuses on HCI in the context of the work/organization and marketplace [81], compared to the surge of interest in non-work contexts in the so-called third wave [15, 16] in computer- and design-oriented ACM HCI. Furthermore, in business-oriented AIS HCI, most of the studies address the use of IT artefacts (80% of studies), rather than the design and construction of new artefacts (20%) [81] which are the central research foci in ACM HCI.

As for the integration of UX in organizations, it has been highlighted for some time that there is a need for ways to rethink the user-centric approach throughout the organization in order to embed it in business strategies [112]. UX professionals should have or develop an entrepreneurial mindset [110]. Familiarity with UX work and UX professionals in upper management should be supported and further investigated, which can be supported through cost-benefit analysis models to communicate usability work to upper management [93]. Besides the challenges of integrating the UX profession into traditional organizations, there are also issues specific to the emerging types of organizations and development processes and practices, such as open-source development, distributed and virtual global teams, and agile computing [6]. For example, Bach and Carroll [6] analyzed the socio-technical complexities of integrating UX activities into open-source projects and found that UX professionals applied different UX strategies of disseminating UX knowledge, rather than asking for UX feedback, to manage UX awareness in open source communities.

In brief, similarly to research in other professions [87], HCI research on the UX professional tend to enact several splits in perspectives: 1) between research in the classic UX professional specialist role versus the more recent UX professional managerial role, and 2) between the occupation of a UX professional versus the UX-oriented organization. These splits in perspectives may make it tempting to propose too simple solutions of either focusing on the UX specialist (return to professionalism) or focusing on the manager and other stakeholders with more or less sympathy for UX (going beyond professionalism). At the same time, various studies on the UX professional presented above seem to highlight the dynamics of UX professional services and reinterpret the meaning and boundaries of the UX occupation. The research indicates how the UX professional role is only emerging in some developing countries, such as Malaysia while being incorporated into design thinking in other contexts, how standards of usability and UX are continuously challenged, and how UX professional are gradually moving into management positions. As the UX professional becomes integrated into the organizational setting, it becomes harder to maintain an isolated research focus only on their specific skills and knowledge about usability evaluation methods. Organization and management must increasingly be approached as issues to be addressed in relation to the UX profession.

3   Research Model

In this section, we propose a descriptive research model to define Organized UX Professionalism. At the center of this model stands the integration of UX work into organizations. Such integration is shaped by the perception of UX professionals concerning their own expertise and work integration in the organization and system development process. Other stakeholders, such as managers, designers, developers, marketing, and customers may also have various perceptions and experiences about the degree to which UX is known within and integrated in the organization. Thus, we propose that the notion of Organized UX Professionalism is described by the extent to which the UX work and expertise are integrated in the organization. This integration can be observed and measured in various ways such as self-perception by UX professionals and perception by other professional roles. The conceptual model of Organized UX Professionals consists of seven factors shown in Fig. 1, namely: basic understanding of UX, management-minded work orientation, innovative tool use, professionals' best practices, organizational user centeredness, community participation, and maturity of UX in the country. The seven factors of Organized UX Professionalism are described in the propositions P1–P7 below.

P1. UX professionals' management-minded understanding of usability and UX as well as their use of broad range of UX theories and methods is associated with Organized UX Professionalism. We maintain that Organized UX Professionalism entails UX professionals becoming more management-minded. This includes them approaching usability as 'organizational usability', rather than adhering to the classic usability definition, as well as defining UX in a 'human-oriented' manner. We also consider the use of different theoretical approaches and UX methods indicating management minded innovation in UX, enabling tailoring the activities to specific needs of the situation at hand and reorganizing their work to become more effective. However, we also acknowledge there may be challenges in this respect: UX professionals may live by their privileged and basic understanding of classic usability and UX, which they may not want to change. The UX professionals may also be resistant to change, and they may not easily become management-minded [86].

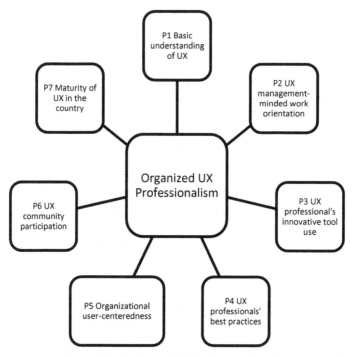

Fig. 1. Seven-factor model of Organized UX Professionalism (Propositions P1–P7).

P2. Having UX professionals higher up in the organizational hierarchy due to their many years of experience in UX work is associated with Organized UX Professionalism. We maintain that management mindedness of UX professionals may include them occupying actual management positions (i.e., with profit responsibility). Along these lines, a UX professional moving up in the organizational hierarchy may contribute through creation of familiarity with UX within the organization, especially so if UX or usability is maintained in the new job title. We also interpret the management-mindedness to relate to the number of years of work experience as a UX professional. On the other hand, we acknowledge that young professionals may have a different sense of professional 'calling' and less 'fixed' occupational identities compared to the past [86] and young UX professionals may respond to the call for becoming entrepreneurs [110] and start managing their own business, or if working within a large organization, they may see themselves in opposition to senior management.

P3: Use of novel UX tools is associated with Organized UX Professionalism. Professionals must organize their work efficiently to offer valuable services on time. Especially when such services are delivered by large organizations, professional work needs to be structured, while in fast digitalizing society adaptability and flexibility are also significant. Hence, UX professionals should continually seek new ways of creating and structuring their services. One important example of this is tool innovation, which includes adoption of new UX tools) for improved quality of user feedback [107], remote testing, and low and high-fidelity prototyping, as well as integration with Artificial Intelligence

(AI), robotics and IoT (Internet of Things). The development of UX work should, thus, be driven by novelty and innovation.

P4: Having highly social and multidisciplinary UX practices is associated with Organized UX Professionalism. UX professionals' work practice development entails also other issues than tool innovation. According to the theory of organized professionalism [86] in other professions, having highly social best practices indicates a change in professionalism toward organizational and management contexts. Recent developments in UX point to the direction of end-users/clients increasingly performing activities previously performed by a specialist, such as a UX professional. For example, it is becoming very easy for a client to video-record users having problems when interacting with systems without the requirement of an equipped, dedicated usability laboratory. This technological development means that it becomes easier to have one-to-one relations between professionals and clients, and related development in new digital business models means that the use of multi-agency partnerships and other forms of collaboration increase. Clients are thus empowered, and UX professionals must cooperate with them to provide effective services. The new kind of Organized UX Professionalism involves follow-up work on usability evaluations, use of professional agencies to recruit users, industry level large number of test users rather than the classic 'discount usability's' one to five test users, more iterations of usability tests, and face-to-face contact with real end-users, which leads to multi-disciplinary interactions with higher complexity. HCI educators already point to the increased complexities in networks and configurations involved in UX activities and seek innovative configurations between students, scholars, UX professionals, and other industry practitioners to collaborate on new learning models that can help teach new generations of UX professionals to adapt, learn, and embrace technological innovation [48, 49]. Overall, our fourth proposition predicts a positive relationship between Organized UX Professionalism and increasingly social and multidisciplinary practices of UX professionals.

P5: More user-centeredness across the organization is associated with Organized UX Professionalism. Organizational user-centeredness partly refers to the changing collective composition of the professional workforce. Some IT professional fields, such as UX, have always been known for their human-centeredness while others, including software engineering and programming are technology-dominated but are currently receiving an influx of user-oriented students and employers [78]. With this change in the workforce come proposals to rethink user-centered methods. Thus, for example, some propose that agile system development methodologies are user-centered and will automatically develop usable systems [78]. These agile-oriented software developers can, therefore, contribute to an organization's UX-oriented work force. An organization with software development certifications (e.g., in rapid and agile development methods), more years of experience in UX work, and a higher number of UX professionals working in teams shows signs of having Organized UX Professionalism in the sense of changing the collective composition of the professional workforce.

P6: Active participation in local and global UX professional communities is associated with Organized UX Professionalism. Local and global professional associations aim to organize their members and support their professional development. To achieve this, they coordinate, arrange, hold events, and disseminate information. UX professionals are not unfamiliar to such associations; in particular, UXPA (User Experience Professionals Association) and ACM SIGCHI (Special Interest Group on Computer–Human Interaction) each organize and support thousands of UX professionals around the world. More HCI communities are emerging throughout the world, with the most recent examples appearing in countries in Africa [89]. With Organized UX Professionalism come new organizational arrangements, such as multi-disciplinary and multi-agency teams and partnerships, inter-professional collaboration, multi-disciplinary practices, and integrated services. Participating in community events may, thus, be a sign of this new approach to UX professionalism.

P7: The maturity and awareness of usability and UX in a country and by its government is associated with Organized UX Professionalism. Organized UX Professionals that meet new service realities at clients, companies, and in society, need to collaborate not only with each other in their UX community but also with professionals and managers from other fields in order to generate acceptance and ensure high quality of their services. This requires the development of laws, regulations, and standards, which enable UX professionals to link their professional practices to a mature understanding of the UX field at a broader society level. The maturity and awareness of usability and user experience in societies worldwide are indicated by the state of global usability and UX. The awareness of usability as a design issue and a professional area of research and education was developed in North America and Europe since the 1980s and is now spread across the world. However, it was only after the 2000s that usability and UX emerged as a global concern [42], and there is still variation between countries; for example, at the time of writing this paper, usability awareness was limited in the local IT industry of Pakistan [3]. We consider country and government maturity and awareness as signs of Organized UX Professionalism.

4 Method

To empirically evaluate the proposed model, we conducted a survey among UX professionals using a questionnaire developed for this purpose. Each construct in the propositions was operationalized using various items derived from the literature (see Sect. 2. Related work). The collected data was then used to describe the concept of Organized UX Professionalism using formative structured equation modeling.

4.1 Participants

To reach a large number of professionals, we conducted the study in countries representing geographic and cultural diversity and where researchers have shown interest in the study, namely Turkey, Malaysia, France, Finland, and Denmark. In these countries, we identified the UX communities and contacted them via social media, mailing lists and direct email to answer the survey questionnaire. Thus, the selection of participants was based on convenience and purposive sampling. The sample included UX professionals from countries characterized by extensive background in HCI (Finland and

Denmark), extensive background in ergonomics (France), and relatively recently established UX communities (Turkey and Malaysia). The sample included practitioners who self-identified as usability/UX professionals and who were members of local UX/HCI associations or communities. Participants had to be knowledgeable about usability and UX to be able to answer the questions about their background. The demographic and professional profiles of the participants as well as their perspectives on usability and UX are detailed in two articles [64, 92]. Below we describe briefly the local UX communities from which the participants were sampled.

In Turkey, the dominant UX community is the UXPA, which was launched in 2014 in İstanbul as a non-profit local chapter of the global UXPA to serve interaction designers, usability/UX professionals, HCI specialists, etc. The email list of UXPA Turkey has more than 500 recipients, representing professionals from a variety of areas.

In Malaysia, there is a recently established Human Computer Interaction Special Interest Group (SIGHCI) under the Human Factors and Ergonomics Society of Malaysia. SIGHCI works with other technical committees and institutions in the development of usable products and services. In addition, UX Malaysia is an active and the largest UX-related social media group in Malaysia, comprising UX practitioners in the country. Founded in 2012, the group currently has 3,300 members on Facebook. Another group is the Kuala Lumpur ACM SIGCHI chapter with 130 members.

In France, the Luxembourg User Experience Professionals' Association (FLUPA) was founded in 2008 as the France-Luxembourg branch of UXPA. In the email list, there are more than 500 recipients. Ergo IHM is another mailing list available in the French community, which reaches more than 800 HCI professionals and students.

In Finland, the ACM SIGCHI Finland was founded in 2001 as a scientific association that gathers researchers and practitioners in HCI, usability, and UX throughout the country. The email list consists of approximately 450 recipients. In addition to SIGCHI Finland, there are several practitioner-oriented communities operating in the country: IxDA Helsinki, IxDA Tampere, and KäytettävyysOSY, all having dedicated Facebook and LinkedIn groups with several hundreds of members.

In Denmark, the dominant UX community is UX Denmark (formerly SIGCHI.DK), which is associated with ACM SIGCHI and UXPA, but not a formal chapter of either. UX Denmark was launched in 1999 as a website for interaction designers, usability professionals, HCI specialists, and so forth. The website uxdanmark.dk has 1261 registered interested persons from the industry, government, and academia. Furthermore, the UX Denmark social media groups are LinkedIn UX Denmark with currently 551 members and Facebook UX Denmark page with 1221 followers.

A total of 422 UX professionals participated in the study, of whom 91 (21.6%) were from Turkey, 51 (12.1%) from Denmark, 68 (16.1%) from France, 88 (20.9%) from Finland, and 124 (29.4%) from Malaysia. Of the participants, 213 (50.5%) were male, 188 (44.5%) were female, and 21 (5%) chose not to state their gender. The mean age of the participants was 35.2 years (standard deviation [SD] = 8.3).

4.2 Questionnaire Development, Data Collection and Analysis

Thorough Literature Review with Theoretical Grounding for Measures

We constructed the questionnaire items based on the data from previous studies presented and reviewed in the related work section and added some more questions that we deemed important. We chose indicators that were theoretically relevant based on their previous use in surveys on UX and usability professionals or other relevant research, and also novel indicators from related work that we believed were key to modeling the Organized UX Professionalism. During this process, we followed recommendations for developing items for formative modeling [57]. The questionnaire is described in detail by Inal et al. [64].

Content Specification (Built on Rigorous Previous Studies and Qualitative Data)

The research model and the questionnaire were developed using a protocol over a year of monthly Skype discussions among the researchers participating in this research. At each meeting, we discussed the literature on previous surveys of UX professionals, refined the theoretical research model to incorporate the findings from the literature, and developed themes/propositions to explore.

Experts' Assessment (Local Experts from Five Countries)

Our aim was to create a research model and then define a set of questions that would not only measure the constructs in the developed model to seek answers to the research questions but also provide meaningful results for each country and local UX community from which the participants were sampled. In our Skype discussions, we prioritized developing meaningful question items over their discriminatory value, since our research was exploratory and involved five very different countries, and there was a risk that calibrating questions could mean endless iterations of little value. Furthermore, we conducted pilot tests of the questionnaire, reviewed the results of the pilot tests in each community, and reached an agreement on the wording of questions. The final questionnaire included items that measured the theoretical constructs using binary, semantic differential and Likert scale items in English language (Table 1). The questions were then translated into the five local languages by the researchers from the respective countries. The questionnaires were back-translated to ensure the accuracy of the translations.

Measures

The questionnaire thus constructed included in total 62 questions of which 33 questions measured the constructs in the research model (Table 1), while the other questions were aimed at collecting background information and other quantitative and qualitative data (see [64]). The main construct Organized UX Professionalism was captured by 4 items namely, asking the respondents to rate the integration of UX in their organization, the management familiarity with UX, the integration of UX in the development cycle, and the self-reported level of expertise. The other items measured the 7 factors in the proposed model of Organized UX Professionalism (Fig. 1 and Table 1). For each construct, we aimed to have a minimum of three questions.

Data Collection and Analysis

The questionnaire was administered using online survey tools over a period of eight weeks. It was distributed through local UX associations, communities, mailing lists, and personal networks of researchers. The participants were given the option to choose a questionnaire in English or their local language. Reminder emails were sent two and four weeks after the initial emails. In total, more than 1,000 people accessed the survey.

Table 1. Assessment of the formative measurement and structural model.

Construct	Items	Item scales	Item previously used by	VIF	Weights	P-value
Organized UX Professionalism	Management familiarity with UX	(1) Not known, (2) Probably not known, (3) Not sure if known, (4) Probably known, (5) Very well known	*Novel*, see [24, 25, 44]	2.09	.004	.477
	Development phase including UX	(1) None, (2) Late, (3) Early, (4) All	[19, 25, 28, 30, 39, 50, 61, 69, 118]	1.14	.168	.001
	UX integration	(1) Not at all integrated, (2) Mostly not integrated, (3) Medium, (4) mostly integrated, (5) Fully integrated	[23, 28, 30, 39, 54, 70, 101, 124]	1.44	.148	.005
	UX professional's sense of expertise	(1) Novice, (2) Little expertise, (3) Moderate expertise, (4) Considerable expertise, (5) Expert	[55, 61, 62, 70, 84, 90, 96, 117, 118, 124]	1.22	.87	.000
P1 Understanding of UX	Usability definition	Individual (Def1) vs. organizational (Def2) definition - (1) Def1 most, (2) Def1 Somewhat, (3) Equally, (4) Def2 Somewhat, (5) Def2 most	[39, 82, 96]	1.02	−.137	.013

(*continued*)

Table 1. (*continued*)

Construct	Items	Item scales	Item previously used by	VIF	Weights	P-value
	UX definition	Product (Def1) vs. human (Def2) definition - (1) Def1 most, (2) Def1 Somewhat, (3) Equally, (4) Def2 Somewhat, (5) Def2 most	[66, 80]	1.03	.017	.394
	Theories, frameworks, and methods used	1,2,3...N	[32, 33, 69, 84, 98, 117, 124]	1.33	.294	.000
	Interaction design activities	1,2,3...N	[13, 19, 23, 28, 30, 39, 55, 56, 70, 96, 98]	1.33	.806	.000
P2 UX management minded work orientation UX	Current position in the organization	(1) Outside hierarchy (Not applicable, e.g., unemployed), (2) Other (e.g., student, intern), (3) Entry level, (4) Specialist (including academic specialists), (5) Lower/middle management, (6) Top management	[61, 90]	1.03	.149	.025
	Current job title	(1) Neither UX nor usability in the job title, (2) Either UX or usability in the job title	[13, 17–19, 23, 28, 30, 32, 33, 39, 50, 52, 55, 56, 62, 66, 69, 70, 80, 82, 84, 90, 94, 96, 98, 117, 118, 124]	1.01	.729	.000
	UX work experience	1,2,3...N	[18, 30, 33, 52, 55, 62, 70, 80, 84, 117, 124]	1.03	.64	.000

(*continued*)

Table 1. (*continued*)

Construct	Items	Item scales	Item previously used by	VIF	Weights	P-value
P3 UX professionals' innovative tool use	Tools for quick user feedback	1,2,3…N	*Novel*, [17, 51]	1.28	.199	.012
	Tools for remote usability testing	1,2,3…N	*Novel*, [51, 124]	1.15	.139	.068
	Tools for low-fidelity prototyping	1,2,3…N	*Novel*, [26, 32, 51, 55, 115]	1.63	.701	.000
	Tools for high-fidelity prototyping	1,2,3…N	*Novel*, [26, 32, 51, 55, 115]	1.62	.225	.006
P4 UX professionals' social best practices	Face-to-face contact with end users	(1) No, (2) Yes	[19, 23, 28, 39, 52, 96]	1.25	.174	.069
	Usability testing	(1) No, (2) Yes	[2, 8, 18, 19, 23, 39, 55, 96, 118]	1.35	.754	.000
	Number of usability tests conducted	(1) No test, (2) Single round, (3) Two rounds, (4) Three or more rounds	*Novel*, [50, 79]	1.12	.011	.455
	Number of users involved in usability tests	(1) Discount usability testing 1–5, (2) Research level usability testing6–50, (3) Large, multinational industry level > 50	[23]	1.02	− .186	.028
	User recruitment method	(1) Organization itself, (2) Through an agency	[2, 23, 39, 70]	1.02	.086	.160
	Follow-up usability process	(1) No, (2) Yes	[18, 30, 56]	1.06	.339	.001

(*continued*)

Table 1. (*continued*)

Construct	Items	Item scales	Item previously used by	VIF	Weights	P-value
P5 Organizational user centeredness	Number of UX professionals	(1) One, (2) Two to five, (3) More than five	*Novel*, [103]	1.07	−.098	.260
	Organization's years of experience in UX	(1) < 5 years, (2) 5–10 years, (3) > 10 years', Missing (Do not know)	[63]	1.03	.445	.000
	Number of UX professionals per team	(1) One, (2) Two to five, (3) Five to ten (4) More than ten	[13, 18, 56, 70, 94, 118]	1.08	.004	.485
	System development method	(1) Waterfall, (2) Rapid, (3) Agile	[2, 23, 55, 56, 62, 70, 118]	1.00	.915	.000
	Software maturity	(1) No awareness, (2) Not certified, (3) Certified	* Novel*, [85, 119]	1.02	−.032	.415
P6 UX community participation	National community membership	(1) No, (2) Yes	* Novel*, [33, 42, 94]	1.24	.558	.000
	International community membership	(1) No, (2) Yes	* Novel*, [33, 42, 94]	1.19	.283	.006
	National UX event attendance	1,2,3…N	* Novel*, [33, 46, 94]	1.27	.359	.001
	International UX event attendance	1,2,3…N	* Novel*, [33, 46, 94]	1.50	.451	.001
P7 Maturity of UX in country	Years since usability first used in country	1,2,3…N	* Novel*, [42, 105]	1.43	.128	.232
	Years since UX first used in country	1,2,3…N	* Novel*, [38, 47]	1.06	.733	.000
	Information about government regulations	(1) Yes, (2) No	* Novel*	1.12	.252	.024

At the end of the data collection process, the data from each country were merged and cleaned, and the responses to the open questions were translated to English to allow all researchers to take part in the analysis. The final data set consisted of the valid responses of 422 participants. The data was analyzed using structural equation modeling utilizing SmartPLS3 [95].

5 Results

5.1 Formative Measurement Model Assessment

We assessed the formative measurement model by assessing the collinearity of the indicators, the effect of the indicators on the construct, and their basis in the literature (Table 1 and [57]). The indicators were theoretically relevant and key to modeling the Organized UX Professionalism as indicated by the questionnaire development (see Sect. 4). Table 1 shows the constructs, items, and item-scales used in modeling, publications that previously used these items, and publications reporting findings that support our novel items; for example, those about innovative tool use, which has not been previously measured with a specific focus.

Regarding collinearity, Table 1 shows that for all items, the variance inflation factor (VIF) was below 3, which indicates no problematically high correlation between two formative indicators and supports the idea that our indicators together captured their constructs [57].

Table 1 also provides information on the significance and relevance of the formative indicators in terms of their weights on their constructs and the p-values. The overall results suggest that the items previously used in the literature had significant effects on their constructs. Of the novel items, some did not significantly correlate with their constructs or only did so when relaxed criteria were used while others correlated with their constructs significantly. We did, however, keep the novel items that we considered to be important indicators of their constructs even if they did not have significant effect on their constructs, if we had theoretical reason to believe that they would be key to modeling Organized UX Professionalism, again following the recommendations in Hair et al. [57].

5.2 The Formative Model of Organized UX Professionalism

The proposed seven-factor research model of Organized UX Professionalism is supported by the formative modeling of the responses from 422 UX professionals across five countries (Fig. 2). The model in Fig. 2 should be seen as an initial proposal based on formative indicators. The model has enough indicators to capture the constructs, and the inclusion of these items are supported by the research literature.

5.3 Organized UX Professionalism

The proposed research model for Organized UX Professionalism hypothesizing that seven factors describe the integration of UX professionals into an organization is supported by the data obtained from the study (Fig. 2). The percentage of variation in

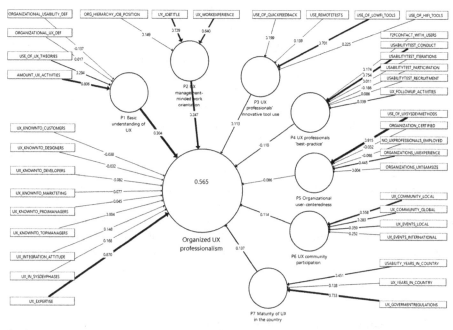

Fig. 2. Holistic modeling with formative indicators of Organized UX Professionalism. The model shows the inner model path coefficients, outer model weights or path coefficients, construct R squared, and the relative contributions of the formative indicators and factors as the paths' widths [57].

the response that is explained by the model is considerable (R squared = 57%). We measured Organized UX Professionalism as a mixture of familiarity of UX across the organization's hierarchy and departments, UX expertise, overall UX integration, and the embeddedness of UX professionals in the system development processes of the organization. This was positively associated with a basic understanding of UX (path coefficient = .30, p < .001) (supporting P1), management-minded work orientation (path coefficient = .25; p < .001 (supporting P2), innovative tool use (path coefficient = .11; p = .01) (supporting P3), organizational user-centeredness (path coefficient = .1; p = .02) (supporting P5), UX community participation (path coefficient = .11, p = .001) (supporting P6), and maturity of UX in the country (path coefficient = .14, p < .001) (supporting P7). P4 was also supported as the UX professionals' best practices appeared to have an impact on Organized UX Professionalism (path coefficient = −.11, p = .01), though the impact was negative.

The relative paths between the constructs in Fig. 2 suggest that individual factors (P1, P2, P3) and the factors at the society level (P6, P7) were important factors for our dataset. However, the lack of a strong effect of organizational-level factors (P4, P5) may reflect a relative low degree of maturity of the UX profession in parts of our data (see also Sect. 5.3). Nevertheless, the path coefficients of all seven factors were significant at the .05 level, which, we consider, will support future attempts to further consolidate the proposed seven-factor model of Organized UX Professionalism.

5.4 Management-Minded UX Professionals

Qualitative findings in our data supported the quantitative results given above. We asked the respondents to report and prioritize their main frustrations in being a UX professional using open-ended questions about UX professionals' frustration with both organizational issues and professional tools, skills and knowledge, and their needs for more organizational resources and better tools and knowledge. Four of five top frustrations were organization-related (insufficient resources: time, money, equipment; lack of understanding and knowledge about UX in the organization, team or project; low priority of UX issues in the organization; and communication problems with developers). Only in place number five came the need for better professional qualifications. A classic usability professional frustration (i.e., lack of knowledge about the user) was only mentioned in seventh place on the list. A similar pattern of responses emerged when we inquired about the means to improve UX work. Among the top five responses, three were directly organization-related (improved work environment, more support from upper management, and more internal collaboration), while the remaining were more associated with professional work (easier access to quantitative user data, education/training of usability/UX professionals).

5.5 Cross Country and UX Community Findings

To investigate the possible differences between the participants from each country, we did a multi-group analysis [57]. The relation between Basic understanding of UX and Organized UX Professionalism (P1) was significantly stronger in Denmark (path coefficient .28) compared to Finland (path coefficient $-.04$; path coefficient difference $= .32$, $p = .03$) and to Malaysia (path coefficient $-.19$; difference $= .46$, $p = .03$). The relation between the basic understanding of UX and Organized UX Professionalism was also significantly different ($p = .01$) in France (path coefficient $= .34$) compared to Malaysia (path coefficient $= -.19$). Further analysis is needed to clearly identify the reasons for these differences, but some possible explanations are as follows: Having ownership of Nokia and related industries, Finland may have more business-oriented UX professionals compared to Denmark. For the Malaysian UX community, it may distinguish itself by being oriented toward certified engineering approaches, rather than business or design. However, such speculations require further research to be sustained.

In addition, we found that the relation between UX management-minded work orientation and Organized UX Professionalism (P2) had a significantly different direction ($p = .01$) in Malaysia (path coefficient $= -.23$) compared to Finland (path coefficient $= .33$) and compared to France (path coefficient $= .21$; $p = .03$). Furthermore, the relation between UX professionals 'social best practices' and Organized UX Professionalism (P4) was significantly different ($p = .02$) in Malaysia (path coefficient $= .21$) compared to Turkey (path coefficient $= -.21$). Finally, the relation between Maturity of UX in the country and Organized UX Professionalism (P7) was strong in Finland (path coefficient $= .30$) and statistically significantly different compared to France (path coefficient $= -.14$; $p = .01$), Malaysia (path coefficient $= .08$; $p = .04$), and Turkey (path coefficient $= .10$; $p = .05$). Note that these multi-group differences should be considered rather tentative since group sizes are small. Further research is required.

6 Discussion

6.1 Organized UX Professionalism

Overall, our findings suggest that a new kind of Organized UX Professionalism may be emerging and point to some of the issues that support or hinder this development. According to our results, the issues that have a positive impact on Organized UX Professionalism include an open and wide basic understanding of UX, management-minded work orientation, organizational user-centeredness, UX community participation, and maturity of UX in the country.

Surprisingly, our respondents tended to choose the individual focused ISO standard usability definition, resisting to shift their perspective toward a more organization-oriented definition of usability [65], [for a detailed discussion see 92]. Organization science researchers have suggested that it is important to analyze professional resistance to organizational control to understand professionalism [86]. Perhaps the ISO standard definition of usability is the core of UX professionals' identity [35]. In contrast to the consensus we found on usability, we found no consensus among our respondents about the newer concept of UX, a finding that is supported by other recent surveys [76]. The standard notion of usability as individual effectiveness and efficiency has been challenged, unsuccessfully, by organizational usability many years ago [72], whereas similarly organizational definitions of UX, for example, quantified UX [75], have only just recently appeared.

According to the theory of organized professionalism [86] in other professions, having highly social best UX practices should indicate a change toward organizational and management contexts. However, we found that UX professionals' best practice actually had a negative impact on Organized UX Professionalism, which may be because the social practices we inquired about in this study belonged to the tradition of the certified usability profession (usability testing, face-to-face meetings with users, etc.), rather than the new social media-mediated and fluent collaboration recommended by organization science research [86].

Participation in local and global UX communities and their events did have a significant influence on Organized UX Professionalism. To some degree, however, it may be natural that a professional community does not support its members in becoming more management- and less profession-oriented. In addition, Sari and Wadhwa [102] pointed out that the development of the UX profession was not considered as a top priority in developing countries, such as Indonesia, which may also be the case in some of the countries included in our study. Furthermore, studies of older professionals suggest that when IT professionals get older, this has a negative impact on the number of activities that older professionals do to keep their skills updated [104]; we did not find this relation in our data. Further research into this issue may investigate the nature of UX events and UX communities.

A high level of general maturity of UX in our respondents' countries did have a positive impact on Organized UX Professionalism. While this may require further analysis, it can be speculated that some countries that only recently familiarized with UX could be faster in directly adopting a network-connected organized professionalism. In our study, Turkey and Malaysia were the newest in the UX field. Malaysia may also have a government-driven approach to UX that somewhat placed it in front of UX-mature countries, such as Finland.

Our qualitative results indicate that our respondents really had a great deal of interest in the so-called 'secondary' aspects of service treatment, namely efficiency, communication, cooperation, safety, and reputation management. This again supports the use of our proposed notion of Organized UX Professionalism as a means to further develop the UX profession.

6.2 Return to the (Certified) Usability Professional?

Usability in classic terms proved to be very important for the respondents in our study. The qualitative data clearly revealed the respondents' demand for standardized concepts and services. The statements from the participants, such as "General understanding of how much value (efficiency and error minimization) good UX provides" [Participant ID 110, Denmark], indicated a strong belief in the value of UX tools and skills. The certified usability professional issue [120] is important, considering that 30% of our respondents referred to a 'lack of qualified usability/UX professionals in the organization, team or project' as a frustration related to being a UX professional. Perhaps the early HCI days' description of usability professionals 'being too late in the system development process and achieving too low-level solutions' days remains or the founders of HCI never imagined that UX professionals would become more than specialists [83]; in either case, our findings suggest that UX professionals today still have a strong focus on specialist knowledge and skills.

6.3 Beyond UX Professionalism?

Alternatively, we could abandon focusing on individual UX skills and knowledge, and instead turn toward organizational capabilities. Our data clearly supports that organizational issues influence UX Professionalism, and to an extent, rethinking a user-centric approach throughout the organization so that it becomes embedded in business strategies, as has already happened or is happening in many organizations [112]. Another frontier challenging the notion of UX professionals is the call for them to have an entrepreneurial mindset; that is, not only solving user problems in their contexts but also transforming them into business problems by considering solution dimensions, i.e., products versus services, target segments, competitive edge, competition, market size, scalability, etc. [111]. This mindset was only indirectly indicated in our data in terms of the respondents' innovative tool use and use of a broad set of HCI theories and methods. Finally, not all usability work takes place in organizations with a clear hierarchy, and the socio-technical complexities of integrating UX activities into flat organizations, such as open-source projects may call for rethinking UX work practices, such as the dissemination of UX knowledge to maintain UX awareness [6].

Another reason for turning more toward organizational capabilities (rather than certified professionalism) could be the impact of emotional labor and conflict handling at the core of UX professionals' work tasks. The frustration expressed by our participants about being a UX professional pointed to more or less open conflicts with management; e.g., "There is a lack of design thinking in leadership; the management sets the direction for the final solution, without the managers knowing that they are already in the process of designing the solution" [Participant ID 113, Denmark], "Management interferes with decision making" [Participant ID 248, Malaysia], and "It is difficult for users to meet more regularly. My [company's] hierarchy sees reaching out [to users] as 'political' and almost always slows my progress" [Participant ID 413, France]. Such comments from our participants testify to a level of job frustration and work exhaustion resulting from a negative organizational climate [99], which may lead to high turnover [71, 100] among UX professionals. However, our participants also had many ideas about how to improve UX work practices within their organizations. For example, "There is a need for more money for user studies in customer organization" [Participant ID 156, Finland] and "I need to have time for UX activities in the product development life cycle and think about time, budget, force, etc." [Participant ID 65, Turkey]. While these comments may be of little surprise, such issues need to be well addressed to support the development and maintenance of UX Professionalism in organizations.

6.4 Future Research

Further research is required into the notion of Organized UX Professionalism in order to navigate between the 'return to the certified usability professionalism' to retain the specialist role and 'giving up UX Professionalism' to become a business entrepreneur'. Szóstek [113], who reported on UX management practices in Microsoft, revealed a number of issues, some of which we addressed in the current study, but there remain further questions to be discussed in future studies, in particular those related to the extended social side of Organized UX Professionalism: Is UX work included in the standard invoice issued for customers (and even when it is included in the invoice, are the amount and ratio sufficient)? If yes, how do customers react to their invoice including a fee for UX? What are the key challenges in managing UX methods in complex, dynamic and cross-border settings (language, culture, time, face-to-face, physical, social tensions, and deliverables)? Do managers and specialists view UX methods from different perspectives? What are bad practices in UX management? How does a UX manager establish clear accountability within and between UX teams? What is the perfect UX development team in terms of skill composition and size? Finally, how can a perfect UX team be created and managed?

Organized UX professionals may work in organizations that go across borders. The differences between countries and UX professional communities indicated by our data should be taken seriously. HCI education should train UX professionals not only in traditional usability and UX skills but also in organizational and cultural competence and knowledge [1]. Business schools with an IS department may be in a good position to provide this kind of training. UX professionals will have to learn how to (re)organize their professionalism and become more management-minded, social, and connective, familiarize with new digital work and organizational forms, and create new kind of usability and UX standards that work in the many emerging HCI communities in many different geographical and cultural settings throughout the world.

Returning to age and gender, Barkhuus and Rode [10] pointed out that embarrassingly, only few HCI studies report the distribution of gender of their participants (respondents). In our study, we had nearly an equal number of female and male respondents.

Thakkar et al. [114] found that the proportion of women working in HCI in India was far less compared to the U.S., where it was already low. Furthermore, they found that familial pressures and workplace discrimination, e.g., from management, often prevented women in the HCI field from reaching management positions. This is something that should be analyzed in detail in future research. Things start to happen when the gender composition of a workforce changes [86, 87].

Finally, we would like to point out the recent developments in technology, including AI, robotics and IoT based solutions, and how they may be transforming the work of UX professionals, among other professionals, and impacting their work experiences and well-being (e.g., [14]). These tools may be used by the professionals as part of their UX work practices or UX professionals may be involved in designing such tools for other professionals. In either case, such intelligent technologies pose novel challenges for the HCI research community (e.g. [21, 43, 123]), which requires further studies.

7 Conclusion

In this paper, we proposed a seven-factor model of Organized UX Professionalism as a way of navigating the development of the UX profession between on one hand a return to certified UX specialism and on the other hand dissolving UX professional knowledge and skills toward organizational development approaches and management values. We hope that the model we propose guides further research in UX Professionalism in general and across AIS HCI, IFIP HCI, ACM CHI, UXPA, and other HCI communities. We consider the model and the concept highly valuable for HWID research and practice, enabling consideration of professional UX practices as well as their management and integration at different levels (organizational, national, professional). Our findings strongly support the idea that a new type of Organized UX professionals may be emerging, which differs not only from the classic certified usability professional but also from the software developer with skills in user-centered design. This new version of Organized UX Professionalism consists of organizational integration of UX expertise into all phases of system development, and it is positively influenced by management-minded work orientation, innovative tool use, highly social best practices, organizational user-centeredness, UX community participation, and the general maturity of UX and usability concepts in the local society.

Acknowledgments. We thank Amélie Roche for collecting the data from the French participants. We thank Kerem Rizvanoglu and Yavuz Inal for collecting the data from the Turkish participants and for their contributions to the theoretical model and questionnaire design.

References

1. Abdelnour-Nocera, J., Michaelides, M., Austin, A., Modi, S.: An intercultural study of HCI education experience and representation. In: Proceedings of the 4th International Conference on Intercultural Collaboration (ICIC 2012), pp. 157–160 (2012). https://doi.org/10.1145/216 0881.2160909

2. Ardito, C., Buono, P., Caivano, D., Costabile, M.F., Lanzilotti, R., Bruun, A., Stage, J.: Usability evaluation: a survey of software development organizations. In: SEKE, pp. 282–287 (2011)
3. Ashraf, M., et al.: A study on usability awareness in local IT industry. Int. J. Adv. Comput. Sci. Appl. 9(5), 427–432 (2018). www.ijacsa.thesai.org
4. Austin, A.: The differing profiles of the human-computer interaction professional: perceptions of practice, cognitive preferences and the impact on HCI education. The University of West London (2017). https://repository.uwl.ac.uk/id/eprint/5327/7/AnnAustinfinalPhDsubmission.pdf. Accessed 7 Sep 2018
5. Austin, A., Nocera, J.A.: So, who exactly is the HCI professional? In: CHI EA 2015, pp. 1037–1042 (2015). https://doi.org/10.1145/2702613.2732906
6. Bach, P.M., Carroll, J.M.: Characterizing the dynamics of open user experience design: the cases of Firefox and OpenOffice.org (2010). https://aisel.aisnet.org/cgi/viewcontent.cgi?article=1563&context=jais. Accessed 7 Sep 2018
7. Baets, W.: Aligning information systems with business strategy. J. Strateg. Inf. Syst. 1(4), 205–213 (1992)
8. Bak, J.O., Nguyen, K., Risgaard, P., Stage, J.: Obstacles to usability evaluation in practice: a survey of software development organizations. In: Proceedings of the 5th Nordic Conference on Human-Computer Interaction: Building Bridges, pp. 23–32 (2008)
9. Bangor, A., Kortum, P., Miller, J.: Determining what individual SUS scores mean: adding an adjective rating scale. J. Usability Stud. 4(3), 114–123 (2009)
10. Barkhuus, L., Rode, J.A.: From mice to men - 24 years of evaluation in CHI. In: Proceedings of the SIGCHI Conference on Human Factors in Computing Systems (CHI 2007) (2007). https://doi.org/10.1145/1240624.2180963
11. Barricelli, B.R., et al. (eds.) Human Work Interaction Design. Designing Engaging Automation: 5th IFIP WG 13.6 Working Conference, HWID 2018, Espoo, Finland, 20–21 August 2018, Revised Selected Papers. Springer, Cham (2019). https://doi.org/10.1007/978-3-030-05297-3
12. Bassellier, G., Benbasat, I.: Business competence of information technology professionals: conceptual development and influence on IT-business partnerships. MIS Q. 28(4), 673 (2004). https://doi.org/10.2307/25148659
13. Bekker, M.M., Vermeeren, A.P.O.S.: An analysis of user interface design projects: information sources and constraints in design. Interact. Comput. 8(1), 112–116 (1996)
14. Benbya, H., Pachidi, S., Jarvenpaa, S.: Special issue editorial: artificial intelligence in organizations: implications for information systems research. J. Assoc. Inf. Syst. 22(2), 10 (2021)
15. Bødker, S.: When second wave HCI meets third wave challenges. In: Proceedings of the 4th Nordic Conference on Human-computer Interaction: Changing Roles (NordiCHI 2006), pp. 1–8 (2006). https://doi.org/10.1145/1182475.1182476
16. Bødker, S.: Third-wave HCI, 10 years later-participation and sharing. ACM Interact. 22(5), 24-31 (2015). http://delivery.acm.org/10.1145/2810000/2804405/p24-bodker.pdf?ip=130.226.41.20&id=2804405&acc=OPEN&key=36332CD97FA87885.35BC399B9BC88DC5.4D4702B0C3E38B35.6D218144511F3437&__acm__=1536396774_db9697dc1630234ec28b3eec70bfb21. Accessed 8 Sep 2018
17. Boivie, I., Åborg, C., Persson, J., Löfberg, M.: Why usability gets lost or usability in in-house software development. Interact. Comput. 15(4), 623–639 (2003)
18. Boivie, I., Gulliksen, J., Göransson, B.: The lonesome cowboy: a study of the usability designer role in systems development. Interact. Comput. (2006). https://doi.org/10.1016/j.intcom.2005.10.003
19. Borgholm, T., Madsen, K.H.: Cooperative usability practices. Commun. ACM 42(5), 91–97 (1999)

20. Bornoe, N., Stage, J.: Active involvement of software developers in usability engineering: two small-scale case studies. In: Bernhaupt, R., Dalvi, G., Joshi, A., K. Balkrishan, D., O'Neill, J., Winckler, M. (eds.) INTERACT 2017. LNCS, vol. 10516, pp. 159–168. Springer, Cham (2017). https://doi.org/10.1007/978-3-319-68059-0_10
21. Bratteteig, T., Verne, G.: Does AI make PD obsolete? Exploring challenges from artificial intelligence to participatory design. In: Proceedings of the 15th Participatory Design Conference: Short Papers, Situated Actions, Workshops and Tutorial, vol. 2, pp. 1–5 (2018)
22. Brooke, J.: SUS: a quick and dirty usability scale. In: Jordan, P.W., Thomas, B., Weerdmeester, B.A., McClelland, A.L. (eds.) Usability Evaluation in Industry. Taylor & Francis, Milton Park, vol. 189 (1996). https://doi.org/10.1201/9781498710411
23. Bygstad, B., Ghinea, G., Brevik, E.: Software development methods and usability: perspectives from a survey in the software industry in Norway. Interact. Comput. **20**(3), 375–385 (2008). https://doi.org/10.1016/j.intcom.2007.12.001
24. Cajander, Å.: Usability–who cares? The introduction of user-centred systems design in organisations. The Faculty of Science and Technology, Uppsala (2010). Accessed from http://www.diva-portal.org/smash/get/diva2:310201/FULLTEXT01.pdf
25. Cajander, Å., Gulliksen, J., Boivie, I.: Management perspectives on usability in a public authority. In: Proceedings of the 4th Nordic Conference on Human-Computer Interaction: Changing Roles - Nord. 2006, pp. 38–47 (2006). https://doi.org/10.1145/1182475.1182480
26. Cajander, Å., Larusdottir, M., Gulliksen, J.: Existing but not explicit-the user perspective in scrum projects in practice. In: INTERACT, pp. 762–779 (2013)
27. Carroll, J.M., Dourish, P., Friedman, B., Kurosu, M., Olson, G.M., Sutcliffe, A.: Institutionalizing HCI. In: CHI 2006 Extended Abstracts on Human Factors in Computing Systems - CHI EA 2006, p. 17 (2006). https://doi.org/10.1145/1125451.1125457
28. Catarci, T., Matarazzo, G., Raiss, G.: Driving usability into the public administration: the Italian experience. Int. J. Hum. Comput. Stud. **57**(2), 121–138 (2002). https://doi.org/10.1016/S1071-5819(02)91014-1
29. Chan, S.S., Wolfe, R.J., Fang, X.: Teaching HCI in is/EC curriculum. In: AMCIS 2002 Proceedings (2002). Article 142. http://www.pitt.edu/~isprogs/graduate.html. Accessed 6 Aug 2019
30. Chilana, P.K., Ko, A.J., Wobbrock, J.O., Grossman, T., Fitzmaurice, G.: Post-deployment usability: a survey of current practices. In: Proceedings of the SIGCHI Conference on Human Factors in Computing Systems (CHI 2011), pp. 2243–2246 (2011). https://doi.org/10.1145/1978942.1979270
31. Clark, J.G., Walz, D.B., Wynekoop, J.L.: Identifying exceptional application software developers: a comparison of students and professionals. Commun. Assoc. Inf. Syst. (2018). https://doi.org/10.17705/1cais.01108
32. Clemmensen, T.: Usability professionals' personal interest in basic HCI theory. In: INTERACT 2003, pp. 639–646 (2003)
33. Clemmensen, T.: Community knowledge in an emerging online professional community: the case of Sigchi.dk. Knowl. Process Manag. **12**(1), 43–52 (2005). https://doi.org/10.1002/kpm.206
34. Clemmensen, T.: Human Work Interaction Design: A Platform for Theory and Action. Springer, Cham (2021). https://doi.org/10.1007/978-3-030-71796-4
35. Clemmensen, T., Hertzum, M., Yang, J., Chen, Y.: Do usability professionals think about user experience in the same way as users and developers do? In: Kotzé, P., Marsden, G., Lindgaard, G., Wesson, J., Winckler, M. (eds.) INTERACT 2013. LNCS, vol. 8118, pp. 461–478. Springer, Heidelberg (2013). https://doi.org/10.1007/978-3-642-40480-1_31
36. Clemmensen, T., Orngreen, R., Pejtersen, A.M.: Describing users in contexts: perspectives on human-work interaction design. In: Workshop Proceedings of Workshop 4, held in

Conjunction with the 10th IFIP TC13 International Conference on Human-Computer Inter-action, INTERACT 2005, Rom, Italy, vol. 60 (2005). http://citeseerx.ist.psu.edu/viewdoc/download?doi=10.1.1.123.7265&rep=rep1&type=pdf

37. Clemmensen, T., Plocher, T.: The cultural usability (CULTUSAB) project: studies of cultural models in psychological usability evaluation methods. In: Aykin, N. (ed.) UI-HCII 2007. LNCS, vol. 4559, pp. 274–280. Springer, Heidelberg (2007). https://doi.org/10.1007/978-3-540-73287-7_34

38. Diefenbach, S., Kolb, N., Hassenzahl, M.: The Hedonic in human-computer interaction: history, contributions, and future research directions. In: Proceedings of the 2014 Conference on Designing Interactive Systems, pp. 305–314 (2014). http://dl.acm.org/citation.cfm?doid=2598510.2598549

39. Dillon, A., Sweeney, M., Maguire, M.: A survey of usability engineering within the European IT industry-current practice and needs. People Comput. **1993**, 81 (1993)

40. Dinger, M., Thatcher, J.B., Treadway, D., Stepina, L., Breland, J.: Does professionalism matter in the IT workforce? An empirical examination of IT professionals. J. Assoc. Inf. Syst. **16**(4), 1 (2015)

41. Djamasbi, S., Galletta, D.F., Nah, F.F.H., Page, X., Robert, L.P., Jr., Wisniewski, P.J.: Bridging a bridge: bringing two HCI communities together. In: Extended Abstracts of the 2018 CHI Conference on Human Factors in Computing Systems (CHI EA 2018), pp. W23:1–W23:8 (2018). https://doi.org/10.1145/3170427.3170612

42. Douglas, I., Liu, Z.: Global Usability. Springer, London (2011). https://doi.org/10.1007/978-0-85729-304-6

43. Dove, G., Halskov, K., Forlizzi, J., Zimmerman, J.: UX design innovation: challenges for working with machine learning as a design material. In: Proceedings of the 2017 Chi Conference on Human Factors in Computing Systems, pp. 278–288 (2017)

44. Eshet, E., De Reuver, M., Bouwman, H.: The role of organizational strategy in the user-centered design of mobile applications. Commun. Assoc. Inf. Syst. **40**(1), 14 (2017)

45. Friedland, L.: Culture eats UX strategy for breakfast. Interactions **26**(5), 78–81 (2019)

46. Galletta, D.F., et al.: If practice makes perfect, where do we stand? Commun. Assoc. Inf. Syst. **45**(1), 3 (2019)

47. Gerea, C., Herskovic. V.: Measuring user experience in Latin America: an exploratory survey. In Proceedings of the Latin American Conference on Human Computer Interaction (CLIHC 2015), pp. 19:1–19:4 (2015). https://doi.org/10.1145/2824893.2824914

48. Getto, G., Potts, L., Gossett, K., Salvo, M.J.: Teaching UX: designing programs to train the next generation of UX experts. In: SIGDOC 2013, 30 September–1 October 2013, Greenville, NC, USA (2013). https://doi.org/10.1145/2507065.2507082

49. Ghazali, M., Sivaji, A., Hussein, I., Yong, L.T., Mahmud, M., Md Noor, N.L.: HCI practice at MIMOS berhad: a symbiotic collaboration between academia and industry. In: Proceedings of the ASEAN CHI Symposium 2015, pp. 11–14 (2015). https://doi.org/10.1145/2776888.2780360

50. Gould, J.D., Lewis, C.: Designing for usability: key principles and what designers think. Commun. ACM **28**(3), 300–311 (1985)

51. Gray, C.M.: It's more of a mindset than a method: UX conception of design methods. In: Proceedings of the 2016 CHI Conference on Human Factors in Computing Systems (CHI 2016), pp. 4044–4055 (2016). https://doi.org/10.1145/2858036.2858410

52. Grudin, J., Poltrock, S.E.: User interface design in large corporations: coordination and communication across disciplines. In: ACM SIGCHI Bulletin, pp. 197–203 (1989)

53. Gulliksen, J.: Institutionalizing human-computer interaction for global health. Glob. Health Action **10**(sup3), 1344003 (2017). https://doi.org/10.1080/16549716.2017.1344003

54. Gulliksen, J., Boivie, I., Göransson, B.: Usability professionals—current practices and future development. Interact. Comput. **18**(4), 568–600 (2006). https://doi.org/10.1016/j.intcom. 2005.10.005

55. Gulliksen, J., Boivie, I., Persson, J., Hektor, A., Herulf, L.: Making a difference: a survey of the usability profession in Sweden. In: Proceedings of the third Nordic Conference on Human-Computer Interaction, pp. 207–215 (2004)

56. Gunther, R., Janis, J., Butler, S.: The UCD decision matrix: how, when, and where to sell user-centered design into the development cycle (2001). http://www.ovostudios.com/upa 2001/

57. Hair, J.F., Hult, G.T.M., Ringle, C., Sarstedt, M.: A primer on partial least squares structural equation modeling (PLS-SEM). Sage (2017). https://uk.sagepub.com/en-gb/eur/a-pri mer-on-partial-least-squares-structural-equation-modeling-pls-sem/book244583. Accessed 9 Sep 2018

58. Herrmann, T., Tscheligi, M.: Institutionalizing mobile user experience. In: Proceedings of the 8th Conference on Human-Computer Interaction with Mobile Devices and Services - MobileHCI 2006, p. 285 (2006). https://doi.org/10.1145/1152215.1152290

59. Hertzum, M.: Images of usability. Int. J. Hum-Comput. Interact. **26**(6), 567–600 (2010). https://doi.org/10.1080/10447311003781300

60. Holmes, M., Spence, W., Tan, B., Wei, K-K., Wu, J.: A preliminary cultural comparison of information systems professionals in Singapore and Taiwan: a field survey. In: PACIS 1995 Proceedings, December 1995. https://aisel.aisnet.org/pacis1995/39. 6 Accessed 2019

61. Hussein, I., Mahmud, M., Md Tap, A.O., Jack, L.: Does user-centered design (UCD) matter? Perspectives of Malaysian IT organizations. Management **14**, 24 (2013)

62. Hussein, I., Mahmud, M., Tap, M., Osman, A.: User experience design (UXD): a survey of user interface development practices in Malaysia (2012)

63. Iivari, N.: 'Representing the user' in software development—a cultural analysis of usability work in the product development context. Interact. Comput. **18**(4), 635–664 (2006). https:// doi.org/10.1016/j.intcom.2005.10.002

64. Inal, Y., Clemmensen, T., Rajanen, D., Iivari, N., Rizvanoglu, K., Sivaji, A.: Positive developments but challenges still ahead: a survey study on UX professionals' work practices. J. Usability Stud. **15**, 4 (2020)

65. International_Organization_For_Standardization. 2018. ISO 9241-11:2018 - Ergonomics of human-system interaction - Part 11: Usability: Definitions and concepts. https://www.iso. org/standard/63500.html. Accessed 9 Sep 2018

66. Jääskeläinen, A., Heikkinen, K.: Divergence of user experience: professionals vs. end users. Age (Omaha). **25**(59), 18–64 (2010)

67. Jain, J., Courage, C., Innes, J., Churchill, E.: Managing global UX teams. In: CHI 2011 Extended, pp. 527–530 (2011). https://doi.org/10.1145/1979742.1979492

68. Jarzabkowski, P.: Strategy as practice: recursiveness, adaptation, and practices-in-use. Organ. Stud. **25**(4), 529–560 (2004)

69. Jerome, B., Kazman, R.: Surveying the solitudes: an investigation into the relationships between human computer interaction and software engineering in practice. In: Seffah, A., Gulliksen, J., Desmarais, M.C. (eds.) Human-Centered Software Engineering –Integrating Usability in the Software Development Lifecycle, Springer, Dordrecht, pp. 59–70 (2005). https://doi.org/10.1007/1-4020-4113-6_4

70. Ji, Y.G., Yun, M.H.: Enhancing the minority discipline in the IT industry: a survey of usability and user-centered design practice. Int. J. Hum. Comput. Interact. **20**(2), 117–134 (2006)

71. Joseph, D., Koh, C.S.K., Foo, A.C.H.: Sustainable it-specific human capital: coping with the threat of professional obsolescence. In: ICIS 2010 Proceedings - Thirty First International Conference on Information Systems, p. 46 (2010)

72. Kling, R., Elliott, M.: Digital library design for organizational usability. ACM SIGOIS Bull. **15**(2), 59–70 (1994). https://doi.org/10.1145/192611.192746

73. Kuusinen, K., Väänänen-Vainio-Mattila, K.: How to make agile UX work more efficient: management and sales perspectives. In: Proceedings of the 7th Nordic Conference on Human-Computer Interaction: Making Sense Through Design (NordiCHI 2012), pp. 139–148 (2012). https://doi.org/10.1145/2399016.2399037

74. Kyng, M.: Bridging the gap between politics and techniques on the next practices of participatory design. Scand. J. Inf. Syst. **22**(1), 5 (2010)

75. Lachner, F., Naegelein, P., Kowalski, R., Spann, M., Butz, A.: Quantified UX: towards a common organizational understanding of user experience. In: Proceedings of 9th Nordic Conference on Human-Computer Interaction - Nordic 2016, pp. 56:1–56:10 (2016). https://doi.org/10.1145/2971485.2971501

76. Lallemand, C., Gronier, G., Koenig, V.: User experience: a concept without consensus? Exploring practitioners' perspectives through an international survey. Comput. Human Behav. **43**(2015), 35–48 (2015). https://doi.org/10.1016/j.chb.2014.10.048

77. Lantz, A., Holmlid, S.: Interaction design in procurement: the view of procurers and interaction designers. CoDesign **6**(1), 43–57 (2010). https://doi.org/10.1080/157108810036 71890

78. Lárusdóttir, M., Cajander, Å., Gulliksen, J.: Informal feedback rather than performance measurements - user-centred evaluation in scrum projects. Behav. Inf. Technol. **33**(11), 1118–1135 (2014). https://doi.org/10.1080/0144929X.2013.857430

79. Larusdottir, M., Gulliksen, J., Cajander, Å.: A license to kill–improving UCSD in agile development. J. Syst. Softw. **123**(2017), 214–222 (2017)

80. Law, E.L.C., Roto, V., Hassenzahl, M., Vermeeren, A.P.O.S., Kort, J.: Understanding, scoping and defining user experience: a survey approach. In: Proceedings of the ACM SIGCHI Conference on Human Factors in Computing Systems, pp. 719–728 (2009). https://doi.org/10.1145/1518701.1518813

81. Li, N., Scialdone, M.J., Carey, J., Zhang, P., Scialdone, M.J., Carey, J.: The intellectual advancement of human-computer interaction research: a critical assessment of the MIS literature. AIS Trans. Hum. Comput. Interact. **3**(1), 55–107 (2009). http://thci.aisnet.org. Accessed 8 Sep 2018

82. Lizano, F., Sandoval, M.M., Bruun, A., Stage, J.: Usability evaluation in a digitally emerging country: a survey study. In: Kotzé, P., Marsden, G., Lindgaard, G., Wesson, J., Winckler, M. (eds.) INTERACT 2013. LNCS, vol. 8120, pp. 298–305. Springer, Heidelberg (2013). https://doi.org/10.1007/978-3-642-40498-6_22

83. Long, J., Dowell, J.: Conceptions of the discipline of HCI: craft, applied science, and engineering. In: Proceedings of HCI 89, pp. 9–32 (1989). https://dl.acm.org/citation.cfm?id= 92973. Accessed 4 Jun 2018

84. Mao, J.Y., Vredenburg, K., Smith, P.W., Carey, T.: The state of user-centered design practice. Commun. ACM **48**(3), 105–109 (2005)

85. Molich, R., Bevan, N.: How can usability be certified? A practical test of your skills. In: CHI2004 (2004). www.usability.serco.com/trump. Accessed 7 Sep 2018

86. Noordegraaf, M.: Risky business: how professionals and professional fields (must) deal with organizational issues. Organ. Stud. **32**(10), 1349–1371 (2011). https://doi.org/10.1177/017 0840611416748

87. Noordegraaf, M.: Reconfiguring professional work: changing forms of professionalism in public services. Adm. Soc. **48**(7), 783–810 (2016). https://doi.org/10.1177/009539971350 9242

88. Ogunyemi, A., Lamas, D., Adagunodo, E.R., da Rosa, I.B.: HCI practices in the Nigerian software industry. In: Abascal, J., Barbosa, S., Fetter, M., Gross, T., Palanque, P., Winckler,

M. (eds.) INTERACT 2015. LNCS, vol. 9297, pp. 479–488. Springer, Cham (2015). https://doi.org/10.1007/978-3-319-22668-2_37

89. Peters, A., Winschiers-Theophilus, H.: HCI out of Namibia. Interactions **24**(4), 85 (2017). https://doi.org/10.1145/3099120

90. Poltrock, S.E., Grudin, J.: Organizational obstacles to interface design and development: two participant-observer studies. ACM Trans. Comput. Hum. Interact. **1**(1), 52–80 (1994)

91. Putnam, C., Kolko, B.: HCI professions: differences and definitions. In: CHI EA 2012, pp. 2021–2026 (2012). https://doi.org/10.1145/2212776.2223746

92. Rajanen, D., et al.: UX professionals' definitions of usability and UX – a comparison between Turkey, Finland, Denmark, France and Malaysia. In: Bernhaupt, R., Dalvi, G., Joshi, A., K. Balkrishan, D., O'Neill, J., Winckler, M. (eds.) INTERACT 2017. LNCS, vol. 10516, pp. 218–239. Springer, Cham (2017). https://doi.org/10.1007/978-3-319-68059-0_14

93. Rajanen, M., Iivari, N.: Usability cost-benefit analysis: how usability became a curse word? In: Baranauskas, C., Palanque, P., Abascal, J., Barbosa, S.D.J. (eds.) INTERACT 2007. LNCS, vol. 4663, pp. 511–524. Springer, Heidelberg (2007). https://doi.org/10.1007/978-3-540-74800-7_47

94. Rauch, T., Wilson, T.: UPA and CHI surveys on usability processes. ACM SIGCHI Bull. **27**(3), 23–25 (1995)

95. Ringle, C.M., Wende, S., Becker, J.M.: SmartPLS 3. Boenningstedt SmartPLS GmbH (2015)

96. Roche, A., Lespinet-Najib, V., André, J.M.: Use of usability evaluation methods in France: the reality in professional practices. In: User Science and Engineering (i-USEr), 2014 3rd International Conference on, pp. 180–185 (2014)

97. Rohn, J.A., Thompson, C.F.: Leadership beyond the UX box. Interactions **24**(3), 74–77 (2017). https://doi.org/10.1145/3077330

98. Rosenbaum, S., Rohn, J.A., Humburg, J.: A toolkit for strategic usability: results from workshops, panels, and surveys. In: Proceedings of the SIGCHI Conference on Human Factors in Computing Systems, pp. 337–344 (2000)

99. Rutner, P., Riemenschneider, C.: The impact of emotional labor and conflict management style on work exhaustion of information technology professionals. Commun. Assoc. Inf. Syst. **36**(1), 13 (2015)

100. Rutner, P.S., Hardgrave, B.C., McKnight, D.H.: Emotional dissonance and the information technology professional. Mis Q. **32**(3), 635–652 (2008)

101. Sandblad, B., et al.: Work environment and computer systems development. Behav. Inf. Technol. (2003). https://doi.org/10.1080/01449290310001624356

102. Sari, E., Wadhwa, B.: Understanding HCI education across Asia-Pacific. In: Proceedings of the International HCI and UX Conference in Indonesia (CHIuXiD 2015), pp. 65–68 (2015). https://doi.org/10.1145/2742032.2742042

103. Sauro, J., Johnson, K., Meenan, C.: From snake-oil to science: measuring UX maturity. In: Proceedings of the 2017 CHI Conference Extended Abstracts on Human Factors in Computing Systems, pp. 1084–1091 (2017)

104. Schambach, T.: Updating activities of older professionals. In: AMCIS 1999 Proceedings, p. 175 (1999)

105. Shackel, B.: Usability – context, framework, definition, design and evaluation. Interact. Comput. **21**(5–6), 339–346 (2009). https://doi.org/10.1016/j.intcom.2009.04.007

106. Siegel, D.A.: Strategic UX: the value of making the problem bigger. Interactions **24**(1), 68–70 (2016). https://doi.org/10.1145/3012172

107. Sivaji, A., Nielsen, S.F., Clemmensen, T.: A textual feedback tool for empowering participants in usability and UX evaluations. Int. J. Hum. Comput. Interact. **33**(5), 357–370 (2017). https://doi.org/10.1080/10447318.2016.1243928

108. Smith, A., Joshi, A., Liu, Z., Bannon, L., Gulliksen, J., Li, C.: Institutionalizing HCI in Asia. In: Baranauskas, C., Palanque, P., Abascal, J., Barbosa, S.D.J. (eds.) INTERACT 2007. LNCS, vol. 4663, pp. 85–99. Springer, Heidelberg (2007). https://doi.org/10.1007/978-3-540-74800-7_7

109. St-Cyr, O., Jovanovic, A., Chignell, M., MacDonald, C.M., Churchill, E.F.: The HCI living curriculum as a community of practice. Interactions **25**(5), 68–75 (2018). https://doi.org/10.1145/3215842

110. Sturm, C., Aly, M., von Schmidt, B., Flatten, T.: Entrepreneurial & UX mindsets: two perspectives - one objective. In: Proceedings of the 19th International Conference on Human-Computer Interaction with Mobile Devices and Services (MobileHCI 2017), pp. 60:1–60:11 (2017). https://doi.org/10.1145/3098279.3119912

111. Sturm, C., Aly, M., von Schmidt, B., Flatten, T.: Entrepreneurial & UX mindsets: two perspectives - one objective. In: Proceedings of MobileHCI 2017, pp. 60:1–60:11 (2017). https://doi.org/10.1145/3098279.3119912

112. Sward, D.: User experience design: a strategy for competitive advantage. In: AMCIS 2007 Proceedings, pp. 1–14 (2007). Article 163. http://aisel.aisnet.org/amcis2007, http://aisel.aisnet.org/amcis2007/163. Accessed 8 Sep 2018

113. Szóstek, A.: A look into some practices behind Microsoft UX management. In: CHI EA 2012, pp. 605–618 (2012). https://doi.org/10.1145/2212776.2212833

114. Thakkar, D., Sambasivan, N., Kulkarni, P., Sudarshan, P.K., Toyama, K.: The unexpected entry and exodus of women in computing and HCI in India. In: Proceedings of the 2018 CHI Conference on Human Factors in Computing Systems (CHI 2018), pp. 352:1–352:12 (2018). https://doi.org/10.1145/3173574.3173926

115. Tscheligi, M., Sefelin, R., Giller, V.: Paper prototyping–what is it good for? A comparison of paper-and computer-based low-fidelity prototyping. In: CHI2003 Conference on Human Factors in Computing Systems, Extended Abstracts (2003)

116. Tuovila, S., Iivari, N.: Bridge builders in IT artifact development. In: ECIS2007 (2007). Paper 163. http://aisel.aisnet.org/ecis2007/163

117. Vredenburg, K., Mao, J.Y., Smith, P.W., Carey, T.: A survey of user-centered design practice. In: Proceedings of the SIGCHI Conference on Human Factors in Computing Systems, pp. 471–478 (2002)

118. Vukelja, L., Müller, L., Opwis, K.: Are engineers condemned to design? a survey on software engineering and UI design in Switzerland. In: Baranauskas, C., Palanque, P., Abascal, J., Barbosa, S.D.J. (eds.) INTERACT 2007. LNCS, vol. 4663, pp. 555–568. Springer, Heidelberg (2007). https://doi.org/10.1007/978-3-540-74800-7_50

119. Walldius, Å., Sundblad, Y., Bengtsson, L., Sandblad, B., Gulliksen, J.: User certification of workplace software: assessing both artefact and usage. Behav. Inf. Technol. **28**(2), 101–120 (2009)

120. Wichansky, A.: Professional UX credentials: are they worth the paper they're printed on? ACM Interact. **21**(5), 82–84 (2014). https://doi.org/10.1145/2656370

121. Wilson, E.V., Djamasbi, S.: Measuring mobile user experience instruments for research and practice. Commun. Assoc. Inf. Syst. **44**(1), 8 (2019)

122. Yaghmaie, F., Jayasuriya, R.: Development of a scale for measuring user computer experience. In: PACIS 1997 Proceedings of, vol. 49 (1997)

123. Yang, Q., Steinfeld, A., Rosé, C., Zimmerman, J.: Re-examining whether, why, and how human-AI interaction is uniquely difficult to design. In: Proceedings of the 2020 Chi Conference on Human Factors in Computing Systems, pp. 1–13 (2020)

124. Zhou, R., Huang, S., Qin, X., Huang, J.: A survey of user-centered design practice in China. In: 2008 IEEE International Conference on Systems, Man and Cybernetics, pp. 1885–1889 (2008)

Research on the Integration of Human-Computer Interaction and Cognitive Neuroscience

Xiu Miao[1,2] and Wen-jun Hou[2(✉)]

[1] Beijing University of Posts and Telecommunications, Beijing 100083, China
[2] Inner Mongolia University of Science and Technology, Baotou 014010, Inner Mogolia, China
18547290825@163.com

Abstract. This paper aims at reviewing the development of the integration of Cognitive Neuroscience and Human-computer Interaction, and put forward the main directions of the development of Brain-computer Interaction in the future.

Research status and application of Human-computer Interaction based on Cognitive Neuroscience were reviewed by desktop analysis and literature survey, combined with the new research trends of Brain-computer Interface according to domestic and foreign development. According to the brain signal acquisition method and application, the types of BCI are divided into (1) Passive brain-computer interface: exploring and modeling neural mechanisms related to human interaction and on that basis realizing iterative improvement of computer design. (2) Initiative brain-computer interface: direct interaction between brain signal and computer. Then the main development direction of Brain-computer Interface field in the future from three progressive levels are discussed: broadening existing interactive channels, improving the reliability of human-computer interaction system and improving the interaction experience. The deep integration and two-way promotion of Cognitive Neuroscience and Human-computer Interaction will usher in the era of Brain-computer Interface and the next generation of artificial intelligence after overcoming a series of problems such as scene mining, algorithm optimization and model generalization.

Keywords: Human-computer Interaction · Cognitive Neuroscience · EEG · Brain-computer Interface

1   The Evolution of HCI

The development of Human-Computer Interaction (HCI) has experienced the computer-centered command-line Interface (CLI) which used Computer language to input and output information through perforated paper tape, the Graphic User Interface (GUI) represented by WIMP (Windows, Icon, Mouse, Point), the Touch-screen User Interface (TUI) developed with the maturity of intelligent mobile technology. With the boom in perception, computing exchange Interface between human and computer gradually evolved into Multi Model User Interface (MMUI), Perceptual User Interface (PUI),

G. Bhutkar et al. (Eds.): HWID 2021, IFIP AICT 609, pp. 66–82, 2022.
https://doi.org/10.1007/978-3-031-02904-2_3

post-WIMP, non-WIMP, we called them Natural human-computer interaction phase, in which human five senses (vision, hearing, taste, smell and touch) and physical data are sufficiently understood as computer input commands and parameters in real-time. Natural human-computer interaction has the following characteristics:

1.1 Provide Multi-modal Interaction Channels

In addition to supporting traditional input methods such as mouse and touch, intelligent human-computer system also supports eye movement interaction, voice interaction, somatosensory interaction, brain-computer interaction and other operation. Eye movement interactions are common in AR/VR devices, where users interact with them through gaze and blink. Voice interaction is one of the most vigorous development of human-computer interaction technology in recent years, speech recognition and speech synthesis of natural language processing has reached a more mature level, which to a certain extent, the catalytic voice the development of intelligent devices, such as a small degree of intelligent speakers, apple Siri and Microsoft small ice and other household intelligent voice. Somatosensory interaction more applications in the field of entertainment, such as nintendo body feeling game new adventures in fitness ring, on a fitness ring "push" and "stretch", "flat" and a series of actions, to achieve "artillery" and "absorption of gold", "jump", such as operation, hit a monster, complete fitness adventure. In addition to motion-sensing games, AR and VR also support gamepads and gesture. Brain-computer interaction is a new type of interaction technology emerging in recent years. Its principle is to decode the brain neuron activity, interpret the user's intention, emotion, cognitive state and consciousness by implanting chips into the brain or through non-invasive eeg signal acquisition equipment, and realize the direct information communication between the brain and the computer. See Fig. 1.

Fig. 1. Multi-modal interaction channel (from left to right, baidu's Xiaodu smart speaker, Nintendo's Fitness Ring Adventure and Microsoft Hololens)

1.2 Support Discrete and Continuous Information Exchange

Traditional human-computer interaction, such as GUI, can only support users' discrete operations on objects such as pictures and text through mouse and keyboard. The process of information exchange is discrete. Natural human-computer interaction system combines continuous and discrete. Through real-time and continuous acquisition, processing and analysis of multi-channel information of users by multi-sensors, rapid, real-time and adaptive information output can be made in a timely manner. It is a multi-dimensional interaction mode that integrates the time factor into the human-computer system.

1.3 Allowing for Fuzzy Interaction with Uncertainty

Natural interactions allow for user-submitted interactions without certain and definite. In the physical space, not only human beings are constantly changing, but also the spatial and temporal data in the surrounding environment are also updated. How to transform uncertainty into certainty and use it for human-computer system is an important problem in human-computer integration. Take eye-movement interaction as an example, the research shows that the eye-movement behaviors of users are different under different cognitive load conditions [1]. In the mouse click task, the shape, size, distance and other factors of the target will affect the final position of the user's landing point [2]; In speech interaction, natural language is characterized by large amount of information, fuzziness, context and other uncertainties. Natural human-computer interaction supports the exploration and modeling of fuzziness and uncertainty in the process of human-computer interaction, so as to identify and predict the real intention and behavior of users, improve the support of intelligent system for people and improve user performance.

The era of natural human-computer interaction has promoted the prosperity of multi-channel perception and interaction technology, emphasizing the continuous real-time analysis of human motivation, state, intention and behavior and generating appropriate reasoning, with the goal of realizing the natural and intelligent integration and collaboration between human and computer. The brain is in charge of oversees human's acceptance, processing and command of external information. The activity of neurons and the changes of brain network can reflect the most natural cognitive, emotional and behavioral states in real time, fast and truly, which has incomparable advantages to other channels.

1.4 Owning Rich Perceptual Ability

With the development of hardware technology, computers have a variety of sensory abilities similar to human eye, ear, nose, tongue and body. Intelligent system by sensors "look" to the user's facial expressions and body movements and the surrounding environment, "listen" to the user's voice information and the environment, user perception neural networks and brain neurons state, through the voice recognition technology, computing technology such as affective computing and analyzing the characteristic of the user's intention, cognitive and emotional state and situation of information, make intelligent push and judgment, and adaptive adjustment of their own state, give appropriate feedback. The paper mainly describes the development of human-computer interaction and neuroscience after the human-computer interaction channel is expanded to neural signal.

In 2016, Chinese scientists represented by the Institute of Neuroscience, Chinese Academy of Sciences jointly published a paper titled "China Brain Project: Basic Neuroscience, Brain Diseases, and Brain Inspired Computing", which introduced the research progress in Basic Neuroscience, Brain Diseases and brain-inspired Computing in China to the world. The Chinese Brain Project was launched [3]. Brain-computer interaction and brain-computer interface (BCI) have become the emerging representatives of natural interaction in human-computer interaction. Brain-computer interaction refers to the information exchange between human and computer through the direct connection pathway established between the brain and external devices. It is the most natural and harmonious interaction mode in NUI, which aims to realize the control of the brain to the computer by studying the neural mechanism of the brain's electrical activity, or realize the brain-brain connection through the medium of the computer.

2 Human Data and BCI

In human-computer interaction system, the usage behavior of users and performance of computer are influenced by the interplay between computer and users' awareness [4]. So to speak, human plays a vital role in HCI system. However, the complex human system is undergoing complex changes all the time. How to scientifically obtain and analyze human data is an important challenge in human-computer interaction.

2.1 Approach to Obtain Human Data

Generally, we obtain human data from four channels:

Subjective Review. Subjective review refers to the acquisition of users' insights into the system by means of questionnaires, interviews. Subjective data of users are obtained through the outline or scale drawn up in advance. Classical scales in HCI include NASA-TLX scale, SYSTEM availability scale (SUS), USER experience assessment Scale (UEQ), user emotion assessment scale (SAM) and so on.

Behavior Performance Measurement. Behavioral indicators include user performance (completion time, completion rate, number of errors, etc.), and behavioral data such as eye movement, expression, voice, and body. Take eye movement behavior as an example, eye movement behavior includes location-based eye movement and non-location-based eye movement. Positioning eye movement refers to saccadic, smooth tracking, depth information focusing, rhythmical eye movement and physiological tremor of the eye affected by vestibular. Non-stationary eye movements include self-regulating movements such as pupil dilation and lens focus. There are three types commonly used in human-computer interaction: fixation point, saccadic, scanning path, and pupil diameter in non-locational eye movement [5]. Since behavior can be disguised, the above two methods have some problems in authenticity and effectiveness.

Physiological Monitoring. Physiological parameter monitoring equipment appeared in the 1950s, divided into portable, wearable, desktop monitoring equipment, monitoring parameters including blood pressure, blood oxygen saturation, Electrocardiogram, heart rate, electroskin, electromyography, body temperature, respiration and other physiological data.

Neural Signal Detection. Neural data refers to the collection of signals of electrical activity from the brain using devices such as EEG or fMRI. The cerebral cortex is composed of sensory, motor and associative areas. It realizes the perception and coordinated action of events by integrating the neuronal collection of cortical areas of multifunctional areas. It is highly correlated with the inner cognitive process and human behavior including feeling, perception, thinking, consciousness and emotion. The detection method based on neural signal has the characteristics of non-camouflage, authenticity, effectiveness and real-time, it is an ideal way to study what people think and do in human-computer system, and has high research value. In recent years, EEG has gradually begun to cross and integrate with the field of human-computer interaction, focusing on human state evaluation in human-computer system, neural feedback of computer performance to human, and even the emergence of brain-computer interface controlling computer through brainwaves, which has widened the interaction channel in traditional human-computer interaction. To some extent, this has promoted the development of human-computer interaction from the perspective of cognitive nerve.

Compared with the traditional subjective review method, the paper expounds oral physiological index assessment method (heart rate, ECG, EMG, blood pressure, etc.), and the behavior index assessment method (task completion time, completion, wrong number, number of seeking help, eye gaze, twitch, pupil diameter, etc.), the neural detection method interpret the user's EEG data when interacting with the computer through time domain, frequency domain or the time-frequency analysis method, from the aspects of people's cognition, emotion and so on. Regardless of individual differences and complexity of signal analysis, cognitive neural assessment method exhibits superior performance assessment compared to other measures of assessment due to its authenticity and real-time performance.

Many scholars have devoted themselves to the exploration of brain cognitive neural mechanism in the process of human-computer interaction, and are committed to providing cognitive neuroscience basis for brain-computer interface and the next generation of artificial intelligence. Relevant theories, research ideas and methods of cognitive neuroscience can help human-computer interaction establish a more accurate and more powerful cognitive processing function model, so as to evaluate human-computer interaction process and predict user interaction behavior, and finally design a suitable human-computer interaction system [6].

Among many brain signal acquisition technologies like fMRI, fNIRs and EEG, EEG is widely used due to its low cost, portability, non-invasive, and high temporal resolution. Electroencephalogram (EEG) is the overall reflection of the electrophysiological activity of brain nerve cells on the surface of the brain's cortex or scalp. Sophisticated instruments record the potential difference between electrodes and reference electrodes on the scalp as voltage, which amplifies and yields the waveform of an Electroencephalogram over time. EEG is regarded as the first technology to realize brain-computer interaction and in this paper, EEG technology is the main technology being discussed.

According to the integration degree of Cognitive Neuroscience and Human-Computer Interaction, the research on brain-computer systems can be divided into two directions: Passive brain-computer interface and Initiative brain-computer interface.

2.2 Classification of BCI

Passive Brain-Computer Interface. This kind of brain-computer interface mainly provides the identification and judgment of user state and computer design. This type of brain-computer interface requires constant, dynamic and continuous assessment to user without participation of user consciousness. (1) From the computers' perspective, evaluate existing systems or prototypes using neuro data evidence to improve computer design and propose iterative design solutions and implement adaptive design; (2) From the users' perspective: assess the user' cognitive state when interact with human-computer system such as workload and emotion state, experience level, and exploring users' neural model related to the human-computer system.

Initiative Brain-Computer Interface. Initiative brain-computer interface provides direct interaction between brain signal and computer. This type of brain-computer interface is used when the user intends to operate the computer. The integration of human neural model and computer design emphasizes the one-way input or two-way interaction and cooperation between brain and computer, as well as the brain-brain interconnection between unilateral control or multiple computers.

3 Three Progressive Levels of Cognitive Neuroscience Used in HCI

Through secondary data research and desktop analysis, according to the degree of integration of human and computer in HCI system, the application of cognitive neuroscience to human-computer interaction can be divided into three progressive levels shown in Fig. 2.

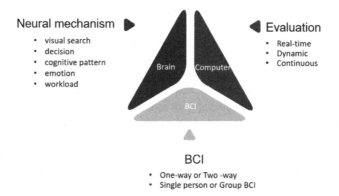

Fig. 2. Brain computer system

3.1 Explore Neural Mechanisms Related to HCI

In addition to measuring people's cognitive and emotional performance when using human-computer systems to assess the rationality of human-computer system design, cognitive neuroscience can also be used for "brain reading", i.e. analyzing EEG data to determine the user's current mode. At present, the recognition of human patterns in human-computer interaction based on cognitive neuroscience mainly includes the recognition of cognitive patterns, interactive intention and affective states. Exploration of neural mechanisms and the construction of cognitive neural models is as important to brain-computer interaction as the user's mental model is to design modeling in design discipline.

User Intent Inference Before Interaction Occurs. Another exploration direction of cognitive neuroscience in human-computer interaction contexts is to distinguish the differences in brain electrical activity under different intentions, such as click-unclickable intention, aimless browse-finding intention, decision intention, motor imagination intention and so on. Research results have been applied to the design of BCI system selection intention, AI system browsing pattern monitoring, intelligent recommendation system and adaptive computing.

Human-computer interaction intention refers to the goals and expectations of users when operating the computer system. It is important to improve the efficiency of human-computer interaction to avoid consuming a lot of resources and time in human-computer information exchange for the inference of uncertain information of users in terms of behavior and perception of intelligent system. Intent modeling and recognition are used to create human-robot Interaction and human-robot Interaction (HRI) Interaction paradigms in cognitive psychology. In psychology, human intention is divided into explicit intention and implicit intention. Explicit intention through facial expression, voice and gestures to express, implicit intention is vague and difficult to understand, electrical neural electrical activity can be a very good response user intent state, because of the cerebral cortex is the commander of the central nervous system, responsible for upload, give orders, on the time series of neural activity should come before the other mode. Therefore, the intention prediction dynamic model is established with the EEG data, and the real intention of the user can be inferred according to the neural activity time series, and the behavior of the intelligent system can be adaptively adjusted, which has certain advantages in terms of time and efficiency.

At present, intentional reasoning has a wide range of applications, including human-service robot interaction, traffic monitoring, vehicle assisted driving, military and flight monitoring, games and entertainment, helping the elderly and disabled system, virtual reality and other fields with potential application value. For example, by observing users' information browsing behavior and brain electrical activity when using e-commerce websites, we can judge whether users are searching targets with goals or browsing without goals. In the intelligent driving system, the EEG characteristics of users during flexible braking and emergency braking are obtained to judge the braking intention of users. In an emergency, the intelligent driving car can take braking measures first to help users avoid danger [7]. The power of EEG in human-computer interaction intent reasoning can be carried out from three aspects: visual search intent, decision intent, and behavioral intent.

Visual Search Intent Reasoning. Visual search intention refers to the user's intention to search for information when browsing the website. Most scholars classify this process into aimless exploration intention, targeted search intention and transactional intention.

In the case of aimless exploration intention, the user is not clear about the target, the search method is uncertain, and the target domain is unknown. The user scans the whole scene to obtain a general picture, and the process is open and dynamic, and the search process lacks obvious boundaries. Under the search intention with goals, users search for specific goals with interest and motivation for specific goals. The transactional intent is when the user needs to accomplish something, such as modifying the remark name. EEG signals corresponding to different visual search intentions are also different. scholars have proposed that the reasoning of visual search intention from the perspective of functional connection can obtain higher accuracy. For example, the PLV difference between browsing and searching intentions and the characteristics of intention transition period can be used for the user's intention reasoning when browsing the interface [8] for specific targets, obtained phase locking value (PLV) of EEG data, extracted significant electrode pairs as characteristic values, and classified browsing intention using SVM, GMM and Bayes.

Decision Intention Reasoning. Decision intention includes user preference prediction (like/dislike), next click behavior prediction (click/don't click, combined with eye movement signal can predict the click location) and next action prediction (action decision or action direction), etc.

In terms of preference decision-making, when users observe the goals with different preference levels, the EEG will show significant difference. Rami N. Khushaba's team, for example, uses EEG and ET data to quantify the importance of different shapes, colors, and materials to interpret consumers from neuroscience perspective. They found that there were clear and significant changes in brain waves in the frontal, temporal and occipital lobes when consumers made preference decisions. Using the mutual information (MI) method, they found that the Theta band (4–7 Hz) in the frontal, parietal and occipital lobes was most correlated with preference decision. Alpha (8–12 Hz) in the frontal and parietal lobes and beta (13–30 Hz) in the occipital and temporal lobes were also associated with preferred decision. Based on neuroscientific evidence, this paper classifies consumers dominated by color and consumers dominated by pattern, compares the differences in mutual information and brain activity between different channel pairs, and builds a decision model to deduce user preference [9]. According to this feature, users' preferences for target objects can be judged by analyzing EEG data, so as to assist decision-making and reasoning.

In terms of click decision reasoning, studies have shown that when users browse websites, the EEG generated by clicking behavior is significantly different from the EEG without clicking behavior. The temporal statistical characteristics, Hjorth characteristics and the pupil diameter in eye movement can well classify users' click intention [10]. Combining the fixation position of eye movements, the user's click intention and click target can be inferred prior to the click behavior. Park et al. fused EEG and eye movement signals to identify the implicit interactive intention in the process of visual search, and found that the recognition accuracy of fused EEG and eye movement signals was about 5% higher than that of single physiological signal, which confirmed that the intent reasoning accuracy of fused EEG data better. This provides theoretical support for brain-computer interface technology [11].

In the aspect of behavioral decision prediction, the classical motor imagination paradigm is mainly combined. When users imagine the movement of different limbs or tongue, the EEG signals generated are significantly different, and then the intention of the user's next movement direction is inferred. Classical motor imagination paradigm can induce the corresponding behavior of the EEG, through neural modeling to find the corresponding behavioral intention mapping. It has been widely and successfully used in complex systems and to help people with disabilities interact naturally, such as brain-controlled drones, brain-controlled aircraft turning left and right and shooting, and brain-controlled wheelchairs moving or turning. Gino Slanzi et al. explored EEG differences in click intentions in the experimental design of different information-seeking tasks on five website. Using EEG mean, standard deviation, maximum, minimum, Hjorth characteristics such as energy, mobility and complexity of time-frequency characteristics of approximate entropy, Petrosian fractal dimension, Higuchi, Hurst index, fractal dimension and nonlinear dynamic characteristics, combining with the pupil diameter of maximum, minimum, average and poor eye movement characteristics, such as using the Random Lasso algorithm for feature selection, get a linear classifier 71% classification accuracy [12].

Cognitive Pattern Classification. Researchers designed tasks with different cognitive patterns in advance, collected EEG differences of subjects under different tasks, selected appropriate eigenvalues after data processing, and classified task patterns through computer learning or deep learning algorithms to realize pattern recognition for different cognitive tasks.

The most classic task types are from the experiments of Keirn et al. [6], which include resting state, complex task, geometric rotation task, letter combination task and visual counting task. The general classification accuracy can reach 75–90%. Different scholars have carried out studies on the basis of the five-cognitive task EEG dataset constructed by Keirn et al. Although Palaniappan achieved a classification accuracy of 97.5% in the classification of the task dicclassification with the best discrimination, its model generalization ability was insufficient [13]. Anderson et al. also obtained classification results up to 70% by using neural network and time averaging method [14]. Johnny Chung Lee used Keirn's experimental mode, P3 and P4 brain electrode channels, and Weka's CFSSubsetEeval operator feature selection method to screen out 23 features of the triclassification task and 16 features under the classification task, and found that the mean spectral power, alpha and beta-low power features played a crucial role in the cognitive classification task [15].

Recognition of User Physiological State During and After Interaction

Affective Pattern Recognition. Affective pattern recognition is a part of Affective Computing. Certain areas and neural circuits in the brain are responsible for processing and processing emotional information. Studies have shown that emotion recognition based on EEG signals is more accurate than verbal evaluation, because brain signals do not "camouflage". Therefore, it is of great significance to study the neural mechanisms associated with emotional states for affective computing and artificial intelligence. FM-Theta waves in the midfrontal cortex and FAA (Frontal Alpha Asymmetry) were associated with emotional expression in the brain. FM Theta is not only associated with attention, but also with pleasurable emotional experiences. Hemispheric Pleasure Hypothesis proposes that the alpha drop in the left frontal lobe represents positive emotions, while the alpha drop in the right frontal lobe indicates negative emotions. Therefore, the alpha asymmetry index FAA in the frontal lobe is often used for affective valence recognition. By processing and calculating the emotion-related EEG features, the result is mapped into the emotion space to realize emotion recognition and classification.

Koelstra et al. used DEAP database to classify emotions in two dimensions of VA, and proposed that arousal was negatively correlated with theta, alpha and gamma, while pleasure was correlated with all bands of EEG. Zheng et al. used computer learning method to study the stability pattern of EEG over time, and proposed that in terms of pleasure, temporal lobe Beta and Gamma were more active in pleasure state, alpha was more active in inferior occipital region in neutral emotion, beta was more active in inferior occipital region in negative emotion, and Gamma was more active in prefrontal lobe in negative emotion [16]. M. Stikic waiting 10 bandwidth according to the standard of the EEG in 20 electrodes and the power spectral density (PSD) in 10 regions, a total of 300 eigenvalues and coiflet function based wavelet analysis to extract the characteristic values of 6 bands 20 electrode 120 through F test, finally extracted 48 characteristic value, and found that most of the eigenvalues of the emotional good prediction effect comes from the frontal lobe, the frontal lobe and temporal lobe, most prediction effect is gamma frequency band, followed by theta and beta [17].

Cognitive State Calculation. In the process of human-computer interaction, with the aggravation of human fatigue factors, there will be a series of physiological reactions, such as increased sensory threshold, decreased movement speed and accuracy, inattention, decreased memory ability, and thinking disorder, which will lead to decreased working ability, increased mistakes, and then lead to a series of human accidents. EEG can be used to assist in monitoring the physiological state of the user in human-computer system. Take the human-autonomous vehicle system as an example, fatigue detection can help the intelligent vehicle judge the state of the human in real time and take over the operation of the vehicle at the necessary time, so as to ensure the safety of the user and complete the intelligent collaboration between man and computer. For example, some scholars compared the EEG of human in normal state and physiological fatigue state (no sleep for 40 h), and found significant differences in brain networks, and proposed the method of EEG fatigue detection and applied it to the physiological fatigue detection of aircraft pilots. In addition, a number of studies have confirmed the role of EEG in early diagnosis and intervention in Alzheimer's disease, depression and personality disorders.

The support of EEG technology to human-computer system during interaction is mainly reflected in the real-time monitoring and evaluation of the cognitive load of users during interaction with the system. By observing the EEG data related to the cognitive load generated by the interaction between the user and the human-computer system, the usability of the human-computer system is evaluated and the design errors are mined, and the design optimization of the human-computer system is finally helped. Cognitive load includes internal cognitive load, external cognitive load and related load. Internal load refers to the requirement of the inherent complexity of information on working memory ability, which is an indicator reflecting the difficulty of using human-computer system. External load refers to the form of information presentation, which is generated by the presentation mode of human-computer interface. Related load is the process of schema building and automation when users use the system. High cognitive load indicates problems in the use of the system and causes psychological stress to users. Cognitive load is expressed by specific spectral energy increases in different brain region. Results show that when the cognitive load increases, the activity of delta wave increase. Theta and alpha waves are related to the cognitive process of processing new information, and higher working memory load will lead to the enhancement of Theta and Beta [18]. Prefrontal gamma waves are correlated with task difficulty, and the more difficult the interactive task, the more active the prefrontal gamma waves are [19].

3.2 Improve Computer Performance Based on Neural Assessment

Among the systematic design methods of Human-Computer Interaction, besides the goal-oriented method and user-centered design method, the design method based on assessment is also widely used because of its efficiency, accuracy and low cost.

Designers usually organize subjective assessment, physiological assessment or neural assessment on the design prototype or the old version, dig out the inconformity of human behavior and needs in the current design, and carry out iterative design on the basis of the original design. The general process diagram see Fig. 3. On the one hand, evaluation is used to verify the rationality of a design, on the other hand, iteratively improve the design by means of evaluation [18].

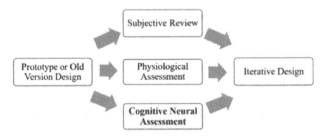

Fig. 3. Design method and process based on assessment

In the process of human-computer interaction, the performance of intelligent system is evaluated by brain neural signals, such as usability, visual aesthetic and user experience.

Real-Time Evaluation. From the time dimension, EEG based assessment can be divided into post-stimulus assessment and real-time assessment. Post-stimulus assessment refers to the analysis of EEG differences between the stimulus state and the resting state after a given human-computer interaction related stimulus, and then draw conclusions about the difficulty, aesthetic feeling, experience and other aspects of the stimulus objects. Real-time evaluation is based on the characteristics of high spatial and temporal resolution of EEG, and the real-time feedback of EEG on the subject materials can be obtained by real-time detection of EEG changes in the process of human-computer interaction. Take human-computer interface design evaluation as an example, ICONS with different design colors, shapes, text and graphics combinations were presented to the subjects, and EEG signals were used to analyze which design form better. By looking at different looks of smartphones, the brain electricity was used to assess which design was more acceptable to users [20].

Dynamic and Continuous Evaluation. In terms of the type of results, neural data based evaluation can not only obtain independent judgments about the stimulus materials, such as difficult-easy, Beautiful-ugly, but also obtain continuous time series of neural signals if the stimulus materials are dynamically changing time series. Combining with Bayesian and hidden Markov algorithms, time series can also be predicted, which is the content of intent reasoning mentioned above.

3.3   Direct Interaction Between Brain Signal and Computer

Brain-computer interface, also known as "Brain-machine interface", is a direct one-way or two-way communication connection between human and external devices. In the case of a one-way brain-computer interface, the computer either receives commands from the brain or sends signals to the brain, but cannot send and receive signals at the same time. Bidirectional brain-computer interface (BCI) allows the bidirectional information exchange between the brain and external devices to achieve human-computer cooperation.

In the aspect of unidirectional brain-computer interface, the EEG is connected with other external devices as a recording device of neural activity signal, and the external devices are directly controlled based on the neural activity signal. Five sensory channels of eye, ear, nose, tongue and body each perform their respective functions, and the absence of any interactive channel will bring inconvenience to basic life. In a sense, brain-computer interface can make up for the regret caused by the lack of channel. For example, the research on motor imagination in cognitive neuroscience provides relevant evidence of brain regions, frequency bands and components related to movement, which provides research basis for controlling movement through imagination. Intelligent medical wheelchair controlled by brainwave can realize the forward stopping and steering function of the wheelchair by real-time detecting the energy value of α wave, β wave, θ wave and δ wave. BCI also implements mind-control machinery for paralyzed people, for example, using brainwave-controlled robotic arms to help patients with physical disabilities complete specific tasks, as shown in Fig. 4.

Fig. 4. Brain-computer interface cases: brain-controlled robotic arms from Carnegie Mellon University and the University of Minnesota

4   Directions of HCI Research Based on Cognitive Neuroscience

The current research achievements in the field of cognitive neuroscience provide a large number of cognitive neural mechanisms for researchers in the design of BCI brain-computer interfaces and the design of the next generation of Artificial Intelligence (AI). The efficiency of BCI recognition and control can be greatly improved by selecting appropriate brain region channels and EEG characteristics according to the task type to be complete. In terms of AI, based on studies on basic cognitive functions related to attention and cognitive load and neural mechanisms related to advanced cognitive functions such as emotion recognition and empathy, the AI system is more humanized in terms of self-adaptation, personalization and human-computer collaboration.

4.1   Broaden Existing Interactive Channels

Traditional human-computer interaction relies on human's visual, auditory, voice and tactile channels. These four-sense collaboration completes basic human-computer interaction and brings real experience, such as the interaction between human and touch-screen mobile phones. With the advent of the era of natural interaction, AR, VR and other intelligent devices have entered people's lives. Eye movement interaction, somatosensory interaction and voice interaction have gradually become the mainstream interaction mode. As a natural interaction mode based on neuroscience, brain-computer interface (BCI) has attracted extensive attention. Brain-computer interface creats a direct connection between brain and external devices and provides a new interactive channel to implement two-way information exchange for the human-computer interaction system.

    The use of brain-computer interfaces is generally considered in three situations. First, for patients lost basic interaction channels, such as patients with total paralysis, BCI provides them a path to control computers, products and assistant robots with neural signals, helps paralysis patients achieving the basic skills they need for daily life. By using BCI technology, products become the extension of the human body, such as brain-controlled wheelchairs. Second, when the user is in a complex work context such as operate with complex information systems with large amount of information input, operation is complex and each operation is critical, though all users' multi-sensory channels are occupied, it is still difficult to complete the interactive tasks. In this case, BCI operation is a good choice. For example, studies have realized pilots control military aircraft, using the brain to control the aircraft to fly left and right and firing artillery shells, and achieved high identification accuracy [21]. Thirdly, some human-computer interaction tasks require people's quick response. For example, in the military, the recognition and judgment of real and virtual scenes require quick action. At this time, the user's intention is automatically judged by the brainwave, so that the computer can respond quickly and complete the target.

4.2   Improve the Reliability of Human-Computer Cooperation

Interaction based on the cognitive neuroscience provides fast and real user status and help the computer to judge the situation of human-computer system. Through the adaptive design and enhanced cognitive design, realize automatic control, determine under what circumstances give users help based on cognitive neuroscience evidence. When people deal with tasks of different cognitive difficulty, they consume different cognitive resources and carry different cognitive loads. For example, from the perspective of neuroscience, ratio of brain beta to alpha band power can reflect cognitive load to some extent. Under different task difficulty, the changes and differences of brain electrical activity can be used as the basis for human-computer cooperation, such as determining the weight of human-computer division of labor in human-computer interaction process, that is, in which scene the intervention of computer is needed and in which scene the decision of human is needed. To improve the reliability, safety and efficiency of human-computer system by recognizing, sensing and monitoring EEG state.

For example, intelligent driving systems that incorporate intelligent computing use EEG to monitor physical sleepiness to ensure safe driving; By monitoring the cognitive attraction, cognitive load and emotion of learners' brain wave characteristics, the online learning system can adjust the learning plan and progress individually. Intelligent recommendation system realizes accurate recommendation through brainwave interest points; Persuasion robots use emotional computing to obtain people's cognitive models and emotions, help people timely resolve bad emotions, and effectively persuade users to engage in a healthy lifestyle with real-time strategies. Alicia Heraz et al. [22] used the normalized peak characteristics of the four frequency bands of EEG to classify 8 emotions including anger, boredom, confusion, contempt, curiosity, delay, surprise and frustration by WEKA, and designed an intelligent system for emotion detection and intervention. The system consists of four modules: EEG signal acquisition module, signal processing module, emotional state induction module and emotion classification module. The intelligent system will have a certain positive impact on learners with disabilities, who are silent or have no interest in learning.

4.3 Optimize the Experience of Human-Computer Interaction

Brain-Computer Interface, the new human-computer interaction way, brings people new feelings and experiences. User experience is the actions, sensations, considerations, feelings and sense making of a person when interacting with a technical device or service [23]. User experience is composed of two main dimensions: hedonic and pragmatic aspects. Brain-computer interface bring natural and novel experiences from functional and social psychological level.

Especially in the field of entertainment, through novel interactive way brought by BCI to enhance the experience of players. For example, using the brain's attention condition to control the flight of the drone. Under attention condition, users can control the drone to continue to fly in the sky. Laurent Bonnet et al. designed a two-player soccer game based on motor imagination potential. Players push the ball toward the left (or right) goal by imagining the movement of the left (or right) hand. This game also involves competition mode and cooperation mode, which expands the channel of multi-brain computer interaction design [24]. The brain-computer device represented by the NextMind with 8 electrodes and 60 g of weight converts the signals from the cerebral cortex into computer-readable digital commands through the brain-wave reading and analysis device, which can control the TV, input passwords, switch the color of lights according to the attention of color blocks, play duck games and VR games and so on.

Open source platform allows researchers to enter, and in the near future, brain-computer games will become another NUI emerging game field after AR/VR.

5 Conclusion

Interdisciplinary integration is the general trend in today's world. Due to the authenticity, timeliness and maturation of acquisition and analysis techniques of brain signal, cognitive neuroscience has been relatively applied in Human-computer interaction through the efforts of scholars from many fields in more than 30 years.

At the same time, after going through the development stage of CLI, GUI, MMUI, PUI and NUI, human-computer interaction has gradually stepped into the phase of multi-perception, rich modes and real-time continuous natural two-way information exchange, and there is a more urgent need for other natural and real data support besides human views and physiological data. This article take a non-invasive, high time resolution and low cost cerebral cortex signal collection method-EEG technology as an example to state crossover and fusion of EEG and Human-computer interaction not only brings the physiological, cognitive, emotional and intentional data of the user to the intelligent human-computer system from the perspective of neuroscience, but also provides the neural basis for the adaptive adjustment of the operating state and user-centered iterative improvement of the intelligent systems. What's more, deep fusion of brain and computer leads to the birth of BCI technique. This seamless direct connection between human brain and intelligent system widens the human-computer interaction channel. Especially in the complex human-work interaction contexts, the additional interaction channel from neural signals can well solve the occupation of human interaction channels in complex environment and provide additional information output channel. High spatial and temporal resolution and authenticity of BCI, to some extent, guarantee the timeless and smooth completion of the work. Besides that, cognitive neuroscience is of great significance in the evaluation and adaptive work system design, it evaluates the work environment in real-time, continuously and dynamically from both human and computer aspects and provides neuroscience evidence for the design of adaptive human-work systems.

Today, design of HCI system based on cognitive neuroscience is one of the most popular directions in the field of NUI. At present, the cognitive functions such as attention, memory, emotion, decision of neural mechanism studies have been comparative maturity, the neural mechanism model and neural assessment method has been widely used in the design of human-computer collaboration system, especially the noninvasive brain-computer interface is preliminary already put into practical application, achieve the expand human-computer interaction channels, improve system reliability and improve the human-computer interaction experience.

However, due to individual differences in brain signal, the existing cognitive neural mechanism from individual dependent calculation to model generalization is still the focus and difficulty of the research. In addition, in the human-computer interaction process, more detailed neural loop working principle, feature extraction, algorithm optimization and more scene mining are challenges and opportunities for the development of human-computer interaction based on cognitive neuroscience in the future NUI, BCI and AI era. In general, the basic research and application of cognitive neuroscience in human-computer interaction are still in their infancy, and there is still a long way to go for the two to merge in nature.

Acknowledgments. This study was supported by the Foundation of Education Department of Inner Mongolia Autonomous Region, CHINA (No. ZSZX21098).

References

1. Kosch, T., Hassib, M., Woźniak, P.W., et al.: Your eyes tell: leveraging smooth pursuit for assessing cognitive workload. In: Conference on Human Factors in Computing Systems – Proceedings (2018)

2. Ahn, M., Lee, M., Choi, J., Jun, S.C.: A review of brain-computer interface games and an opinion survey from researchers, developers and users. Sensors (Switzerland) **14** (2014). https://doi.org/10.3390/s140814601

3. Mu-ming, P., Du, J.L., Ip, N.Y., et al.: China brain project: basic neuroscience, brain diseases, and brain-inspired computing. Neuron **92**, 591–596 (2016)

4. Qin, X., Tan, C.-W., Clemmensen, T.: Unraveling the influence of the interplay between mobile phones' and users' awareness on the user experience (UX) of using mobile phones. In: Barricelli, B.R., et al. (eds.) HWID 2018. IAICT, vol. 544, pp. 69–84. Springer, Cham (2019). https://doi.org/10.1007/978-3-030-05297-3_5

5. Cheng, S., Hu, Y., Fan, J., Wei, Q.: Reading comprehension based on visualization of eye tracking and EEG data. Sci. China Inf. Sci. **63**(11), 1–3 (2020). https://doi.org/10.1007/s11432-019-1466-7

6. Keirn, Z.A., Aunon, J.I.: A new mode of communication between man and his surroundings. IEEE Trans. Biomed. Eng. **37** (1990). https://doi.org/10.1109/10.64464

7. Wang, X., Bi, L., Fei, W., et al.: EEG-based universal prediction model of emergency braking intention for brain-controlled vehicles. In: International IEEE/EMBS Conference on Neural Engineering, NER (2019)

8. Kang, J.S., Park, U., Gonuguntla, V., et al.: Human implicit intent recognition based on the phase synchrony of EEG signals. Pattern Recogn. Lett. **66** (2015). https://doi.org/10.1016/j.patrec.2015.06.013

9. Khushaba, R.N., Greenacre, L., Kodagoda, S., et al.: Choice modeling and the brain: a study on the Electroencephalogram (EEG) of preferences. Expert Syst. Appl. **39** (2012). https://doi.org/10.1016/j.eswa.2012.04.084

10. Slanzi, G., Balazs, J.A., Velásquez, J.D.: Combining eye tracking, pupil dilation and EEG analysis for predicting web users click intention. Inf. Fusion **35** (2017). https://doi.org/10.1016/j.inffus.2016.09.003

11. Park, U., Mallipeddi, R., Lee, M.: Human implicit intent discrimination using EEG and eye movement. In: Loo, C.K., Yap, K.S., Wong, K.W., Teoh, A., Huang, K. (eds.) ICONIP 2014. LNCS, vol. 8834, pp. 11–18. Springer, Cham (2014). https://doi.org/10.1007/978-3-319-12637-1_2

12. Ko, K., Yang, H.C., Sim, K.B.: Emotion recognition using EEG signals with relative power values and Bayesian network. Int. J. Control Autom. Syst. **7** (2009). https://doi.org/10.1007/s12555-009-0521-0

13. Palaniappan, R.: Brain computer interface design using band powers extracted during mental tasks. In: 2nd International IEEE EMBS Conference on Neural Engineering (2005)

14. Anderson, C.W., Sijercic, Z.: Classification of EEG signals from four subjects during five mental tasks. Advances (1996)

15. Lee, J.C., Tan, D.S.: Using a low-cost electroencephalograph for task classification in HCI research. In: UIST 2006: Proceedings of the 19th Annual ACM Symposium on User Interface Software and Technology (2008)

16. Zheng, W.L., Zhu, J.Y., Lu, B.L.: Identifying stable patterns over time for emotion recognition from EEG. IEEE Trans. Affect. Comput. (2019). https://doi.org/10.1109/TAFFC.2017.271 2143

17. Stikic, M., Johnson, R.R., Tan, V., Berka, C.: EEG-based classification of positive and negative affective states. Brain Comput. Interfaces 1 (2014). https://doi.org/10.1080/2326263X.2014. 912883

18. Kumar, N., Kumar, J.: Measurement of cognitive load in HCI systems using EEG power spectrum: an experimental study. Procedia Comput. Sci. 84, 70–78 (2016)

19. Bouzekri, E., Canny, A., Martinie, C., Palanque, P., Gris, C.: Using task descriptions with explicit representation of allocation of functions, authority and responsibility to design and assess automation. In: Barricelli, B.R., et al. (eds.) HWID 2018. IAICT, vol. 544, pp. 36–56. Springer, Cham (2019). https://doi.org/10.1007/978-3-030-05297-3_3

20. Ding, Y., Guo, F., Zhang, X., et al.: Using event related potentials to identify a user's behavioural intention aroused by product form design. Appl. Ergon. 55 (2016). https://doi. org/10.1016/j.apergo.2016.01.018

21. Zhao, M., Gao, H., Wang, W., Qu, J.: Research on human-computer interaction intention recognition based on EEG and eye movement. IEEE Access 8 (2020). https://doi.org/10. 1109/ACCESS.2020.3011740

22. Heraz, A., Frasson, C.: Predicting the three major dimensions of the learner's emotions from brainwaves. Int. J. Electric. Comput. Eng. 2, 3 (2007)

23. Schrepp, M., Held, T., Laugwitz, B.: The influence of hedonic quality on the attractiveness of user interfaces of business management software. Interact. Comput. 18 (2006). https://doi. org/10.1016/j.intcom.2006.01.002

24. Bonnet, L., Lotte, F., Lécuyer, A.: Two brains, one game: design and evaluation of a multiuser BCI video game based on motor imagery. IEEE Trans. Comput. Intell. AI Games 5 (2013). https://doi.org/10.1109/TCIAIG.2012.2237173

HCI Four Waves Within Different Interaction Design Examples

Arminda Guerra Lopes$^{(\boxtimes)}$ (iD)

ITI/LARSyS and Polytechnic Institute of Castelo Branco, Castelo Branco, Portugal
aguerralopes@gmail.com

Abstract. The several approaches available on literature regarding the origins of the universe conduct us to remove certainty concerning what we know about the world: the things (artifacts), theories, and behaviors among other effects. Making an analogy with it and some constructs of Human Computer Interaction, we face that the waves or paradigms have been concentrated on different focus, however, ontologically in intersection and complementarity with each other. To illustrate these connections, several creative design case studies, developed in different eras are described. The results and discussion about the waves characteristics, the theoretical concepts and those practical cases, will probably, take us to think better on a less bumpy road that leads to more positive user experiences.

Keywords: Waves in human computer interaction · Creative design · Culture · Interaction design

1 Introduction

According to literature, there are four waves (paradigms) that Human Computer Interaction (HCI) has jumped, which correspond roughly historically to how HCI has developed in terms of the academic discipline that have most prevailed as inputs to its pluridisciplinary character. The first wave was focused on technical patterns; the second wave was concentrated with the cognitive paradigm; the third, on the ethnographic paradigm. Research in the third wave challenged the values related to technology in the second wave (e.g., efficiency) and embraced experience and meaning making (e.g., [29]). Then, a fourth, namely the trans disciplinary design paradigm or fourth wave was added [20]. Other contributions about this wave were presented by Blevis [5] who argued that: the trans disciplinary (see for example, [28, 31] paradigm may be defined as a focus on insisting on a values-orientation for interactivity design as a higher order concern than collections of methods or domains of expertise. They added that the trans disciplinary design is distinguished from the other paradigms by its primary cardinality of focus is on politics and values and ethics. The four waves were considered the 4th 'Gratifying' Wave by Cabrero [9]. Lately, Ashley et al. [37] argued that the four waves must push harder, beyond measured criticism for actual change in institutions.

© IFIP International Federation for Information Processing 2022
Published by Springer Nature Switzerland AG 2022
G. Bhutkar et al. (Eds.): HWID 2021, IFIP AICT 609, pp. 83–98, 2022.
https://doi.org/10.1007/978-3-031-02904-2_4

This paper is organized as follows: Author presents a snapshot on HCI waves, then, examples of serious and silly creative artifacts design, followed by the design cases analyzed according to each wave characteristics. Finally, a discussion and contributions are presented before the conclusions.

2   A Snapshot on HCI: The Waves

After the initial HCI wave of technical rationality, Grudin began to focus on the cultural barriers that separate HCI and IS [17]: HCI discovered the limitations of laboratory studies and surveys to understand discretionary use of methods and the focus of Information Systems (IS) in research has grounded on the economic, organizational, and marketing theory and practice [18].

The first wave was based on cognitive science and human factors. Bannon [1] argued that it was model-driven and focused on the human being as a subject to be studied through strict guidelines, formal methods, and systematic testing.

In the second wave, according to Bannon [1] the emphasis is "from human factors to human actors." In the second wave, the focus was on groups working with several applications. Theory focused on work settings and interaction within well-established communities of practice [33]. Other important aspects and concepts for reflection were situated action [38] and distributed cognition [23, 32].

The third wave of HCI explores the several interdisciplinary inquiries within the HCI field. This includes the extensive compilation of aims at understanding the design, methods and applications of forms of interaction with new technologies and the varieties of human knowledge and experiences. This wave claimed to expand from the working and computer-based context into a broader environment of the mobile and the home, the everyday lives and into culture [6]. This, then, meant to break the boundaries between work and leisure, arts, and the home: in other words, between rationality and emotion.

A contemplation of a fourth wave in HCI emerge from, for example, problematizing methods, tools, and techniques [12]; also, by propositioning to solidly moving from User-Centered Design (UCD) philosophies of professional designer into a more Participatory Design (PD) involvement of laypeople [36] in the construction of sustainable and gratifying futures. What seems clear is that there must be a liaison and a human attuning in the adoption of human values towards a gratifying UX [19], as well as a carefully drafted agenda toward an HCI research and practice based on human needs and social responsibility [30]. Bødker's [6] challenge to 'identify' a fourth wave HCI, on a new vision that places 'politics and values and ethics' at the forefront without abandoning the strengths of previous waves. Ashley agrees, while they go deeply on the discussion stating that a fourth wave must push harder, beyond measured criticism for actual (e.g., institutional) change [37].

After these views about different authors and their considerations about each wave's characteristics, we focus on a deeper engagement with the existing literature from Grudin and Bodker. Bødker [6] has initiated the three waves of HCI captured and presented the challenges faced by HCI in the past three decades.

Harrison, Tatar [20] postulated an almost similar idea in categorizing the development of HCI into 3 stages. Bødker [6] referred to it as three waves of HCI while Harrison (2007) referred to it as three paradigms of HCI development based on the phenomenological matrix they created. These prove that Bødker [6] was not alone in this effort and both studies apprehend an almost similar timeframe of the HCI development.

Referring to the history of HCI publications, Bødker [6] assumed the challenges in HCI research which the HCI community has broadened intellectually from its root in engineering research to cognitive science, sociological studies, emotional design as well as social participatory research.

According to Bødker [7], the three waves timeframe is: first wave - from the early years of HCI to 1992, second wave – 1992 to 2006 and third wave – 2006 and beyond. The transition of first wave to second wave was discussed by Bannon [2] in his paper From Human Factors to Human Actor. The first wave was pitched towards cognitive science and human factors. It was model driven and focused on the human being as a subject of rigid research with formal guidelines and systematic texting, and most of the studies were conducted in a closed scientific lab setting. Bannon [2] observed there was a significant change in the second wave as there was a transition from human factor to human actor in the HCI research. User studies were carried out from the enclosed scientific labs to the real-life environment as anthropology ethnographic research approaches were adopted. Concept of context became important. This signified the beginning of user entered design (UCD). Theories and research approaches from non-computer science disciplines were applied. Proactive methods, such as a variety of participatory design, prototyping and contextual inquiries, started to emerge in this wave [7, 16]. In the third wave, the success of consumer technology was observed, integration of multiple devices such as desktop, laptop, iPad and mobile. Multiple user experience-based situations become evident when the devices are used in different environments. Ubiquitous computing increased whereby computing is made to appear anytime and everywhere [7]. Research in the third wave challenged the value related to the second wave and embraced experience and meaning making [12]. User created content, common artifact and shared artifact caused the boundary between user and designer to become ambiguous in the realm of social network service (SNS). Scopes of proactive methods such as participatory design as well as the argument of the ability of such methods from existing practices to the need of emergent use were broadened.

The fourth wave is governed by two fields: positive psychology (well-being beyond humans defined as needy) and cognitive neuroscience (human irrationality), which leads to calls to consider an even more "human-centered perspective" [3] such as human values [8] and ethical aspects [34], embodiment [20, 24], and well-being [10].

In summary, the first wave approach is based on the formulations of engineering; where the second was focused on the human mind's mental and cognitive aspect, information processing and general communication between man and machine. In contrast, the third highlights the relationship in the impact of society, culture, value and social changes. The fourth focuses on the transdisciplinary design paradigm, which means, on politics and values and ethics.

3   Creative Design

The analysis of the different approaches of HCI waves can help us to have more understanding of human behavior and its interaction with artifacts. Design has a central position in HCI. It is the medium to fix a problem. Thus, the HCI waves concerns are reflected in the different design perspectives. If we look around us, we see things. Those things have been designed following one or more of four wave characteristics on HCI. They were designed as models-driven and focused on the human being, developed by groups working with a collection of applications. They use contexts and application types broadened, and intermixed, relative to the second wave's focus on work. They challenged the values related to technology in the second wave and they embraced experience and meaning making. From the fourth wave we notice, for example, a more participatory design involvement. The design is refined as matters of rigor, openness and tolerance.

Design, making and intervening in the world have captured the attention of communication scholars in recent years. From explaining algorithmic bias on social media to the creation of online storytelling platforms, contemporary questions of communication require an understanding of the affordances, biases and constraints of communication devices, interfaces and systems - as well as an understanding about the work of designers that create these technologies.

Furthermore, there is also growing interest in using design as an inventive method in order to inquire about the world and build theory through the making of media, things and prototypes. Design is the reflection on the transformative power of doing, making and knowing as strength for positive change in the world. It connects us to the surrounding world and the society of which we are part; good things can happen, and new realities are possible, we just have to work for them. People design with a purpose since pretty much everything we do now has a purpose. However, sometimes things are created by hazard (some of the great discoveries happened by hazard) or even as a result of a creativity process. Other times design was inspired by nature.

This section presents three types of output designs: those that were invented with or without a purpose (engines of our ingenuity), those that were born useless and those that reflected the value delivered by design thinking, which is almost always seen having improvements in the creativity and usefulness of the produced solutions. It reflects the type of creativity in engineering and technology, and in what way, it communicates to innovation in art and science.

3.1 Engines of our Ingenuity

Engines of our ingenuity" was a radio program, where stories of how our culture is formed by human creativity. Lienhard [11] looked at history, art, technology and the epic failures and successes that human curiosity had led us to. He registered his reflections about the nature of technology, culture and human inventiveness in a book with the same name as the radio program. Lienhard observes that the interactions between society and technology result in machines that reflect social needs while also acting as the instruments of social change; he also stated that "the history of technology is a history of us – we are the machines we create" [11]. If we look back to some of those engines, we stay astonished with them, either because of their aesthetic appearance or the absence of remote technology integration, for example, cars, bicycles, airplanes and so on. However, we learned, and those artifacts contributed to the technology development, and to the research on several areas. All together subsidized to the things we have now, and to those that are in groundwork for tomorrow. The way artifacts were developed and improved along the years, permitted us to understand the nature of creativity in engineering, technology, art or in science domains.

3.2 Chindogu Philosophy

Chindogu [11] means a 'weird tool'. The Japanese comedian Kenji Kawakami, who termed the idea in his book, in the mid-nineties, 101 Useless Japanese Inventions, invented the term: "The Art of Chindogu". "Every Chindogu is an almost useless object, but not every almost useless object is a Chindogu. In order to transcend the realms of the merely almost useless, certain vital criteria must be met. These criteria, is a set of ten fundamental tenets, that define the art and philosophy of Chindogu, as outlined by the International Chindogu Society to bear in mind: A Chindogu cannot be for real use; A Chindogu must exist; Inherent in every Chindogu is the spirit of anarchy; Chindogu are tools for everyday life; Chindogu are not for sale; Humor must not be the sole reason for creating a Chindogu; Humor must not be the sole reason for creating a Chindogu; Chindogu is not propaganda; Chindogu are never taboo; Chindogu cannot be patented; Chindogu are without prejudice. As an illustration, the next figure presents some of the Chindogu products. These pictures are taken from a Chindogu website with authorization from the International Chindogu Society (Fig. 1).

Fig. 1. Chindogu pictures [https://www.chindogu.com]

This philosophy was considered as a motivation source to put working together multidisciplinary professionals and researchers on a research workshop as it is described in Sect. 4.

3.3 Culture Creativity and Interaction Design

Leonardo Network (Leonardo-Net) [26] was an international interdisciplinary research network, led by the UK, established to define a program of research in culture, creativity, and interaction design. Within this network several workshops took place.

Authors present two case studies from two workshops as examples of creativity in design. The first one was based on the Chindogu philosophy as a motivation source to put working together multidisciplinary professionals and researchers. The second one had a different purpose. The goal was to examine human-computer interaction (HCI) and the theory, design and application of interactive technologies, specifically, in relation to the arts. Conversely, it is permitted to define a research agenda at the interface between the two. The project included among other outputs, an arts/science interactive digital artwork, the execution of which was planned as part of the collaboration of the nodes. The involvement of artists and scientists brought to the design practice different perspectives. Designers with an arts perspective look at design differently from those with engineering perspective. The objectives were to involve the participants to think and to materialize the design thinking process with only drawings and words.

Human Beans (HB), two creative designers, who made fictional products by hacking commercial culture, designed new services by working with real people. They were the facilitators. Their aim was to challenge assumptions. Some of their presented developed projects were: "Hearwear – hearing augmentation for the hearingable"; "What's Cooking Grandma? – a media platform to reconnect with grandmothers" and "Neighbours TXT – a service platform to help neighbors to help each other." [21, 22].

4   Results

In the Chindogu Challenger, three artworks were constructed following the Chindogu tenets and the theory, design and application of interactive technologies, specifically, in relation to the arts including the definition of a research agenda at the interface between the two. In the second case study, the researcher chose two representative draws from one of the work rounds. Participants were obliged to choose from a given table, a technology, a context and a problem. Then, the goal was to use drawings and words to create ideas to explore in future HCI research. They were representative of the materialization of the design thinking process.

We provide an overview of some of the interaction design examples within the frame of the HCI waves and consider their impact on the design process.

1st wave – technical and theoretical aspects, focusing on the interaction between a specific user with a specific computer. First design example - Engines of our ingenuity - the interactions between society and technology result in machines that reflect social needs.

2nd wave – value choices rather than technical ones because of the endless technological possibilities. Second design example - Engines of our ingenuity.

3rd wave – elements of human life are included in the human-computer interaction such as culture, emotion, and experience. Third design example – Chindogu - Society to bear in mind.

4th wave – well-being beyond humans defined as needy and human senselessness, which leads to consideration of "human-centered perspective" such as human values and ethical aspects, embodiment, and well-being. Fourth design example – Leonardo network - The objectives were to involve the participants to think and to materialize the design thinking process with only drawings and words. The design of new services by working with real people. Also, an example of a university teaching method in HCI.

4.1 Case Study 1

The program was composed of about twenty multidisciplinary researchers. From these, sixteen participated in the Chindogu Scrapheap Challenge. One day was given (about five hours) to each team to build a solution to the challenge using either the materials and equipment provided or material that each team brought to the competition. The event included mainly two stages: one to find ideas, mainly conceptual; and the other to implement ideas, essentially practical in nature. These were preceded by an opening session and concluded with a final session, in which each group presented the work developed. Mind, body and spirit – how does diversity impact?

4.1.1 Findings

Team 1 - The group discussed some ideas about electric chairs, addictive things, automatic cleaners, electricity and mobile phones, and the material they needed for the artwork was defined: kitchen foil, a piece of carpet, transformer, etc. Participants described the use of the device ("What we have here is a stack of CDs cases. The critical thing is the plastic access of the dialectic for those who remember from the school physics. On one side, we have a foil going inside and outside…"). It addressed the ideas of connection to a person and that kind of problems could arise in the wild: it was stylish but useless (Fig. 2).

Teams used a set of methods, which consisted of a large body of knowledge and techniques (design thinking). This was the start of the design process – an innovative one, then, the thoughts were put into action by the design doing process.

Fig. 2. A static mobile phone charger [19]

Team 2 - The project "Remote Wild Animal – Interaction Device – Using Petting, Enabling Technology" (P.etting E.nabling T.echnology), was made of: a back scratcher; a Lego robot; a mechanical tickling hand; a computer mouse; a rubber bands; sheets and plastics for a tent; a computer for voices and a toy dog. They addressed the problem – interacting with animals. Along with the HCI themes: interaction without connection, interaction not only in, but also with the wild. A demonstration of the scratching, tickling and calling of the animal with the robotic hand that cuddles him was presented (Fig. 3).

Fig. 3. Remote wild animal – interaction device [19]

Team 3 – Participants decided on using cats after the suggestion "interaction in the wild, that could be, cat computer interaction" and the analogy from the Chindogu tenets: "Can't it be for real use – cat computer interaction?". The notions of death, remembrance, dreams and "their realization in pillows" were then introduced. The chosen name was: "Nine Lives dot dot Question Mark" (Fig. 4). Authors explained how they had arrived at the concept. ("we built an installation for capturing memories and dreams and the layers left behind to replay them...)". The artwork story was: (...) "Sinbad lays on his cushion and he dies. So, the owner takes the cat to the graveyard, lays him down in the graveyard, takes his collar, and places the collar on the cushion to remind the owner of the cat... Jess visits the cushion to remember his dear friend (...)".

Fig. 4. Nine lives dot question mark [19]

The Chindogu philosophy tenets were the standpoint and the research approach used was the design thinking process. The results mirrored in the presented figures are examples of the future research areas identified as the interface between Human Computer Interaction and the arts. It reveals the work of each team's creativity. The funny results, the non-obvious and innovative projects, exposed the concern about people, technology, arts and the contribution to people's quality of life improvement.

4.2   Case Study 2

This case study had twelve participants who worked together for six hours. Human Beans initiated the project. Then, participants split into two groups: one went to visit the exhibition "Front Page" at the British Library and the other group went to visit the exhibition "Michelangelo" at the British Museum. The goal of these visits was an inspiration hunt for the participants' work during the day. People met in the workshop after the visits. They presented what they found inspirational to work from their morning visit.

The second part of the presentation consisted of an interactive exploration of HB's fictional products and inspirational material including: cleanliness, wellbeing, crime, gaming, virtual worlds, experiments in interaction, food, new digital crafts, and death, among others. After that, they posed two questions to the audience: "What you have learned from this morning; from what you looked at what inspired you at most?" and "Think about a problem that you think you would like to solve or an issue that you would like to explore or a technology that you would like to exploit." Participants had ten minutes to create the project.

4.2.1   Findings

The project ideas were created in response to three factors set by HB: a good problem to be solved in future research; a good issue to explore in future research and a good technology or combination of technologies to be explored in future research. There were four rounds of work. After the project concluded, each team presented feedback to the audience. At this workshop, other challenges were proposed following the same context. The results were presented, and the main concerns focused on: Mental Wellbeing; Climate Change; Street Crime; Energy Consumption; Online World; Migrant Communities; Social Exclusion, among others.

In the first-round, team 1 chose a project based on: Problem: "lack of sleep; Technology: reality television; and Context: supermarket" (Fig. 5).

Fig. 5. Lack of sleep, reality TV, and supermarket [19]

Team 2 did the project based on: Problem: "physical fitness; Technology: "any related to simulations"; Context:" a seven-year-old dog that had been mistreated by owner".

Team 3 had: Problem: "binge drinking"; Technology: "camera phones"; Context: "a 68-year-old that used to work in science". Team 4 used: Problem: "world peace"; Technology: "Sony PSP"; Context: "a nurse who worked shifts and was planning a family". In another round, following the same procedures, we underline the "Social Exclusion" theme (Fig. 6).

Fig. 6. Social exclusion [19]

The source to inspire the participants was the "look around" in London city. The participants were researchers from different fields, art, engineering, computer sciences, musicians, psychologists, filmmakers, and ethnographers, among others. According to the presented work description and the obtained results we may conclude that every day we may apply knowledge from a variety of sources to resolve problems, to manage relationships, and to contribute to a better-quality of communities' life. Participants did the whole work in teams. Human Beans were the facilitators and the people who settled the challenges.

The main participants' preoccupation was with people's daily life and with the problems we face around us: mental wellbeing, dementia, street crime, migrant communities, family life, online world, cultural community, remote surveillance, etc. These challenges happened about ten years ago. However, in literature we find that the quality-of-life improvement keeps being a concern for research and for the technology development plan. The themes discussed on the workshops, advocated by participants, reflect several tenets influences concerning the four HCI waves, especially, the transdisciplinary design which enables each designer to articulate her or his vision of what truly matters in design with the materials of digital technologies: social networking, the concern of using different devices, with accessibility and sustainability which are areas in constant development.

5 Discussion

The four waves of HCI follow a chronological order, but the emergence and acceptance of a newer one does not replace the existing ones. They coexist in the same communities. Different research paradigms can underlie the HCI wave. Table 1 presents the four waves differences according to diverse authors.

Table 1. Four waves differences.

1st Wave	2nd Wave	3rd Wave	4th Wave
Steams directly from engineering roots of HCI	Steams from cognitive science.	The topics culture and values are marginalized	Problematization of methds, tools and techniques
The focus is on human factors and ergonomics.	The emphasis in on theory and the focus is on what happens in the human mind in terms of information processing	Interaction is seen as a form of creation of meaning in which both artifacts and its context employ mutual influence	User centered design to more Participatory design involving laypeople
Human being as a subject to be studied	Focus on groups working with several applications	Several interdisciplinares inquires with HCI field	Adoption of Human values towards a gratifying UX
Interaction is perceived as a form man machine coupling	Interaction is perceived as metaphor of mind and computer.	Interaction with new technologies	Practice based on human needs and social responsibility
This wave is pragmatic and focused on practical results	The concept of context is a focus	Human Experiences	Placing politics and values, integrety and ethics at the forefront
		Technology connected with human body and soul	More push for change
		Rationality and emotion	HCI and IxD

Each researcher or community uses the waves characteristics the way they consider more adequate for the work in hands or according to their own understanding and experience. In our view, the important thing is the sharing of knowledge, the exchange of experiences, the collaboration, the revision of methods, the creativity, and the solutions for the problems that need to be solved at a given time.

There is an overabundance of creative theories and models and no one is generally accepted [4, 35]. The main reason is probably due to the multidisciplinary nature of the subject. Creativity is becoming an intrinsic part of working life. It is a quality that is highly regarded, but not always well understood [14]. Creativity denotes a person's capacity to produce new or original ideas, insights, inventions, or artistic products, which are accepted by experts as being scientific, aesthetic, social or technical value [13]. Creative activity grows out of the relationship between an individual and the context of his or her work, as well as, out of the relations between an individual and the other human being. Much human creativity arose from activities that took place in the context in which interaction and the artifacts that embodied group knowledge were important providers to the process. Moreover, creative thinking is not so much an individual feature but rather a social phenomenon involving interactions among people within their specific group or cultural settings [27].

The three approaches of design presented, in this paper, are exemplified with artifacts that were designed to solve problems (e.g., engines of our ingenuity). Some of them were the results of the use of theories and practices from sciences, art or technology. The intention could have been the invention of something, with a purpose or created by hazard, to improve people's quality of life (cars, airplanes, boats, clocks, bicycles, etc.).

The Chindogu Japanese invention, which means valuable or priceless tools are genius, but people would look silly using them out in public. Following this philosophy or art, the useless inventions at first glance, seem a bit reasonable. Then, people realize they are just no better than the usual way of doing things. However, being silly and useless the gadgets are designed to solve everyday problems. They are solutions to a particular everyday problem.

Using some design research techniques such as observations, interviews and activities analysis, the researcher investigated designers in specific environments in order to learn more about them through what they said, how they behaved and the objects they designed. The design thinking process involved multiple stages, and in some cases, brainstorming and discussions. During data gathering and data analysis it was demonstrated that there were some aspects of interaction design that were common to all case studies: design is an interdisciplinary process by its own nature which was verified by the different teams' background and design contains social interactions. Social interaction design integrated communication capabilities, and dynamic changing sequences of social actions between individuals and groups, who adjusted their actions and responses according to the actions of others' interaction. People attached meaning to situations, and interpreted what others were meaning. This overall attached meaning was reflected in the designed artworks [27].

In one of the cases studies it was demonstrated that the goal was not to build an artwork or artifact, but to practice design thinking. Design thinking is a way of applying methodologies to any of life's social situations. It is a creative process based around the building up of ideas and it encourages people to provide maximum input and participation. It is a process for a practical and creative resolution of problems or issues.

The researcher concluded that designers, in general, and design thinkers, in particular, shared a common set of values: these values were mainly creativity, collaboration and culture. The value delivered by design thinking is almost always seen to be improvements in the creativity and usefulness of the produced solutions.

Moreover, technology was always a medium or a tool during the development of all the artifacts. Neither better than using the words from [25]: "As technology strives to connect with the human body and soul, we must now think about the world as a small portion of the Universe, thus act with responsibility in developing life and the human race with a set of values, ethics, and integrity that are coherent with Gaia and all things in the world being interconnected".

Conversely, technology is both a practice and a creative idea, and not simply the concrete manifestation of a solution for human problems. This challenges the idea that technology is only created by exigencies – it also requires human objective and imagination to materialize and achieve it.

As a professor at the university (X) teaching HCI classes, we engage informatics' students to do practical projects by presenting interactive artifacts, which could make part of those that we have at our disposal in our daily life. However, for different reasons they do not. The students made the role of designers and they are free to use different characteristics of each HCI wave. They have a proposed challenger to accomplish. Normally, they are satisfied with their ability to innovate, to develop their creative skills, and to present powerful ideas. In the 'real' world sometimes these ideas win: design prizes, academic results, motifs for discussion, and topics for research. Conversely, the rate at which these ideas achieve commercial success is low. Many of the ideas die within the university never becoming a product. Among those that become products, a good number never reach commercial success. This is a concern because, such as the engines referred to on the paper, even the chindogu's artifacts and creative designs from the described cases, almost all of the student projects stay saved in a room or on a computer file. If we try to guess the reasons why, it will take us to several complex roundabouts to discuss in this paper. This example serves to illustrate that HCI concerns are considered in different places and teams' work. In this case we are talking about design thinking process and design doing.

5.1 Contribution

The main contribution of this paper is to underline the several waves' features that have served as guidelines for HCI researchers and followed as methodological approaches, especially when they develop artifacts, independently of their backgrounds, behaviors, beliefs, values, interests, and considerations about technology experiences.

Then, we presented different perspectives and examples concerning interaction design, since the appearance of the things that are part of our daily life, such as the car, the mobile phone, the plane, the clock, (some engines created, in some cases, initially, by naivety). Next, we offered illustrations of artifacts, created to be useless even though one can find them in daily use. We also settled on artworks resulting from the creative work of research teams, coming from different areas of knowledge, professional experiences, cultures, age. The main objective was the use of design techniques aligned with technologies and with HCI methodologies, to contribute to improve people's quality of life, digital social inclusion and to identify new areas of investment in HCI. Complementarily, in other arenas, such as, at universities, it was presented a narrative and description about the learning by doing method that have been used on the studying/learning process undertaken with informatics' students. They used their creativity and the available technology in the school's laboratories and made prototypes of artifacts that could become products of quotidian use in our daily lives. The design process and the development methods were followed similarly with those from the examples presented before as well as the waves' characteristics. However, in this case, some of the outputs are drivers to fail due to several constraints. Probably, because we do not have an agreement about, for example, the concepts that are the basis of something's generation. The transdisciplinary approach (the fourth wave) focuses on design frameworks, values and ethics, design for important themes such as sustainability, equity, adaptation, justice, and social responsibility which were found values on the designed outputs.

Finally, we intended to highlight that, probably other waves will come soon, containing other focus. Those focuses, whatever it may be, should be aligned with the scope of research groups, academia and industry in order to have a nearby consensus when these people collaborate in the development of artifacts development and on the universal application of methods and techniques. Conversely, the social changes we are facing – the new normal – will irreversibly change the way we think and work in HCI and design. The recollection of waves characteristics and the presented creative designs take us to say that: We don't think that we are diving into the surf in search of a wave to ride back to the shore. So, the debate about HCI, in general, or about design, in particular, will lead us to discover or improve the way we work doing research. probably, the focus should be on the social value plan, starting to understand the others, each other, and ourselves.

New approaches have been used by different authors. For example, Xiangshi et al. [39] proposed a new approach or (wave) or future directions to HCI which goal is to synergize interaction between humans and technologies under the appellation—Human Engaged Computing (HEC) which specifically identifies, promotes, enhances, and synergizes innate human capacities and technological capabilities by maximizing synergism and minimizing antibiosis. They call for a coherent understanding which gives priority to human outcomes, with technologies serving humans as stewards in nature.

Frauenberger argues that our intimate entanglement with digital technologies is challenging the foundations of current HCI research and practice. It is also considered that the relationships to virtual realities, artificial intelligence, neuro-implants or pervasive, cyberphysical require to consider evolving the current research paradigm. The called Entanglement was developed from the following four perspectives: (a) the performative relationship between humans and technology; (b) the re-framing of knowledge generation processes around phenomena; (c) the tracing of accountabilities, responsibilities, and ethical encounters; and (d) the practices of design and mattering that move beyond user-centered design [15].

6 Conclusion

The goal of this paper was to review the literature about HCI waves characteristics and to understand if, over the years, the artifacts were designed under each paradigm either chronologically or according to the researchers' interest and needs. We concluded, based on the presented design examples, that designers chose the wave's characteristics independently of the historical chronology. They adapt it according to the best guidelines that fit the artifact process or fitting the broader perspective on how technology relates to us.

Design is about people. It is about our hopes and dreams, our lives and joy. How we perceive aesthetics and how it makes us satisfied with the artifact leads to creating symmetrical conclusions and reproducing them in different forms, helping each other and advancing research to better humankind.

Some of the ideas offered by the designs seemed foolish in the whole presented cases. Although, the designers, at some point, believe that they did a solution to sort a kind of problem or what they express in an artifact had only a creativity to propose. Others may not accept either as such. However, if we consider great ideas of the past and how they were generated, and if we judge them by appearance, we will arrive at the conclusion that some of the ideas were engines of ingenuity. Nevertheless, those design ideas and discoveries permitted the development and evolution of our society and the artifacts contributed to improve some of our quality of daily life. The main goal of this paper was attained since we settled the waves characteristics and searched examples that have been focused on them during the design process development.

Probably, the contribution for a next wave or wavelet will come from the results of an interesting discussion among several researchers and professors concerning, for example, standard concepts' meaning, terminologies and their translations across languages. The top of discussion in research/academy communities is about: translation of the word affordances on the design of interfaces. The goal is to understand, in the different languages, if all over the world they are referring to it with the same meaning. Authors are also discussing their preoccupations concerning terminology about design and plan, since in some disciplines and or/situations the term is used almost interchangeably. And an interesting debate is appearing around design thinking, design doing, and design driven transformation.

References

1. Bannon, L.: From human factors to human actors: the role of psychology and human-computer interaction studies in system design. In: Greenbaum, J., Kyng, M. (eds.) Design at Work: Cooperative Design of Computer Systems Erlbaum, pp. 25–44 (1986)
2. Bannon, L.: From human factors to human actors: the role of psychology and human-computer interaction studies in system design. In: Design at Work, pp. 25–44. L. Erlbaum Associates Inc. (1992)
3. Bannon, L.: Reimagining HCI: toward a more human-centered perspective. Interactions **18**(4), 50–57 (2011). https://doi.org/10.1145/1978822.1978833
4. Barbot, B., Besançon, M., Lubart, T.: Assessing creativity in the classroom. Open Educ. J. **4**(Suppl1), 58–66 (2011)
5. Blevis, E., et al.: Transdisciplinary interaction design in design education. In: Proceedings of the 33rd Annual ACM Conference Extended Abstracts on Human Factors in Computing Systems, pp. 833–838. ACM, New York (2015). https://doi.org/10.1145/2702613.2724726
6. Bødker, S.: When second wave HCI meets third wave challenges. In: Proceedings NordiCHI 2006, pp. 14–18. ACM, New York (2006). https://doi.org/10.1145/1182475.1182476
7. Bødker, S.: Third wave HCI, 10 years later—participation and sharing. Interactions **22**(5), 24–31 (2015)
8. Borning, A., Muller, M.: Next steps for value sensitive design. In: Proceedings CHI 2012, pp. 1125–1134 (2012). https://doi.org/10.1145/2207676.2208560
9. Cabrero, D.G., Lopes, A.G., Barricelli, B.R.: HCI within cross-cultural discourses of globally situated rhetorical and etymological interactions. In: Rau, P.-L. (ed.) CCD 2016. LNCS, vol. 9741, pp. 16–25. Springer, Cham (2016). https://doi.org/10.1007/978-3-319-40093-8_2
10. Calvo, R., Peters, D.: Positive Computing: Technology for Wellbeing and Human Potential. The MIT Press, Cambridge (2014)
11. Chindogu: The Art of "Unuseless Idea". RingTones, Gamesville, Rhapsody, Wired (2001). https://www.chindogu.com. Accessed 1 Sept 2020
12. Cockton, G.: A load of Cobbler's children: beyond the model designing processor. In: Proceedings of the CHI 2013, pp. 2139–2148. ACM Press (2013)
13. Eysenck, H.J.: The Measurement of Creativity. In: Boden, M.A. (ed.) Dimensions of Creativity, pp. 199–242. The MIT Press (1994)
14. Florida, R.: The Rise of the Creative Class: and How It's Transforming Work, Leisure, Community and Everyday Life. Basic Books (2012)
15. Frauenberger, C.: Entanglement HCI the next wave? ACM Trans. Comput. Hum. Interact. **27**, 1–27 (2020). Article No.: 2. https://doi.org/10.1145/3364998
16. Grudin, J., Pruitt, J.: Personas, participatory design and product development: an infrastructure for engagement. In: Proceedings of the Participatory Design Conference, Malmo, Sweden (2002)
17. Grudin, J.: Three faces of human-computer interaction. IEEE Trans., 2–18 (2005)
18. Grudin, J.: A moving target—the evolution of human-computer interaction. In: Jackson, J. (ed.) Human-Computer Interaction Handbook, 3rd edn. p. 40. Taylor & Francis (2012)
19. Harper, R., Rodden, T., Rogers, Y., Sellen, A. (eds.): Being Human: Human-Computer Interaction in the Year 2020 (A3). Microsoft Research Ltd. (2008)
20. Harrison, S., Tatar, D., Sengers, P.: The three paradigms of HCI. In: Proceedings of CHI 2007. ACM, New York (2007)
21. Human Beans: (2001–2006). Accessed 6 Jan 2008. http://www.humanbeans.net/
22. Iedema, R.: Analyzing film and television: a social semiotic account of Hospital: an unhealthy business. In: van Leeuwen, T., Jewitt, C. (eds.) Handbook of Visual Analysis, pp. 183–206. Sage, London (2001)

23. Hutchins, E.: The Distributed Cognition Perspective on Human Interaction (2006)
24. Kuutti, K., Bannon, L.J.: The turn to practice in HCI: towards a research agenda. In: Proceedings CHI 2014, pp. 3543–3552 (2014). https://doi.org/10.1145/2556288.2557111
25. Laurel, B.: Gaian IxD. Interactions **18**(5), 38–46 (2011). http://dx.doi.org.ezproxy.uwl.ac.uk/10.1145/2008176.2008187
26. Leonardo Net – The Theory, Design and Application of Interactive Technologies (2005). Alan Dix and Hiraeth Mixed Media. http://www.leonardo-net.org/leonardonet.php. Accessed 29 Aug 2020
27. Lopes, A.: Design as Dialogue: Encouraging and Facilitating Interdisciplinary Collaboration. VDM Verlag Dr. Muller, Springer (2009). ISBN: 978-3-639-11713-4
28. Max-Neef, M.A.: Foundations of Transdisciplinarity. Ecol. Econ., 5–16 (2005)
29. McCarthy, J., Wright, P.: Technology as Experience. MIT Press, Cambridge (2004)
30. Muller, M.J., Wharton, C., McIver Jr., W.J., Laux, L.: Toward an HCI research and practice agenda based on human needs and social responsibility. In: Proceedings of the ACM SIGCHI Conference on Human Factors in Computing Systems, pp. 155–161 (1997)
31. Nicolescu, B.: Manifesto of Transdisciplinarity. State University of New York Press, New York (2002)
32. Perry, M.: Distributed cognition. In: Carroll, J.M. (ed.) HCI Models, Theories and Frameworks: Toward a Multidisciplinary Science, pp. 194–233. Morgan Kaufmann, San Francisco (2003)
33. Pyrko, I., Dörfler, V., Eden, C.: Thinking together: what makes communities of practice work? Hum. Relat. **70**, 389–409 (2017). https://doi.org/10.1177/0018726716661040
34. Rogers, Y.: HCI Theory: Classical, Modern, and Contemporary. Morgan & Claypool Publishers, San Rafael (2012)
35. Runco, M., Jaeger, G.: The standard definition of creativity. Creat. Res. J. **24**(1), 92–96 (2012)
36. Sanders, E.B.-N.: From user-centered to participatory design approaches. In: Frascara, J. (ed.) Design and the Social Sciences: Making Connections, pp. 1–8. Taylor & Francis (2002)
37. Ashby, S., Hanna, J., Matos, S., Nash, C., Faria, A.: Fourth wave HCI meets the 21st century manifesto. In: Proceedings of the Halfway to the Future Symposium 2019 (HTTF 2019), pp. 1–11. Association for Computing Machinery, New York (2019). Article 23. https://doi.org/10.1145/3363384.3363467
38. Suchman, L.: Plans and Situated Actions: The Problem of Human-Machine Communication. Cambridge University Press, New York (1987)
39. Ren, X., Silpasuwanchai, C., Cahill, J.: Human-engaged computing: the future of human–computer interaction. CCF Trans. Pervasive Comput. Interact. **1**(1), 47–68 (2019). https://doi.org/10.1007/s42486-019-00007-0

Workplace and Work Experience Analysis for Interaction Design

Design and Deployment Considerations for Ethically Advanced Technologies for Human Flourishing in the Workplace

Judith Molka-Danielsen[1]([⊠]) ⓘ, Jazz Rasool[2] ⓘ, and Carl H. Smith[2] ⓘ

[1] Molde University College, Britvn. 2, Postboks 2110, 6402 Molde, Norway
j.molka-danielsen@hhimolde.no
[2] Ravensbourne University London, 6 Penrose Way, Greenwich Peninsula,
London 10 OEW, UK
{j.rasool,c.smith}@rave.ac.uk

Abstract. Advanced technologies are increasingly integrated in to modern workplaces in situations to automate mundane tasks, improve safety, increase speed and efficiency in work production. Artificial Intelligence (AI) is playing an increasingly central role in advanced technology design. In parallel, there may be growing concern from workers that AI in workplace technologies will take away jobs and autonomy from humans. This paper proposes how to include key ethical factors in technology design processes and discusses future implications for AI in the workplace. Key ethical factors considered are privacy, security, integrity and equity. We reflect on employee experience factors of belonging, purpose, achievement, happiness and vigour that can underpin discretionary efforts of workers and discuss how these factors relate to low desire behaviours. We review application areas and propose a layered model approach and design and deployment considerations needed for cultivation of ethically advanced technology (ETHAD), that give potential for human flourishing.

Keywords: Human code of conduct · Smart workplace · Intelligent workplace · Artificial intelligence · Discretionary efforts · Employee experience · Human Work Interaction Design · Ethical advanced technology

1 Introduction

In the age of automation and use of Artificial Intelligence (AI) the nature of the workplace and work are changing. Employees may feel challenged by the threat to their existing jobs and the needs to develop new skill sets. Additionally, external forces can exert pressure on workforces, such as production complexities in global supply chains and global competition. Organizational culture may also exert pressure on commitment of workers. The heightened pressures on workers can have negative impact on the workers' psychological health and well-being and can trigger worker behaviour that has been recently labelled as "low-desire" behaviour, a term that was first introduced by management scientist, Kenichi Ohmae [1]. The workers psychological response may be characterized by

© IFIP International Federation for Information Processing 2022
Published by Springer Nature Switzerland AG 2022
G. Bhutkar et al. (Eds.): HWID 2021, IFIP AICT 609, pp. 101–122, 2022.
https://doi.org/10.1007/978-3-031-02904-2_5

low-trust or low-expectations in their relationship with the employer. Recent research has explored the connection between engagement in work and employee experience. Employee experience and well-being, as described in the literature review, are found to be underpinned by factors of *belonging, purpose, achievement, happiness* and *vigour*. In this paper we propose that AI, if ethically designed and employed in the workplace, can play a positive role in contributing to worker well-being. AI offers affordances, in that it can take away the dull and dangerous work, the technology at the same time may provide opportunities for more engaging work, support workers with greater autonomy in shaping their daily work, and enable workers to develop a greater sense of mastery.

However, the method of design and use of advanced technology in the workplace will play a pivotal role in employee experience. The risks are that AI if it has been applied, scaled up, and in some cases utilised in ways beyond what it was originally proposed for, that it may demonstrate consequences of ethical liabilities. To prevent ethical liabilities, in the case of algorithms and programming associated with machine learning and AI, the concept of ethically advanced technologies (ETHAD), could be introduced into intelligent workplaces. A design approach for ETHAD would embody the consequences of the technology use as it is being selected, designed or even as it is being coded. The advantage of addressing these considerations in the design process is that the first ripple effects of such a potentially disruptive technology that has ethical features incorporated, will be seen at prototyping stages, rather than later in its adoption cycle when the technology in use is a scaled-up implementation and diversified for use by many user or application demographics. Ethical liabilities can be detected and compensated for within the very first prototypes to deliver a novel experience. This will ensure that with general release and implementation, the technologies, especially those to be used in the workplace, cultivate human flourishing in their use of resultant technologies.

This paper will present a design strategy for designing ethically advanced technology (ETHAD) for human flourishing in the workplace. In Sect. 2 we review former research on the meaning of concepts such as smart workplaces and the role of AI in the workplace. We review literature on the factors that comprise discretionary effort and how they relate to low desire behaviours. The contribution of the paper will develop as follows. In Sect. 3, we introduce application areas and explore the potential of ETHAD. In Sect. 4, we propose a practical approach for encoding ETHAD principles into technology, considering layers of design and deployment needed to encourage the creation of technology that facilitates human flourishing. In Sect. 5, we discuss practical considerations for deployment of ethically advanced technologies through intervention of a Value Engine that utilizes ethical algorithms. In Sect. 6 we explore future and emerging impact areas. Section 7 brings focus on the contribution of this paper and recommends directions for future work.

2 Literature Review

This section presents the fundamental concepts and former research, including smart technologies in the workplace, ethics in the workplace, employee experience and human flourishing in the workplace.

2.1 Smart Workplaces

The concept of intelligent or smart workplaces at its core provides automation or tools for efficiency in the workplace [2]. Automation through AI can provide opportunity to free up workers time from mundane tasks and instead allow workers to gain autonomy in shaping their ways of working and co-creating their workspaces to allow more collaboration. For example, an AI tool that allows workers to perform self-time-tracking or scheduling can give them increased ability to be masters of their own time. Some argue that automation is driving a need for social and emotional skills in the workplace [3]. This is because emotional skills such as advanced communication, creativity, and empathy are needed to drive the complex activities that cannot be automated [3].

The intelligent workplace should become a humanized system that senses and adapts to human needs. It should promote responsiveness, flexibility, and adaptability to the needs of the worker promoting their comfort and well-being [4]. As a starting point, workplaces, according to European Agency for Safety and Health at Work (EU-OSHA), have the obligation that they should be safe and secure for workers' physical and psychological well-being, by upholding individuals' information security and privacy [5]. It is important to stress that there is a change in the concept of the intelligent workplace whereby the goals are for a stronger emphasis on the needs and choices of the human worker. Smart or intelligent workplaces should be able to collect data and react responsively to the conditions in the workplace environment that may indicate harm to workers or other threshold needs [6]. Through a variety of technologies for monitoring and response, AI should pave the way to safe and secure workplaces.

2.2 AI and Ethics in the Workplace

In recent years, industry and business leaders have come to increasingly agree on the importance of ethics with the advent of AI and its embodiment as Industry 4.0 practices [7]. In order to minimise risk or prevent it, ethics cannot be applied in hindsight.

In this paper, we identify four key factors of ethical deployment that are privacy, security, integrity and equity. The factors *privacy* and *security* ensure utilization of workplace technologies are done in a protected, safe way. *Integrity* and *equity* ensure it happens in a sound way while providing appropriate access and affordances that respect diversity and inclusion of the workers. As will be expanded in Sect. 4 these factors are key contributing components of empowerment and enablement through technology. We propose that, to ensure responsible implementation, ethical factors cannot be acted on in hindsight. Rather, ethical pillars must be integrated with a foresight mind-set. Ideally, they need to be extrapolated into business processes and strategies. Importantly, there needs to be ethical integration embodied in research and development that drives product or service innovation. Selection of AI technologies in the workplace cannot be done simply as a consultation or participatory design exercise. Ethical considerations must be formally embedded as a moderating feature within designs of organizational hardware, software and applications as well as developmental and implementation life cycles. We propose the future of ETHAD technologies in the workplace could begin by understanding the employee experience and by applying a different methodological approach to designing AI.

2.3 The Role of Discretionary Effort

"Discretionary effort is the level of effort people could give if they wanted to, but above and beyond the minimum required."—Aubrey C. Daniels, Ph. D [8].

This quote leads us to reflect, what factors comprise discretionary effort and how do they relate to low desire behaviours? Employees in companies or citizens in society typically will have a low desire to comply with the rules they have to work and live by if the only reason to follow the rules is to avoid getting into trouble [9]. The term of 'discretionary effort' describes the level of desire or effort someone is prepared to put into an activity beyond what is demanded. Low levels of discretionary effort will typically be accompanied by a low desire mind-set to carry out work or align to social norms. Hesketh, Cooper and Ivy [9] studied the link between discretionary effort and levels of worker engagement. They identified the 'stay-out-of-trouble' work effort at 35% and the maximum long-term sustainable work effort at 85%. Therefore, the potential of discretionary work effort for a workforce could potentially expand by 50%. Their findings concurs with other studies that have identified work engagement in extra time, brainpower and energy to have tremendous value to the organization when a critical mass of the workforce are so engaged [10]. However, the mechanism to invoke discretionary effort "cannot be achieved by a mechanistic approach which tries to extract discretionary effort by manipulating employees' commitment and emotions." [11 p. 9]. The study of [11] applied a well-being psychometric instrument, ASSET [12] to identify the drivers for discretionary effort among a Police workforce in northern UK. They found that if workers had "control" - over what they did, had "job security" - permanence of employment, and had positive "job conditions" - e.g. work being challenging and not dull and repetitive, low risk of physical-violence, that workers were more likely to offer more discretionary effort. Alternatively, factors like "resources and communication" – having enough resources to do a good job, e.g. training and equipment, "work relationships" - with leaders or peers, and "balanced workload" – amount of hours worked, unsociable hours, conflict with personal life, deadlines; seemed to not be significant in contributing to greater discretionary effort [11]. This highlights potential of ETHAD principles contributing more desirable workplace conditions that address worker control and positive job conditions, that is ETHAD technologies can be central in achieving the worker control or autonomy, and positive job conditions that afford the worker to address challenging work rather than the mundane.

2.4 The Role of Positive Reinforcement

The approach of motivating people to stay out of trouble, otherwise known as 'negative reinforcement', is not sufficient in itself to prevent the degradation of the desire to work, follow rules or engage in actionable ways with others. Giving someone a reward or a good reason for behaviour, positive reinforcement, is historically seen to work in a more sustainable way to maintain desire to comply or to collaborate. As far back as Pavlov's [13] work showing how dogs would salivate in the anticipation of a reward received after a bell would ring, there have been efforts to use reward or remuneration systems to maintain and build desire in human beings to cooperate, collaborate and comply with policies, laws as well as strategies. It is possible through tracking employee engagement metrics to establish patterns which could be used with data science to forecast where desire to work needs to be strategically managed and cultivated.

Pavlov's work illustrates research that formed the basis of understanding of what came to be known as 'classical conditioning'. It is a part of the branch of Behaviourism learning theory. The UK's HR professional's development body, the Chartered Institute of Professional Development (CIPD), also recognises 'Operant conditioning' [14] originally promoted by B.F. Skinner in 1957 [15]. Skinner highlighted that voluntary compliance in development of new skills or aligning to specific behaviours was associated with the use of positive or negative reinforcement, on whether someone was given a reward or punishment for their behaviour. Behaviourism though is one category of learning and development. Others the CIPD recognises include Cognitivism, Humanism, Constructivism and Social Learning as well as Neuroscience informed models such as Rapid Application Development (RAD), SCARF (an acronym standing for Status, Certainty, Autonomy, Relatedness, Fairness) and AGES (an acronym standing for Attention, Generation, Emotion, Spacing) [15].

Of the models the CIPD underpins human resources (HR) practices with, positive reinforcement aligned to practices that could favour employee empowerment and flourishing, are best understood through exploring the importance of an employee's learning environment or 'learning culture' [16]. Nigel Cassidy, in a 2020 CIPD podcast, highlights the relationship between learning cultures and positive learning environments and how the balance helps organisations flourish [17]. Much of current Learning and Development strategy is focussed on an organisation flourishing but not necessarily the employees flourishing without there being a return on investment for the business. As such, modern forms of employee flourishing are an outcome of kinds of operant conditioning where return on investment for an organisation rewards employees. Cassidy's discussion of learning culture with industry leaders highlights important principles that must be embedded in development of future learning culture strategy and its influence on flourishing employee experience.

2.5 The Design Approach and Employee Flourishing

Modern forms of innovation for business products and services adopt a *design thinking* methodology for development following design stages that include *empathise, define, ideate, prototype and test* [18]. This methodology could also be applied to encouraging employee flourishing and amplifying discretionary effort. This can be done in a way that does not involve classical or operant conditioning strategies but instead involves employees in less covert routes to organisational return of investment and pathways which the employees have more conscious agency on how they are being developed. After all, the very first stage of *design thinking* methodology involves the utilisation of empathy to engage in a transparent and authentic way. Using a design thinking mindset will then progress the initial empathic interactions into clearly defined problems that ideas can be prototyped from and tested, using workflows that maintain integrity in employer-employee relationships with the necessary accompaniment of transparent and authentic communications. This approach can lead to flourishing of employees first and provide a more sustainable foundation for subsequent organisational flourishing.

Duke Corporate Education highlights this in an online article [19]. They state that applying design thinking principles to internal processes, organisations can begin to genuinely engage employees and put their needs first. In the article they state that "Design Thinking is a human-centred process 'powered by a thorough understanding, through direct observation, of what people want and need in their lives'". In the article, they discuss how the Nike company has adopted Design approaches in their HR function, "A few progressive companies, like Nike, are starting to see the advantages of viewing their employees as customers. They are applying design-thinking principles to internal processes to reshape their organizations for a fast-changing world. These external and internal efforts require leaders throughout the business who can think and act more like designers [19]." The article goes on to state the importance of several key abilities that align to the stages of the design mindset. Specifically, if employees could be viewed as customers, then the company's HR products and services could be adapted to the employees needs and prospectively cultivate their flourishing as well as the organisations.

2.6 Employee Experience and the Role of Ethical Factors

Employee experience (EX) is a new term that companies are beginning to recently develop strategies for managing [20]. Investments in EX provide both tangible and intangible business value. These include reduced recruiting costs, lower attrition, higher employee work performance, as well as increased discretionary effort. So, any attempt to manage low desire must be encapsulated within such an umbrella strategy. Forrester Research has produced two reports relating to such a strategy, "Introducing Forrester's Employee Experience Index" [21], and "The Employee Experience Technology Ecosystem" [22]. The first identifies three main factors that contribute to employee engagement: empowerment, inspiration, and enablement. The second outlines the variety of technologies that impact employees' daily journeys and identifies the ones that have the greatest impact on EX. Even with their conclusions the factors of privacy, integrity, equity, and security are key contributing components of empowerment and enablement through technology. But can they also be prerequisites for inspiration that could counter low desire states?

In a 2017 IBM report [23] authors refer to a study [24] that states that "the battle for the hearts and minds of employees is played out daily through their workplace experiences." The experience at work for employees is now being re-examined by organizations. In a 2007 paper such experience management is seen as a path to improved job performance [25]. A 2016 Deloitte report shows that such management can lead to sustained competitive advantage [26].

The need to foster empowerment, enablement and inspiration of employees is conceptualized in the 2016 Globoforce report as an employee experience that is a positive and powerful – and ultimately human – experience, in which employees are able to invest more of their whole selves into the workplace [27]. The report highlights employee experience as being at the root of the dynamics relating to such a factor as discretionary effort. Employee Experience is defined in the report as "*A set of perceptions that employees have about their experiences at work in response to their interactions with the organization*". Five dimensions of employee experience are considered to frame its nature and dynamics. (1) Belonging – feeling part of a team, group or organization (2) Purpose – understanding why one's work matters (3) Achievement – a sense of accomplishment in the work that is done (4) Happiness – the pleasant feeling arising in and around work (5) Vigour – the presence of energy, enthusiasm and excitement at work. These are seen as part of a larger context of organizational culture. The report further states that "employee experience has its beginnings in the direction and support of leaders and managers, who drive organizational practices that create the employee experience. Ultimately, a positive employee experience is associated with improved employee outcomes such as better job performance, *increased discretionary effort* and higher retention." [27]. A significant outcome of the report is that discretionary effort is almost twice more likely to be reported when employee experience is positive (95% compared to 55%). In producing data science metrics for low desire contributing factors, such as low levels of positive employee experience and the resultant reduction in discretionary effort, a preliminary spectrum of parameters should include measures of empowerment, enablement and inspiration. It may be that these factors themselves are underpinned by *belonging, purpose, achievement, happiness* and *vigour*.

Engaging employees through initiatives that reduce low desire behaviours at work through the use of strategies which enhance Employee Experience based generation of discretionary effort in ethical ways through the use of technology will be a major area of research and development for occupational psychology professionals. If we have measures of such dynamics that is one thing but if technologies can be designed to facilitate the ethical generation of discretionary effort then employees and employers alike will benefit, not to mention the clients, customers and markets they serve. ETHAD technologies, that are accelerants for discretionary effort generation, can help curb emergence or low desire trends in behaviour in workplaces as well as amongst citizens in society. Key foundations can begin to be laid in adapting existing services for employees and citizens whether that is through employer intranets, social media platforms or government supported services for citizens that operate through state managed public sector digital platforms.

3   Application Areas: Potential of ETHAD Technologies

AI (or machine learning) tools as system elements are increasingly integrated into system solutions for navigating increasingly complex and global problems. Adoption of AI tools that are guided by oversight from ethical frameworks could be the next step in the evolution of intelligent system solutions. As an example, AI tools can be integrated into existing Employer Intranets or Public Sector portals. They can be designed and deployed with discretionary effort cultivation strategies. These ETHAD strategies can be based on methodologies and technologies guided by ethical, AI based algorithms to prevent low desire behaviours emerging amongst employees or citizens.

3.1   Employer Intranet Employee Experience Services

Employer Intranets often focus on providing services relating to Human Resources and internal organisational communications. Their design and content though follow information driven design methodologies rather than ones that enhance engagement, develop employee experience or cultivate discretionary effort. The states discussed earlier in the paper that feed these factors such as empowerment, enablement and inspiration as well as the components they comprise of, *belonging, purpose, achievement, happiness* and *vigour* are not overtly or actively developed. Shivakumar has done a thorough development of methodologies to build platforms for employees that focus on Employee Experience [28].

Shivakumar describes Employee Experience Platforms (EXPs) as "*employee-centric intranet platforms that personalize the experience for all employees and that provide contextual content and services*". He goes on to say that "EXPs offer next generation digital workplaces that engage employees throughout the employment lifecycle and improve their productivity for their day-to-day activities". Shivakumar compares traditional employer intranet platforms to Employee Experience driven platforms in Table 1. There are many factors needed for effective EXP design. Several of these factors we quote from the work of Shivakumar in Table 1 [28, pp 3–4]. These factors can be responsible for contributing to discretionary effort and, if provided, could reduce low desire behaviours.

Table 1. How legacy intranet platforms do not meet modern employee needs and challenges, [28, pp 3–4]

Category	Employees' needs and expectations	Challenges with traditional intranet platforms
User experience	Modern employees expect seamless user experience across all services and information. Employees demand consumer-grade on-the-go mobile and omnichannel experiences. Dashboard experience provides a unified view of all information and transactions	Mainly a desktop-driven user experience. Disjointed user experience across various tools and Intranet applications. Challenges with usability and accessibility. Inconsistent brand identity
Information architecture	Personalized and contextualized information	Difficult to find relevant information
Collaboration	Information should be easily shareable. Instantly collaborate with colleagues. Create interest-based groups and communities. Harness collective intelligence for increased productivity	Challenges with cross-team collaboration. Lacks engagement and motivation for employees. Needs integration of multiple collaboration tools

(continued)

Table 1. (*continued*)

Category	Employees' needs and expectations	Challenges with traditional intranet platforms
Analytics	Employees expect analytics-based insights such as personalized content and information based on past transactions	Minimal or absence of analytics Absence of seamless analytics across various touch points
Tools and features	Employees expect self-service and productivity improvement tools Educate, learning, training tools Usage of gamification features	Minimal or absence of gamification features Minimal self-service tools
Artificial intelligence	Employees expect AI–based continuous learning and improvement of the platform	Minimal or absence of AI-based methods
Information discovery	Organized information; provides contextualized and relevant personalized content	Takes too much time to find relevant information Duplicate and outdated information
Content management	Easier authoring and publishing. Easier content discovery Intuitive content workflows	Lacks targeted and personalized content Lacks localized content

The list, although not exhaustive, includes the user experience, personalized and contextualized information, ability to instantly collaborate with colleagues, create interest-based groups and communities, analytics-based insights such as personalized content and information based on past transactions, education, learning, and training tools, usage of gamification features. And further, tools to harness collective intelligence for increased productivity, AI based continuous learning and improvement of the platform, user participation that allows easier authoring and publishing, easier content discovery as well as intuitive content workflows.

3.2 Public Engagement Portals

There are many state activities that require public participation in order for them to function. These could be as simple as encouraging people to vote, combating crime, or coming together to help manage a community in a crisis such as a natural disaster, pandemic or a decline in economic wealth amongst local businesses. Increasing the desire of citizens to help out as well as contribute to their own self-care to reduce loads on public services, such as healthcare or utilities, has become very predominant in the year of the 2020 COVID19 pandemic. An example of a digital experience platform that serves citizens is provided by Belgium based CitizenLab [29] which focuses on "Introducing local democracies to the digital age". Since 2015, they have been on a mission to strengthen local democracies by using community engagement to increase efficiency and legitimacy. They provide digital participation platforms to local governments to help them consult citizens, increase transparency in decision-making and gather actionable insights.

CitizenLab helped take the Youth for Climate movement inspired by Greta Thurnberg, to get politics to act against climate change. The movement in Belgium led to CitizenLab creating a platform for participants to exchange their views and communication. In a period less than 3 months, users posted over 1,700 ideas, 2,600 comments and voted over 32,000 times for the initiatives they wanted to support. In order to turn these ideas into meaningful actions and recommendations, Youth for Climate needed to process thousands of ideas in a short period of time. This was a perfect use case for the automated data analysis feature of the CitizenLab platform. AI driven Natural Language Processing was used on a wide scale to collect and analyse the thousands of contributions written in a variety of languages. CitizenLab have used their capabilities to provide Digital Experience Platforms for a variety of Belgian initiatives including boosting citizen engagement in Liège, in Lommel to involve citizens in urban planning decisions, crowdsourcing innovative ideas to improve mobility in Brussels as well as helping 24,450 citizens take part in Peñalolén's participatory budget. In their 2020 Impact Report [30] CitizenLab describe how their e-democracy platform has supported 200+ local governments and organisations in more than 15 countries over these past years. This led to the launch of 8,796 projects, which enabled 732,327 citizens to make their voices heard. And they have done so quite convincingly, sharing 134,239 ideas, 330,078 comments, and 4,222 proposals on their platforms.

4   Practical Encoding into ETHAD Technologies - What is Needed? How Can It Be Done?

This section will propose an approach to encourage technology that facilitates human flourishing. To achieve this, the applied empowering strategies must shape behaviours and building of technologies through many layers of design and deployment. Initial attempts at applying ethics to technology have focused on influencing effects on human beings. For example, the 'Ethical OS' approach attempts to mitigate negative effects of lack of integration of human directed ethics in various risk zones, of which we address (1) Truth, disinformation, and propaganda (2) Machine ethics and algorithmic biases, (3) Data control and monetization, (4) Implicit trust and user understanding [31]. These risk zones, amongst others, are risk categories arising from failures in applying human directed ethics. Users generate data and the experience of that data gathering must be respectful of that user's privacy and security. This needs to be done in a way where the integrity or accuracy of the data is not corrupted or compromised. In addition, users must have access to their own data without excessive constraints so commercial companies that harvest data must facilitate equity of access. This is achieved by supporting the *integrity* and *equity* of user data and experience while wrapping the data harvesting process in software and hardware containers that secure trust in the management of *privacy* and *security* [32].

Examples of these deeper layers have been explored in the paper "Transforming TEL for Human Flourishing: Learning Enhanced Technology (LET)" [33]. This includes three layers, (1) Human Directed Ethics, consisting of Privacy, Security, Integrity and Equity (2) Interface and Experience Ethics, including User Experience (UX) Storyboarding and User Interface (UI) Design and (3) Hardware and Software Ethics, comprising of Ethical Operating Systems and Algorithms as well as Ethical Machine Architecture. Applying ethics to workplace technology often is limited in practice to the top Human Directed Ethics layer usually focusing on managing privacy and security as well as data and user integrity and equity.

Companies such as Salesforce and Microsoft have prioritised ethical policy implementation at this human directed ethics level. Consultancy firm Deloitte comments, "Salesforce has appointed a chief ethical and humane use officer to guide the company's use of technology. The function aims to ensure that the company has a clear framework in place to guide technological decisions …" [34]. Further, "leaders at Microsoft recently created an AI and Ethics in Engineering and Research Committee, composed of senior leaders from across the company working together to proactively monitor and address issues that may arise as the company advances development of its AI platform and related solutions. Examples of areas on which the committee has focused include addressing bias in AI systems and implementing requirements of the General Data Protection Regulation" [34].

Ethical advanced technology goes beyond such visible human facing affordances. It ensures more fundamental and primary levels are integrated. These include User Experience (UX) and more primary User Interface (UI) features in application development. These could be as simple as accessibility and language features to personalise the user experience or ethically respectful use of icons, menus or themes. At the most sophisticated levels these interfaces and experiences could be customised for users from a particular culture or learning style. Advanced features would ensure customised privacy and security while ensuring accessibility, integrity and equity of data as well as experiences.

In 2018, Somos of UX Studio, explored a redesign of the Facebook interface towards more ethical interactions. He suggested modifying the Facebook platform [35]. His proposal referenced Aran Balkan's Ethical Design Manifesto that is centred around a pyramid, shown in Fig, 1 that focuses on what design workflows need to become ethical [36].

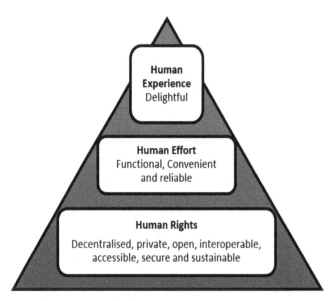

Fig. 1. Ethical design needs [35, 36]

These kinds of features are examples of ethically enhanced technology, focused on UI and UX. To ensure ethical embodiment in the design of applications and their deployment, that is ethically advanced technology, frameworks have to be utilised that provide ethical affordances which are native to computer operating systems, their algorithms as well as the machine architecture that underpins them.

5   Practical Deployment of Ethically Advanced Technologies

The discussions so far have been on the prospective structure of an approach to applying ethics to advanced technology and what is needed in terms of ethic risk zones, layers of ethical integration and ethical design needs. It follows we must move on from what is needed to how technology that is ethically advanced will be designed and implemented in practice. Any proposal that addresses how to design technology that is ethically advanced must consider the two foundations for it, the hard (machine) and soft (human) factors. These include the categories of ethics mentioned earlier, human directed ethics, interface and experience ethics and hardware and software ethics [33]. Also, to be referenced are the layers in Fig. 1. These two aspects need to be brought together into a methodology and workflow that can be deployed in practice. The layers of ethical integration (ethics directed at human beings, user interfaces and user experiences as well as hardware and software domains) must be applied to fulfil ethical design needs of employee experience platforms (employee experiences, efforts, and rights).

5.1   Considerations for Ethics in a High-Level View of an AI Architecture

The practical 'hard' process of embodying ethics into hardware, software and information technology processes must explore how values and virtues, which form the morals that are the foundations for ethics, can be incorporated into the design and deployment of systems and human operations, especially at their interfaces. To do this the structural components of typical computer or information systems that underpin AI operations must be embodied with the values and virtues from the applied ethics factors.

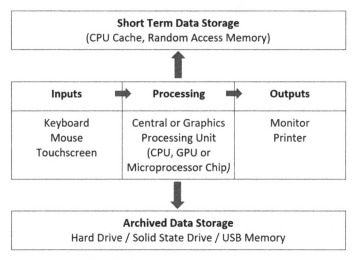

Fig. 2. Typical computer architecture

Figure 2 is a schematic of a typical computer architecture showing how data can flow in through inputs, be processed and then either placed in temporary memory, short- or long-term storage as well as be output to external peripherals or destinations.

Figure 3 expands the typical computer model architecture to consider deployments of these components in modern computing domains that AI operations may be run on, particularly employee experience platforms that may have private walled digital environments as well as exchanges with external public domains especially with streaming and social media channels. Each component must be ethically moderated in a way that is specific to the affordances and operations of that component while remaining congruent to ethics embodied in other components and in the system as a whole.

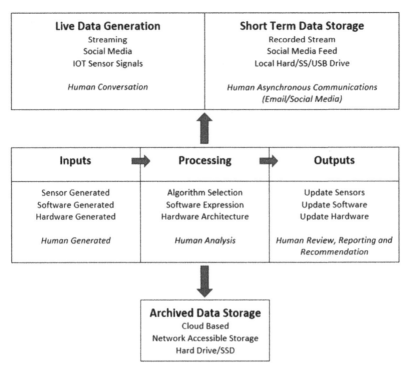

Fig. 3. Sources and flows of data in an AI computing system to be moderated by ethical functions

A prior study by Shneiderman has considered including moderating support functions for ethical oversight of software design practices and associated human activities. Recommendations have been offered for Human Centred AI (HCAI) systems [37]. Of the recommendations [38] the focus on how to 'adapt proven software engineering team practices' is of concern in this discussion [39]. Focusing on employee experience platforms, the first subset of the fifteen recommendations needs to be addressed, which relates to the technology architecture for reliable systems based on sound software engineering practices for a team [38].

This includes recommendations for

1. Audit trails and analysis tools
2. Software Engineering Workflows
3. Verification and validation testing
4. Bias testing to enhance fairness
5. Explainable user interfaces

Not having systems in place to address, embody and enact these recommendations and any lack of system-wide consideration for associated ethical design needs leaves individuals and target groups using employee experience platforms open to vulnerabilities. It can cause potentially harmful outcomes to marginalized target groups. Categories and the descriptions of potential harms in absence of ethical considerations are considered by the Alan Turing Institute's 2019 report on Understanding Artificial Intelligence Ethics and Safety [40, pp. 4–5]. These include.

- *Bias and Discrimination*
  Features, metrics, and analytics structures of AI systems are chosen by their designers. These factors can replicate or reinforce designers' preconceptions and biases.
- *Denial of Individual Autonomy, Recourse, and Rights*
  It may not be possible to hold AI systems accountable for decisions that impact individuals.

- *Non-transparent, Unexplainable, or Unjustifiable Outcomes*
  Complex AI systems can produce outcomes that are non-transparent, unexplainable or appear to be unjustifiable to users regarding how the decisions were reached.

- *Invasions of Privacy*
  AI systems involve the utilization of personal data. This data can be potentially captured and stored and revealed without consent.

- *Isolation and Disintegration of Social Connection*
  Algorithms can reinforce and lock-in patterns of social views, relationships, world views, limiting views that are different.

- *Unreliable, Unsafe or Poor-Quality Outcomes*

Human error in data management, systems design and data deployment can lead to AI systems that produce unreliable, unsafe, or poor-quality outcomes that individuals, organizations, or societies may pre-emptively trust. This can result in damage to wellbeing and welfare.

The report also cites that the implementation of an ethical platform to embody ethical approaches to AI should comprise of a framework of

- ethical values
- actionable principles based on those values
- process based governance framework for operationalizing those actionable principles [40, p 9].

The Turing report safety overview though focuses on the ethical operational delivery of a project to develop AI technology or processes. The process of embodying ethics into the components of AI systems such as hardware and software is implied but not explored. The main operational process consists of a cycle of reflecting on the requirements, acting on them and then justifying those actions -reflect, act, justify. The justification is done after acting whereas this really should happen prior to action. Governance should not follow action, primarily it should be carried out in advance of it as a structural pathway for delivering proposed actions.

Governance should not just happen through human beings, project oversight and enacted policies; it needs to be encoded into hardware and software systems, in the underlying computing code and architecture, to offset flaws arising from a lack in human oversight. Just as a nuclear power plant has hardware and engineering safety monitors and fail-safes such as radioactivity monitors or automatic fire suppression, AI systems must include fundamental, elementary fail-safes that operate without human intervention. These basic fail-safes can then be refined for more complex forms of interventions for higher level, abstract processes, and more complex ethical challenge events.

To scale AI, ethical fail-safes from low level hardware to high level software, alongside the code and data flow driving the AI functions, there must be a parallel governance code and technology set for embodied and encoded ethics to oversee and moderate the AI, there needs to be a partner to the AI, an ethics or 'Value Engine'. The three-part structure of the Turing Institute report, consisting of a values framework, actionable principles, and process-based governance, needs to be made more atomic in its application, down to the scale of generation, modification, and management of raw data as well as how that data progresses through a pipeline of AI software algorithm libraries, computer hardware architecture as well as the local and wider internetworks. Ethics must be applied not just to the humans that use AI but also to the landscape and ecosystems of technologies that run AI and that AI spans its operations across.

Creating a Value Engine that oversees the AI as well as moderate it to optimise for an employee experience platform requires a holistic systems design approach where the technologies that interface with AI, act on its periphery or in its contextual environment as well as comprise its core functions must be included in applying ethical guidelines. A Value Engine will operate much like how an anti-virus software can span its monitoring from Hardware through Operating System to Software and file level operations, preventing harmful events through warnings as well as restricted permissions, in this case relating to prospective emergent threats to ethical operation. However, the engine must also facilitate and inform users much like a spell-check or grammar monitor, highlighting incorrect application of rules as well as provide useful alternative options that might prove to be more understandable, communicable, and aligned to regulations.

5.2 Applying Ethical Design Principles Through a Value Engine

An AI design and deployment framework should apply a value engine that can facilitate a systems design thinking that has checks and balances as part of the workflow. This workflow must apply ethical design principles at every stage of the design process, at every handling point of data. For example, it must be applied in the classic domains of computer and IT architectures such as systems where data is input, output, kept in long term storage, short term memory as well as in system cores where processing is done. Ethical values must Support, Underwrite, and Motivate (SUM) and actionable principles must have behaviours of Fairness, Accountability, Sustainability, and Transparency (FAST) [40] applied not just at high level human operations but also to low level scales of AI systems - to their hardware and software. The Turing report offers a key concept, 'Normativity/Normative':

"In the context of practical ethics, the word 'normativity' means that a given concept, value, or belief puts a moral demand on one's practices, i.e. that such a concept, value, or

belief indicates what one 'should' or 'ought to' do in circumstances where that concept, value, or belief applies. For example, if I hold the moral belief that helping people in need is a good thing, then, when confronted with a sick person in the street who requires help, I should help them. My belief puts a normative demand on me to act in accordance with what it is indicating that I ought to do, namely, to come to the needy person's aid." [40, p. 9].

Should an ethical issue arise that calls a response algorithm, it must have normative functions that can act on an underlying reference ethic, value, or virtue. User Interfaces must adapt to users facing specific challenges unique to their diversity, inclusion, and justice ethical fingerprint.

Ethical Algorithms must be applied across three technology layers

- *Software* - Employee Experience (EX) platform software must answer to the underlying operating system's ethical algorithms.
- *Operating System* - the OS must answer to the atomic level ethical normative functions embodied in the underlying hardware. The existing industry practice is to respond to events and triggers from software or hardware activity so this level of ethical application must be part of the OS event-driven architecture.
- *Hardware* - this must encode normative functions into its drivers, machine code and assembly level firmware, especially hardware that receives direct sensor-based signals relating to wellbeing of employees.

The three layers must be designed to act in coherence with one another but must ultimately answer to the atomic level of ethical normative functions that have morals, values, and actionable principles as their foundations.

- *Software* - at this level an example of someone using software that requires ethical oversight would be an employee reporting stress regarding a workplace experience. The Employee Experience platform software can ensure that, with permission, an appropriate message is logged and reported to the company staff responsible for managing wellbeing and the employee is given some initial guidance to begin the process of ensuring they are helped according to their unique circumstances.
- *Operating System* - an example of an OS level event that would require ethical response would be the registration of the employee stress report in a database as a new record is added for his case. The OS can ensure that the data is monitored so that it gets a verified response within a given time. This ensures accountability and transparency. The employee can provide the final permission for the record to be generated.
- *Hardware* - at this level, some devices could be made available to measure stress, for example relating to heart rate or skin resistance. If any sensors register signals beyond healthy norms the hardware can generate a call for the operating system to record an event in its wellbeing database and register the circumstances in the employee experience platform, raising appropriate flags to accountable staff. Prior to any submission of signal data, the employee can choose which elements can be shared and what permissions are valid for the different layers of communication.

So, the process-based governance that oversees human operations in AI projects must, in a fractal, scaled and parallel way be translated into the operations internal to technologies and their respective partnered hardware, firmware and operating systems as well as human facing software.

6 Future and Emerging Impact Areas

As AI emerges as an integrated part of the smart workplace, present and future efforts need to be made to allow the rise of technologies that moderate that intelligence so they ethically process input data, processing of data as well as output and dissemination of data. In other words, AI must be chaperoned by Artificial Ethics. Machine Learning must be shaped by Machine Ethics algorithms to ensure outcomes are not biased and that cultivate empowering human creativity and flourishing.

Between 2016–2019 the IEEE supported a study on Ethically Aligned Design, to explore these layers of ethical applications to technology. In that study deeper areas of ethical application are explored to "advance a public discussion about how we can establish ethical and social implementations for intelligent and autonomous systems and technologies, aligning them to defined values and ethical principles that prioritize human well-being in a given cultural context" [41, p. 2]. The IEEE study marks a shift in focus to encapsulate design and integration of ethics management features and functions within technology and systems rather than predominantly external to them in human-to-human interactions.

The study [34] has theoretical implications in that it emphasises value-based systems design and the importance of flourishing. It states, 'Eudaimonia', as elucidated by Aristotle, is a practice that defines human well-being as the highest virtue for a society. Translated roughly as *flourishing*, the benefits of Eudaimonia begin by conscious contemplation, where ethical considerations help us define how we wish to live. Whether our ethical practices are Western (Aristotelian, Kantian), Eastern (Shinto, Confucian), African (Ubuntu), or from a different tradition, by creating autonomous and intelligent systems that explicitly honour inalienable human rights and the beneficial values of their users, we can prioritize the increase of human well-being as our metric for progress in the algorithmic age, immunizing people from work-life contexts that trigger low-desire behaviours. In practice, measuring and honouring the potential of holistic economic prosperity should become more important than pursuing one-dimensional goals like productivity increase or GDP growth [36, p. 5]. The IEEE provides a series of recorded webinars on "Ethical Considerations for System Design" that serves as a good starting point for developers in exploring considerations for embodying ethics into systems and their design [42].

7 Concluding Remarks

AI is playing an integral role in emerging smart workplaces. The potential benefits of AI are that it may provide opportunities for more engaging work, support workers with greater autonomy in shaping their daily work, and enable workers to develop a greater sense of mastery. However, there remain many challenges to achieve a positive Employee

Experience that may in turn increase the worker's discretionary effort. The challenges include an ever-growing need for workers to interact with advanced technologies both in and outside of the workplace. Added challenges can be the blurring of work-personal life boundaries, e.g., the uncountable experiences of work-life from home under the COVID 19 pandemic. But, more importantly, supporting worker control (autonomy) and offering challenging work are critical factors in motivating discretionary effort [9]. It is, therefore, not a simple incentive or reward system that can be the foundation of positive EX. Recently publicised cases of Low-Desire society in Japan have pointed to workers losing a sense of expectation towards their employers and towards the work itself [43, 44]. The future workplace environment will need to consider other factors beyond the technology, such as organisational culture, that is a good starting point for future research. However, in this paper we emphasise the critical need for a design approach that does not impose risks of ethical liabilities.

This paper at its core has proposed the need for an increased emphasis on embodying ethical principles into the design and production of the technology itself, especially in its User Interface and User Experience processes. We identified four key factors in ETHAD deployment that are privacy, security, integrity, and equity. Five critical factors that underpin EX have been identified that are belonging, purpose, achievement, happiness, and vigour. We propose there is a critical link between a positive employee experience of these factors and discretionary effort. At the core of successful EX is human flourishing, where the optimal outcome is where human experience is delightful. Such employee experience can only be achieved through technology that respects ethical design needs. The proposal to address this is the design and deployment of a Value Engine that is driven by ethical algorithms that monitor software, operating system and hardware for ethical oversight.

Analogs of components or systems that underpin a future Value Engine are already being innovated. Of these the ones that will need to be capitalised on are those that connect human emotions, affect and underlying value driven motivations with operational activities within an engagement or discretionary effort transformation process. Three examples of efforts demonstrating this in the Human Work Interaction Design field should be mentioned. The first effort, BioStories, a four year project that focussed on uniting affective and ubiquitous computing with context aware multimedia environments real-time generation [45]. This explores how multimedia storylines could be emotionally adapted on the fly, so that end users would unconsciously be determining the story graph. This kind of agency, sourced from emergent human states, is what will be needed to support triggers of Value Engine activity and moderation. The majority of developments will centre on making the Business-IT communication cycle more enriched with benefits for employee experience, engagement and empowerment. The model a business uses to operate must be effectively communicated to ensure employee compliance and engagement. To ensure ongoing discretionary effort availability businesses must be able to identify disruptions or breakdowns in business-IT communication through their business models, something that Ferreira J.J., de Araujo R.M., Baião F.A. have analysed in their 2011 paper [46]. A final example, relating to corporate intranets is worth exploring. Géczy P., Izumi N., Akaho S., Hasida K. in their 2006 paper [47] state that "Knowledge regarding user browsing behavior on corporate Intranet may shed light on general behavioral principles of users in Intranet spaces and assist organizations in making more informed decisions involving management, design, and use policies of Intranet resources." An easy win in developing infrastructure for a workable Value Engine might be able to be achieved through browser-based applications and services.

References

1. Ohmae, K.: The Wealth of a New Country: An Era of Ambition. Japan, Tokyo (2005)
2. Atkin, B.L.: Intelligent Buildings: Applications of IT and Building Automation to High Technology Construction Projects. Wiley (1989)
3. Darino, L.: Employee motivation in the age of automation and agility. McKinsey & Company, McKinsey Organization Blog (2020). https://www.mckinsy.com/business-functions/organi zation/our-insights/the-organization-blog/build-your-organization-identity
4. Zallio, M., Fisk, M.J.: Smart homes. In: Gu, D., Dupre, M. (eds.) Encyclopedia of Gerontology and Population Aging. Springer, Cham (2019). https://doi.org/10.1007/978-3-319-13557-1
5. ECC-OSH: Directive 89/391/EEC - OSH "Framework Directive on Safety and Health at Work", last amendment 2008 (1989). https://osha.europa.eu/en/legislation/directives/the-osh-framework-directive/1. Accessed 30 Jan 2018
6. Strange, R., Zucchella, A.: Industry 4.0, global value chains and international business. Multinatl. Bus. Rev. **25**(3), 174–184 (2017)
7. Hooker, J., Kim, T.W.: Ethical implications of the fourth industrial revolution for business and society. In: Business Ethics, Business and Society 360, vol. 3, pp. 35–63. Emerald Publishing Limited (2019). https://doi.org/10.1108/S2514-175920190000003002
8. Daniels, A.: Discretionary Effort. Aubrey Daniels International, Atlanta GA (2021). https://www.aubreydaniels.com/discretionary-effort. Accessed 22 Feb 2021
9. Hesketh, I., Cooper, C., Ivy, J.: Wellbeing and engagement in policing: the key to unlocking discretionary effort. Int. J. Environ. Res. Public Health **12**, 1–12 (2015). ISSN 1660-4601. https://doi.org/10.3390/ijerph120x0000x
10. Towers-Perrin: Understanding what drives employee engagement. UK Report, Working Today (2003)
11. MacLeod, D., Clarke, N.: Engaging for success: enhancing performance through employee engagement. Report, p. 9, Department for Business Innovation and Skills, UK (2009)
12. Cartwright, S., Cooper, C.: Management Guide: A Short Stress Assessment Tool. Robertson Cooper Ltd., Manchester (2002)
13. Pavlov, I.P.: Conditioned reflexes: an investigation of the physiological activity of the cerebral cortex. Translated and edited by Anrep, G.V. Oxford University Press, London (1927). http://psychclassics.yorku.ca/Pavlov/lecture6.htm
14. Hayden, D.: CIPD, Learning theories for the workplace, 17 August 2020. https://www.cipd.co.uk/knowledge/strategy/development/learning-theories-factsheet
15. Ferster, C.B., Skinner, B.F.: Schedules of Reinforcement. New York (1957)
16. CIPD: Creating learning cultures: assessing the evidence. Chartered Institute of Personnel and Development, London (2020). https://www.cipd.co.uk/Images/creating-learning-cultures-1_t cm18-75606.pdf
17. Cassidy, N.: Evidence-Based L&D: Learning Cultures, Episode 165, 3 November 2020. https://www.cipd.co.uk/podcasts/learning-cultures
18. Behal, C.: How human resources can use design thinking to improve employee engagement, 13 May 2019, Mindhatch. https://www.mindhatchllc.com/design-thinking-human-resources-employee-engagement/

19. Canning, C.: The Benefits of Design Thinking for Employee Engagement. Duke Corporate Education, March 2016. https://www.dukece.com/insights/benefits-design-thinking-employee-engagement/
20. Hewitt, A., Johnson, D.: Introducing Forrester's Guide to Employee Experience Technology (2019). https://go.forrester.com/blogs/introducing-forresters-guide-to-employee-experience-technology/
21. Johnson, D., et al.: Introducing Forrester's Employee Experience Index, Forrester Blogs & Podcasts (2019). https://www.forrester.com/report/Introducing+Forresters+Employee+Experience+Index/-/E-RES137819
22. Johnson, D., et al.: The Employee Experience Technology Ecosystem, Forrester Blogs & Podcasts, 14 February 2019. https://www.forrester.com/report/The+Employee+Experience+Technology+Ecosystem/-/E-RES143517
23. IBM: The Employee Experience Index, IBM Corp. and Globoforce Ltd., Somers NY USA (2017). https://www.ibm.com/downloads/cas/JDMXPMBM
24. Lesser, E., Mertens, J., Barrientos, M., Singer, M.: Designing employee experience: how a unifying approach can enhance engagement and productivity (2017). http://www-01.ibm.com/common/ssi/cgi-bin/ssialias?subtype=XB&infotype=PM&htmlfid=GBE03735USEN&attachment=GBE03735USEN.PDF
25. Wright, T.A., Cropanzano, R., Bonett, D.G.: The moderating role of employee positive well being on the relation between job satisfaction and job performance. J. Occup. Health Psychol. **12**(2), 93 (2007)
26. Deloitte: Global Human Capital Trends 2016: The New Organization: Different by Design. Deloitte University Press (2016)
27. Globoforce WorkHuman Research Institute: The ROI of recognition in building a more human workplace (2016). http://www.globoforce.com/resources/research-reports/roi-recognition-human-workplace/
28. Shivakumar, S.K.: Build a Next-Generation Digital Workplace: Transform Legacy Intranets to Employee Experience Platforms. ISBN-13 (pbk): 978-1-4842-5511-7. ISBN-13 (electronic): 978-1-4842-5512-4. https://doi.org/10.1007/978-1-4842-5512-4
29. Cuau, C.: Applying artificial intelligence to citizen participation on the Youth4Climate platform (2019). https://www.citizenlab.co/blog/civic-engagement/youth-for-climate-case-study/
30. CitizenLab 2020 Impact Report (2021). https://res.cloudinary.com/citizenlabco/image/upload/v1611334323/Impact%20report%202020/CitizenLab%20impact%20report%20%7C%202020.pdf
31. IFTF Ethical OS: Ethical OS Toolkit. A guide to anticipating the future impact of today's technology (2020). https://ethicalos.org/
32. Uria-Recio, P.: Artificial Intelligence & Analytics for CEOs (2018). https://aiforceos.com/2018/06/16/big-data-ethics/
33. Smith, C.H., Molka-Danielsen, J., Rasool, J.: Transforming TEL for human flourishing: learning enhanced technology (LET). In: IEEE TALE2020 Conference (2020). ISBN: 978-1-7281-6942-2(IEEE Xplore®). https://www.researchgate.net/publication/349465496_Transforming_TEL_for_Human_Flourishing_Learning_Enhanced_Technology_LET
34. Bannister, C., Sniderman, B., Buckley, N.: Ethical tech - Making ethics a priority in today's digital organization. Deloitte Insights (2020). https://www2.deloitte.com/us/en/insights/topics/digital-transformation/make-ethical-technology-a-priority.html
35. Somos, A.: 7 Ethical Design Examples to Make Facebook Better for Everyone, UX Studio (2018). https://uxstudioteam.com/ux-blog/ethical-design
36. Balkan, A.: Ethical Design Manifesto (2017). https://2017.ind.ie/ethical-design. Accessed 07 Aug 2020

37. Shneiderman, B.: Human-centered artificial intelligence: three fresh ideas. AIS Trans. Hum. Comput. Interact. **12**(3), 109–124 (2020). https://doi.org/10.17705/1thci.00131
38. Shneiderman, B.: Bridging the gap between ethics and practice: guidelines for reliable, safe and trustworthy Human-Centered AI systems. ACM Trans. Interact. Intell. Syst. (to appear, 2020)
39. Shneiderman, B.: Opinion: the dangers of faulty, biased or malicious algorithms requires independent oversight. Proc. Natl. Acad. Sci. **113**(48), 13538–13540 (2016)
40. Leslie, D.: Understanding artificial intelligence ethics and safety: a guide for the responsible design and implementation of AI systems in the public sector. The Alan Turing Institute (2019). https://doi.org/10.5281/zenodo.3240529
41. IEEE Standards Association: Ethics of Autonomous and Intelligent Systems. Ethically Aligned Design: A Vision for Prioritizing Human Well-being with Autonomous and Intelligent Systems, ver. 2. IEEE (2017). http://standards.ieee.org/develop/indconn/ec/autono mous_systems.html
42. IEEE Standards Association: Ethical Considerations for System Design - Four part webinar on IEEE P700 series of standards (2019). https://www.youtube.com/playlist?list=PL9U5sKt4 P2XpeDuS1Xw1CF3bTQicGCLXm. Accessed 5 Aug 2020
43. Tachibankaki, T., Iwanami, S.: Unequal Society- What is the Problem? (2006)
44. Ohmae, K.: How to Ignite the Low Desire Society. Shanghai Translation Publishing House, Shanghai (2018)
45. Vinhas, V., Oliveira, E., Reis, L.P.: BioStories: dynamic multimedia environments based on real-time audience emotion assessment. In: Filipe, J., Cordeiro, J. (eds.) ICEIS 2010. LNBIP, vol. 73, pp. 512–525. Springer, Heidelberg (2011). https://doi.org/10.1007/978-3-642-19802-1_35
46. Ferreira, J.J., de Araujo, R.M., Baião, F.A.: Identifying ruptures in business-IT communication through business models. In: Filipe, J., Cordeiro, J. (eds.) ICEIS 2010. LNBIP, vol. 73, pp. 311–325. Springer, Heidelberg (2011). https://doi.org/10.1007/978-3-642-19802-1_22
47. Géczy, P., Izumi, N., Akaho, S., Hasida, K.: Extraction and analysis of knowledge worker activities on intranet. In: Reimer, U., Karagiannis, D. (eds.) PAKM 2006. LNCS (LNAI), vol. 4333, pp. 73–85. Springer, Heidelberg (2006). https://doi.org/10.1007/11944935_7

The Influence of Automation and Culture on Human Cooperation

Xuezun Zhi and Ronggang Zhou[✉]

School of Economics and Management, Beihang University, Beijing 100191, China
zhrg@buaa.edu.cn

Abstract. In recent years, intelligent machines which can act on our behalf, such as autonomous vehicles, are in increasing numbers. They follow preset procedures and make decisions for people when certain conditions are reached. These machines improve the efficiency of our daily life as well as bring us a new paradigm of interaction with other people. Setting the program for the machine in advance enables us to make an early decision and provides us with a chance to think more comprehensively from a macro perspective. In this case, how the change of this decision-making paradigm will affect our cooperative behavior with others is the main research question of this study. This article proved that the cooperation rate of participants interacting with others by programming the autonomous vehicle in advance was higher than the direct interaction cooperation rate. A conclusion can be drawn through the experiment that when the system can automatically make decisions and participants can modify the decisions, the higher the initial cooperation rate of the system was, the higher the final cooperation rate of the participants would be. From this, it can be preliminarily concluded that the automation system can guide people to choose cooperation more. In addition, compared with the results of similar studies abroad, it can be found that people's cooperative behavior is different due to different cultural backgrounds. Chinese culture advocates the doctrine of the mean, and the participants' choices of cooperation or betrayal are more balanced. In contrast, western culture is more rational and extreme, in which a large part of the participants chooses to cooperate completely or betray completely.

Keywords: Intelligent interaction · Social dilemmas · Autonomous vehicles · Cooperation

1 Introduction

With the development of science and technology, artificial intelligence has gradually come into people's daily life, such as autonomous vehicles, intelligent speakers and automaton robots, which can act on our behalf. These machines have gradually changed our decision-making mode and provided a new paradigm of interaction and decision for human beings, which may bring new ideas for solving social difficulties.

© IFIP International Federation for Information Processing 2022
Published by Springer Nature Switzerland AG 2022
G. Bhutkar et al. (Eds.): HWID 2021, IFIP AICT 609, pp. 123–140, 2022.
https://doi.org/10.1007/978-3-031-02904-2_6

Social dilemmas represent an inherent time conflict between decisions that bring short-term returns (e.g., betrayal) and decisions that bring long-term returns (e.g., cooperation) [1]. A person chooses to betray because he or she temporarily ignores long-term returns and pays more attention to short-term returns [2]. By programming the autonomous vehicle ahead of time, the temptation of short-term returns can be avoided to some extent [3], in which case, people are more likely to focus on long-term returns and make a favorable choice for the group.

In the field of intelligent machines, the automatic driving vehicle is a hot research topic. The J3016 automatic driving grading standard developed by American International Automaton Engineer Association divides the automatic driving technology into six grades, L0 to L5. The grading method is mainly based on the sophistication of the equipped sensors and the automaticity of perceiving the complex environment and making intelligent decisions. At present, the more popular technology of automatic driving is at L3 level, conditional automatic driving. At this level, the automatic driving system does most of the operation while the driver is supposed to stay focused and answer the requests, which means that on the one hand, when people are designing programs for autopilot, they actually advance the decision time. On the other hand, the autopilot can automatically make decisions in certain situations, while drivers have the final decision-making power, and their final decisions may be influenced by system decisions.

Self-driving cars could change our way of travel to some extent. It would theoretically reduce the mileage, thus reducing environmental pollution, and additionally reduce the number of accidents. However, it may also make people face ethical choices, such as whether to sacrifice the other person or sacrifice oneself in case of danger. In the past, when studying the social dilemmas faced by self-driving cars, most of them have involved the issues of human safety and security, with little focus on directions that do not involve ethical issues, such as whether to choose low-carbon behavior while driving a car.

Considering the above, the research question of this study is how the change of decision-making mode brought by the emergence of an intelligent machine will affect the cooperative behavior of humans in the interaction process.

2 Literature Review

2.1 Social Dilemma

Social dilemma refers to the situation when individual interests conflict with collective interests, which was proposed by Dawes in 1980. In a social dilemma, individual rational behavior would cause collective irrational behavior [4]. In other words, if everyone seeks to maximize personal interests, collective interests will be harmed. In some social dilemmas, people are actually facing social and time dilemmas. From the perspective of time, people prefer immediate gains rather than delayed gains. Individuals with a high level of construal consider the future consequences of their actions very thoughtful, showing a higher level of cooperation [5]. When people describe or explain a situation from a higher psychological level, they tend to focus on a more abstract and comprehensive situation; on the contrary, when people comprehend a situation at a lower level, they tend to focus on more specific aspects related to the environment [6]. When asked to make decisions strategically, participants are more likely to act fairly than participants interacting in real time [7]. This may be because people will consider the opponent's views [8], and people rely on social norms, such as fairness, which provides a consistent metric when people consider all possible outcomes [9].

In social dilemmas, people's decisions may also be related to personal values. In ultimatum games, prosocial people are inclined to cooperate under conditions of high understanding, while individualists tend to compete [10]. Moreover, the same research also puts forward a hypothesis that compared with direct interaction, prosocial people are more likely to let the machine cooperate, while individualists are more likely to make machines betray.

Another aspect is the moral level. Since moral principles are usually more abstract than selfish motives, moral behavior should be seen as having a greater time distance from moral dilemmas [11, 12]. It is found that people will make stricter moral judgments on future moral problems [12], and people are more likely to make moral behaviors when thinking about future events [13].

In summary, time is a critical factor in the issue of social dilemmas. People are more likely to make socially friendly moral behaviors when they make future decisions at a higher level. The intelligent machine provides the possibility to make decisions in advance. Compared with interacting directly with others, interacting through agents may make people behave more fairly. This is because writing an agent program will lead people to adopt a broader perspective, consider each other's position, and rely on social norms (e.g., fairness) to guide their decision-making [14]. In the aspect of self-driving, subjects are more cooperative when setting up self-driving cars than when they are driving by themselves. This is because the selfish short-term rewards become less prominent due to the pre-programming of self-driving cars, and subjects can consider broader social goals. At the same time, it is also proved that programmed behavior is affected by past experience. The final experimental data shows that this conclusion is not limited to the field of self-driving cars. In other words, the design of autonomous machines to make decisions helps build a more cooperative society [15].

From the perspective of the number of participants, the social dilemma can be divided into the two-person social dilemma (only two people participate) and the multi-person social dilemma (more than two people participate). The most typical model of the two-person social dilemma is the prisoner's dilemma, designed by mathematician Albert Tucker according to a game invented by his colleagues. The two prisoners are faced with two choices, cooperation or betrayal, either to testify and report the other party (betrayal) or to remain silent (cooperation). If both parties remain silent, then both parties will go to jail for one year; If one party reports while the other remains silent, the reporting party will be acquitted and the silent party will go to jail for ten years; If both parties report, they will be imprisoned for eight years. It can be seen that no matter whether the other party is silent or reports, their own choice to report can keep their personal interests maximized. If they both make rational choices (seeking to maximize their personal interests), they will eventually choose to betray and go to jail for eight years; however, from a collective point of view, both parties can maximize their collective interests by keeping silent, and they both go to jail for one year.

From an economic point of view, the main problem of environmental damage is that when we consider the impact of a person's behavior at a specific point in time, the damage to the environment is very small [16]. For example, if a person chooses to drive to work tomorrow, the global temperature will not rise significantly, and if a person chooses to use disposable chopsticks, the global resources will not suddenly disappear, and white garbage will not flood the world. However, in the long run, the dependence on cars and excessive use of disposable items has led to the severe environmental challenges we are now facing.

Regarding environmental issues as a social dilemma, when the decision-maker is faced with environmental protection behaviors or non-environmental protection behavior, he faces two kinds of conflicts: social conflicts (individual interests and collective interests) and time conflicts (short-term return and long-term return). At the level of social conflict, the possible reason for a person to cooperate is that he values the happiness of other people, which may be caused by the person's character or his environment, that is, related to his social value orientation. In terms of time conflict, people are more likely to pay attention to a short-term return, but as time goes by, people will realize that cooperation may bring greater personal and collective benefits [17].

2.2 Factors Affecting Cooperation

Decision-making is a basic human activity, and people are making various decisions every moment. Decision-making is essentially a many-to-one mapping relationship, in which people process various information in their brains and finally make a choice. When people process information, it will be related to the person's long-term memory, short-term memory, surrounding environment, emotion, state of consciousness, the reaction of others, etc. These conditions will also affect the outcome of human decision-making. This paper explores the influence of gender, social value orientation, culture, and autonomous machines' assisted decision-making on human cooperative behavior.

There have been many studies on the influence of gender on cooperation for a long time. Eagly et al. showed that men are more inclined to take risks than women [18]. Some experiments show that women tend to be more socially oriented, that is, selfless, while men are more personally oriented [19]. In addition, Eckel also concluded that when the risk level is low, women show more cooperation tendency than men, while when the risk is high, there is no obvious difference between men and women in cooperation tendency [20]. Andreoni et al. have proved through experiments that women show a higher cooperative tendency when cooperative behavior needs to pay a higher price, while men show a higher cooperative tendency when cooperative behavior needs to pay a lower price, and men are more likely to make completely cooperative or completely uncooperative behavior, while women's cooperative behavior is relatively average [21].

Although there are many experimental studies proving that gender affects cooperation, there are still many studies showing that gender has no significant effect on cooperation behavior, especially when using the prisoner's dilemma to investigate whether gender affects cooperation. Simpson argues that previous studies have failed to find differences, mainly because prisoner's dilemmas can trigger people's fear (fear of betrayal) and greed. Simpson conducts experiments on these two emotions respectively and finds that women are more likely to choose betrayal because of fear, and men are more likely to choose betrayal because of greed [22].

To sum up the above contents, it can be known that in some cases, gender has little influence on cooperation, but at the same time, many studies have proved that under certain conditions, such as low risk and less likely to induce fear, women are more inclined to cooperate than men.

People's social value orientation will affect their expectations of the development result of things [23], thus affecting their decision-making choices. Social value orientation can be divided into altruism, prosocial, individualism and competitive orientation. Prosocial people tend to pay more attention to collective interests when encountering conflicts between individual and collective interests, while individualists tend to pay more attention to personal interests in this case. In terms of competitive people, they pursue that their own interests should be more than those of others, rather than maximizing their personal interests. Bogaert et al. show that pro-socialists will cooperate more in social difficulties [24].

From a cultural perspective, cultural backgrounds have important influences on the extent of people's cooperation [25]. The differences between the cultures of Western countries (e.g., Europe and America) and East Asian countries (e.g., China and Japan) are often generalized to individualism and collectivism [26]. The different cultural roots and development processes between China and the West have led to different ways of thinking. The traditional Chinese way of thinking is vague, intuitive, and emphasizes the whole and balance [27], while the traditional western way of thinking is precise and rational, which pays attention to composition and structure. Ho et al. identified no less than 18 different dimensions to make up a more general individualism-collectivism construct (e.g., uniqueness vs. consistency, self-reliance vs. subordination, economic independence vs. interdependence, etc.) [28]. These dimensions are also consistent with traditional Eastern and Western modes of thinking. In summary, these differences make the cooperation choices made by people in Chinese cultural background more average, while the choices made in the Western cultural background may be more extreme.

In addition to the above effects of participants' own characteristics on their cooperative behavior, various factors in human-computer interaction may also influence human decision-making.

During the interaction between humans and intelligent machines, the machine design, specific tasks, and the interaction environment may have an impact on the interaction. In this paper, we focus on the impact of intelligent machine design on human cooperative behavior. The automated systems should be designed to be reliable, dependable, resilient, secure, usable and accessible [29]. One of the important factors to be decided in intelligent design is the level of autonomy. Sheridan et al. developed a scale for measuring the level of computer autonomy during human-computer interaction, which contains ten discrete variables ranked from the lowest to the highest level of computer autonomy [30]. The fifth level is where the computer performs a behavior with the permission of the user, and the sixth level is where the computer allows the user a limited amount of time to veto a behavior before it is automatically performed. Siegel has shown that intelligent machines with different levels of autonomy may have an impact on participants' decision-making [31]. In their experiment, they asked participants to believe that they were dealing with a robot that was either fully autonomous or completely remote controlled by an operator. In the experiment, the robots tried to convince the subjects to donate as much money as possible, and the results showed that the subjects donated more money when the robots were perceived to be completely involuntary. Definitions and rules have been completed on approaches to levels of automation, human-machine cooperation, etc., that aim to better understand the interaction between human operators and more or less "intelligent" assistive tools. However, the impact of intelligent machine decisions on human decisions at higher levels of autonomy remains less studied. This study hopes to investigate this area experimentally and initially.

3   Method

This experiment was adapted from the machine agent decision-making experiment researched by de Melo, Marsella, Gratch. (2019), and the experimental scene was mainly designed according to the prisoner's dilemma. Economic games, like prisoner's dilemmas, are abstractions of typical real-life situations and ideal choices for studying the underlying psychological mechanism in controlled experiments. In a prisoner's dilemma, participants can choose cooperation or betrayal. If they only focus on personal interests, they will choose betrayal. If they pay more attention to collective interests, they are more likely to choose cooperation. According to the choice of cooperation or betrayal of the participants, each participant will get the corresponding score. In this experiment, the final reward of the participants was positively related to their score.

The experimental scene was whether to turn on the air conditioner while driving when the temperature is high. Turning on the air conditioner will increase the comfort, but at the same time, it will consume more energy, emit more harmful gases, and aggravate environmental pollution; if the air conditioner is not turned on, the comfort will be reduced, but it is beneficial to environmental protection. Participants played the prisoner's dilemma game with three other people (as control variables, and the other three people were simulated by computers). They respectively chose to turn on or turn off the air conditioner under the conditions of setting the auto-driving program in advance or making direct manual decisions. Turning on the air conditioner was regarded as a betrayal, while turning off the air conditioner was regarded as cooperation.

Information on the gender of the participants and their social value orientation was collected before the experiment began. There are many methods to measure social value orientation (SVO). In this experiment, we adopted the slider test method [32]. The test consists of 6 primary items and 9 sub-items, and the latter 9 sub-items are designed for those prosocial people. All the projects use the same general formula. Decision-makers choose their own preferred allocation options for each project in turn, and then their SVO angle score could be obtained through the following formula (1):

$$ SVO° = \arctan\left[\sum(P_o - 50)/\sum(P_S - 50)\right] \tag{1} $$

In this formula, P_o is the amount allocated to others for each project, and P_S is the amount of money distributed to oneself. The higher the degree is, the more the decision-maker pays attention to the gains of others rather than their own. 22.45° is the dividing line between prosocial orientation and individualistic orientation. The social value orientations this article focuses on are individualistic and prosocial orientations, so only six primary items are tested on the participants, and their social value orientation is judged with 22.45° as the boundary.

4 Experiments 1: Machine Agent and Direct Interaction

4.1 Participants

A total of 40 participants were recruited to participate in this experiment, 20 men and 20 women. Their ages range from 18 to 20 years old. All the participants signed the informed consent before the experiment, and they participated in the experiment voluntarily. They could give up the experiment for various reasons. The whole experiment process lasted for 15 to 20 min. After the experiment, the participants would get 10 to 15 RMB (according to the experiment results). The results of 40 participants were all valid.

4.2 Design and Procedure

The experiment followed a single factor inter-group design (decision-making method: programming/direct interaction) to explore whether decision-making would affect people's cooperative behavior. The participants made decisions simultaneously without communication for ten rounds, and the dependent variable was the cooperation rate of ten rounds of decision-making.

In this experiment, we hoped that any strategic considerations that may arise due to repeated interactions could be ruled out, so the participants were told before the experiment begins, and they would not know the decisions made by the other three people before the end of the last round. The experimental results of each round and the final scores of the participants were displayed after the end of ten rounds of experiments.

The experimental program was written by scratch, and the interface of direct interaction is shown in Fig. 1(left). The participants control the AV through the left and right buttons on the keyboard for 10 rounds. After each round of selection, the car would turn and move according to the decision of the participants. The game income table would be displayed in the experiment interface (top of Fig. 1(left), bottom of Fig. 1(right)). For example, if the participants and the other three choose to turn on the air conditioning, each of them will get 8 points. If the participant chooses to turn off the air conditioner and the other three choose to turn it on, the participant will get 4 points, and the other three people will get 12 points. If the participant chooses to turn off the air conditioner and One of the other three people turned off the air conditioner and two turned it on, the participant will get 8 points, and The other three people who turned on the air conditioner scored 16 points and so on.

The interface of programming AVs is shown in Fig. 1(right). Participants decided whether or not to turn on the air conditioner in each round by the mouse button, which was the control variable.

Participants conducted the experiment using a computer browser, and the entire experiment was conducted in May in China with weather conditions.

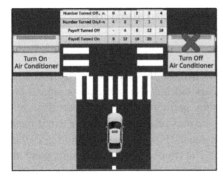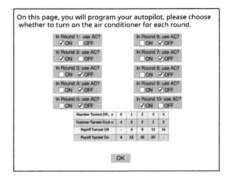

Fig. 1. Experimental conditions in experiment 1: (Left) the interface of direct interaction, (Right) the interface of programming AVs.

4.3 Results

The sample size for this experiment was 40 participants. They were divided into two groups. In this experiment, the average rate of cooperation for decision-making by setting the auto-driving program in advance was 0.5 ($SE = 0.070$), and the average rate of cooperation for decision-making by manual driving is 0.37 ($SE = 0.060$). We can see that participants were more likely to cooperate when programming their AVs than when driving themselves. There was no significant difference in the cooperation rate between the two groups in the one-factor analysis of variance ($F = 1.993, p = 0.166, \eta^2 = 0.05$).

Taking the cooperation rate as the dependent variable, we ran a gender × autonomy between-participants ANOVA. The results showed that the cooperation rate of women ($M = 0.51, SE = 0.063$) was slightly higher than that of men ($M = 0.36, SE = 0.066$). There was no significant difference in one-factor analysis of variance ($F = 2.701, p = 0.109, \eta^2 = 0.066$). The interaction between decision-making mode and gender was significant ($F = 4.930, p = 0.033 < 0.05, \eta^2 = 0.120$). It showed hat women could make AVs more cooperative. From Fig. 2, it can be clearly seen that in the case of direct interaction, the rate of cooperation among men was slightly higher than that of women, but in the case of automatic driving, the cooperation rate of women was significantly higher than that of men. This showed that women were more likely to cooperate when making decisions from a macro perspective.

In this experiment, the average cooperation rate of the participants with SVO of individualism was 0.413 ($SE = 0.076$), and that of prosocial participants was 0.448 ($SE = 0.060$). It can be seen that the cooperation rate of prosocial people was slightly higher than that of individualists. There was no significant difference in one-factor analysis of variance ($F = 0.127, p = 0.724, \eta^2 = 0.003$). It showed that the social value orientation of the participants did not affect their final choice of cooperation. This was not quite in line with the expected conclusion. In order to analyze the reasons for this phenomenon, this paper counted the frequency of cooperation rate of two social value orientations. We found that 4 prosocial participants chose not to cooperate at all, and the cooperation rate of these 12 prosocial participants was less than 0.5.

The reasons for the above phenomenon were as follows: on the one hand, the sample size was small, and it was difficult to offset some accidental cases; On the other hand, it might be related to the measurement method of social value orientation. In this study, we used the slider measurement method. The interest distribution in the measurement was virtual and did not involve the real reward. However, the score in the experiment was directly related to the final reward, which might lead the participants to be more willing to make scores in line with social norms (such as fairness, selflessness, etc.) in the measurement of social value orientation. In the formal experiment, participants were more willing to make decisions that align with their own interests when it came to actual rewards, so the influence of social value orientation on cooperation rate was not obvious.

Taking the cooperation rate as the dependent variable, we ran a two-way ANOVA of autonomy $\times$ SVO. The results showed that the interaction between autonomy and SVO was not significant ($F = 1.353, p = 0.252, \eta^2 = 0.036$). In the case of direct interaction, the rate of cooperation among prosocial people was higher than that of individualists, but in the case of programming AVs in advance, the rate of cooperation among individualists was higher than that of prosocial groups.

There was also a conflict with the theory. In the case of programming the AVs, the proself oriented participants' cooperation rate was higher than that of prosocial oriented participants. The main reason for this is a large number of samples. In the case of programming the AVs, there were 15 prosocial participants, and 5 individualism participants. The sample size of individualism orientation was too small, which made the experimental results deviate from the theory.

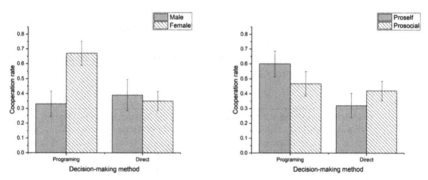

Fig. 2. Results in experiment 1: (Left) cooperation rate for gender, (Right) cooperation rate for SVO. The error bars represent SEs.

In this experiment, the AVs had the minimum degree of automation. If we improve the degree of automation of the automatic driving system and the system has a high initial cooperation rate, can this induce people to choose cooperation more? The next part of this research studied this problem. The initial cooperation rate of the autopilot vehicle system is set to 0.5 and 0.7, respectively. The reason for using 0.5 was based on the results of experiment 1. The reason for using 0.7 was to increase the rate of cooperation on the basis of 0.5, so as to observe whether a higher initial cooperation rate could promote people's cooperation.

5 Experiments 2: The Influence of System Settings on Human Cooperation

5.1 Participants

This experiment adopted an in-group design, so a total of 20 participants were planned to be recruited. There were 22 participants, but two of them did not meet the operation specifications, the data were deleted. Of the remaining 20 participants, 10 were male and 10 were female. Most of the participants were between 18 and 25 years old, and three of them were over 25 years old. All the participants signed the informed consent before the experiment and they participated in the experiment voluntarily. They could give up the experiment for various reasons. The whole experiment lasted for 15 to 20 min. After the experiment, the participants would get 10 to 15 RMB (according to the experiment results).

5.2 Design and Procedure

In this experiment, a single-factor intra-group design was adopted, which required fewer participants and was more sensitive than inter-group design, and could eliminate the influence of individual differences on the experiment. Meanwhile, there was no need for a long recovery period between each experimental condition in this design. All the participants made a decision by programming AVs, and the system had a higher degree of automation. The initial cooperation rates of the two groups were 0.5 and 0.7, and each case was carried out twice. The final cooperation rate was an overall result of the two times. In addition, a trial exercise was added so that the participants could better understand the experimental process.

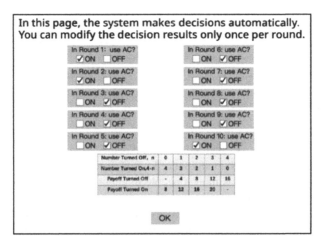

Fig. 3. Experimental conditions in experiment 2. The system generates 0.5 and 0.7 cooperation rates, respectively, and each cooperation rate was presented twice. The figure above showed a cooperation rate of 0.7. Participants could change the decision made by the system.

In order to offset the effect of practice or fatigue, one group of participants adopted the experimental order with system initial cooperation rates of 0.5, 0.5, 0.7, 0.7, while the other group adopted an order with system initial cooperation rates of 0.7, 0.7, 0.5, 0.5. The experimental interface is shown in Fig. 3.

5.3 Results

In this experiment, there were 10 men and 10 women, among which 5 men were individualistic and 5 were prosocial, 3 women were individualistic and 7 prosocial.

When the initial cooperation rate was 0.5, the average final cooperation rate was 0.55 ($SE = 0.043$), and when the initial cooperation rate was 0.7, the average final cooperation rate was 0.593 ($SE = 0.04$). The result of a paired-samples T-test showed that the interaction between paired samples was not significant ($t = -0.732, p = 0.473$).

The final cooperation rate of males was 0.49 ($SE = 0.057$), and the rate of females was 0.61 ($SE = 0.062$) when the initial cooperation rate was 0.5, while the final cooperation rate of males is 0.56 ($SE = 0.052$) and that of females was 0.625 ($SE = 0.062$) when the initial cooperation rate is 0.7. It can be seen that the cooperation rates of women were higher than men in both cases; when the initial cooperation rate was 0.7, the cooperation rates of both men and women were higher compared with the initial cooperation rate of 0.5, and the rate gap between male and female is narrowed (see Fig. 4). A two-way repeated-measures ANOVA was performed to analyze the data, and the results revealed no significant gender $\times$ autonomy interaction ($F = 0.215, p = 0.648$). There were no other relevant effects involving gender ($F = 2.610, p = 0.124$).

There are 8 individualists and 12 prosocial participants. When the initial cooperation rate is 0.5, the average final cooperation rate of individualists was 0.481 ($SE = 0.016$), and the rate of prosocial people was 0.5958 ($SE = 0.069$); when the initial cooperation rate was 0.7, the final cooperation rate of individualists was 0.563 ($SE = 0.061$), and the final cooperation rate of prosocial people was 0.613 ($SD = 0.054$). As shown in Fig. 4, the final cooperation rate of prosocial people was higher than that of individualists in both cases. When the initial cooperation rate was 0.7, the gap between the two groups was narrowed. Taking the initial cooperation rate as the main internal variable, social value orientation as the main inter body variable, and the final cooperation rate as the dependent variable, the results revealed no significant SVO $\times$ autonomy interaction ($F = 0.286, p = 0.600$). There were no other relevant effects involving SVO ($F = 1.916, p = 0.183$).

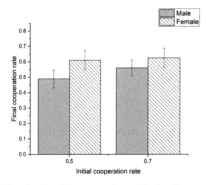
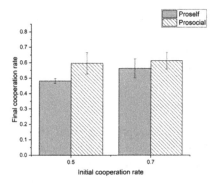

Fig. 4. Results in experiment 2: (Left) cooperation rate for gender, (Right) cooperation rate for SVO. The error bars represent SEs.

To further explore the influence of the initial cooperation rate of the system on human cooperative behavior, this paper conducted a difference analysis, that is, the independent variable was the initial cooperation rate of the system, and the dependent variable was the difference between the final cooperation rate and the initial cooperation rate (hereafter referred to as the difference).

When the initial cooperation rate was 0.5, the average difference was 0.05 ($SE = 0.193$), and when the initial cooperation rate was 0.7, the average difference was -0.108 ($SE = 0.179$). To analyze the data, we did repeated measures and the results showed a significant effect of initial cooperation rate on the difference, $F = 17.000$, $p = 0.025$. It could be seen that at the initial cooperation rate of 0.5, people tended to adjust the cooperation rate upward, while when the cooperation rate was 0.7, people tended to adjust the cooperation rate downward, and the downward adjustment is greater than the upward adjustment.

The difference of males was -0.01 ($SE = 0.181$), and the rate of females was 0.11 ($SE = 0.196$) when the initial cooperation rate was 0.5, while the difference of males was -0.14 ($SE = 0.163$) and that of females was -0.075 ($SE = 0.196$) when the initial cooperation rate was 0.7. At the initial cooperation rate of 0.5, males adjusted their cooperation rate slightly downward while females adjusted it upward and to a greater extent; at the initial cooperation rate of 0.7, both males and females adjusted their cooperation rate downward, and the female downward adjustment was greater. We ran a two-way repeated-measures ANOVA to analyze the data, and the results revealed no significant gender $\times$ initial cooperation rate interaction ($F = 17.000$, $p = 0.728$). There were no other relevant effects involving gender ($F = 1.864$, $p = 0.190$).

When the initial cooperation rate was 0.5, the difference of individualists was -0.019 ($SE = 0.046$), and the rate of prosocial people was 0.096 ($SE = 0.239$); when the initial cooperation rate was 0.7, the difference of individualists was -0.136 ($SE = 0.173$), and the difference of prosocial people was -0.088 ($SD = 0.187$). Taking the initial cooperation rate as the main internal variable, social value orientation as the main inter body variable, and the final cooperation rate as the dependent variable, the results revealed no significant SVO $\times$ initial cooperation rate interaction ($F = 17.000$, $p = 0.667$). There were no other relevant effects involving SVO ($F = 1.229$, $p = 0.283$). It could be seen that individualists tend to adjust the cooperation rate downward at either the initial cooperation rate of 0.5 or 0.7, and the downward adjustment was greater at the initial cooperation rate of 0.5, while pro-socialists tended to adjust the cooperation rate upward at the initial cooperation rate of 0.5 and downward at the initial cooperation rate of 0.7, and the downward adjustment was greater.

In summary, although the final cooperation rate of participants also increased when the initial cooperation rate of the system was higher, the increase was not significant. Participants would be willing to slightly increase their cooperation rate at an initial cooperation rate of 0.5. However, when the initial cooperation rate was 0.7, participants adjusted their cooperation rate downward to a greater extent. Thus, it could be seen that increasing the default cooperation rate of the system was not the best choice, and the initial cooperation rate granularity could be subsequently refined to seek the optimal value of the system.

6   The Influence of Automation on Human Cooperation

When we combined experiment 1 with experiment 2, we ran a one-way ANOVA, which took the decision-making method (direct manual interaction/programming the AVs/system initial cooperation rate of 0.5/system initial cooperation rate of 0.7) as the independent variable, and the final cooperation rate as the dependent variable. The result showed that the final cooperation rates of different decision-making methods had significant differences ($F = 3.117, p = 0.031, \eta^2 = 0.11$).

Taking the final cooperation rate as dependent variable, the data was analyzed in 4 (decision-making method: direct interaction/programming the AVs/initial cooperation rate for 0.5/initial cooperation rate of 0.7) * 2(gender: male/female) two-factor ANOVA. The results showed that gender had a significant effect on the final cooperation rate ($F = 5.486, p = 0.022, \eta^2 = 0.071$), and the interaction between decision-making method and gender was not significant ($F = 2.395, p = 0.075, \eta^2 = 0.091$).

Taking the final cooperation rate as the dependent variable, the data was analyzed in 4 (decision-making mode: direct interaction/programming the AVs/initial cooperation rate for 0.5/initial cooperation rate of 0.7) * 2(social value orientation: prosocial/individualism) two-factor ANOVA. The results of ANOVA showed that social value orientation had no significant effect on the final cooperation rate ($F = 0.323, p = 0.572, \eta^2 = 0.004$), and the interaction between decision-making method and social value orientation was not significant ($F = 0.871, p = 0.46, \eta^2 = 0.035$) (Fig. 5).

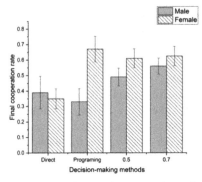 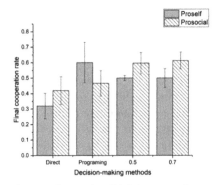

Fig. 5. Results in experiment 1 & 2: (Left) cooperation rate for gender, (Right) cooperation rate for SVO. The error bars represent SEs.

7 The Influence of Culture on Human Cooperation

In order to compare people's cooperative behaviors in different cultural backgrounds, this paper compares the data from the above two experiments with that of literature. The design of the experiment in the fourth chapter was the same as that of the first experiment in the literature (de Melo, C. M., Marsella, S., & Gratch, J., 2019). The experimental procedure was basically restored and the variables studied are the same, which met the comparison conditions.

There were 98 participants in the experiment from the literature. Forty-seven of them programmed the AVs to make decisions, and 51 made decisions through direct interaction. The average rate of cooperation was 0.638 by programming the AVs. The average rate of cooperation in direct interaction was 0.467, $p = 0.022$, which showed a significant difference. The specific cooperation rate distribution is shown in Fig. 6(left). The abscissa represents the cooperation rate, and the ordinate represents the proportion of participants with different cooperation rates in the total number of participants. It turned out that the direct interaction part showed a trend of low in the middle and high on both sides, while programming AVs showed a high on the left side, but the rest is approximately flat.

In this paper, the average rate of cooperation was 0.50 by programming the AVs, while the average rate of cooperation was 0.37 for direct interaction. There was no significant difference ($p = 0.166$). The specific cooperation rate distribution is shown in Fig. 6 (right), the abscissa represents the cooperation rate, and the ordinate showed the corresponding number of different cooperation rates. The two decision-making methods both showed a trend of high in the middle and low on both sides, which meant the cooperation rate of most participants was 0.4 to 0.5.

The overall rate of cooperation in the literature was about 0.1 higher than that in this paper. In the literature experiment, the number of the participants who set up the autopilot vehicle program in advance chose complete cooperation (cooperative rate was 1) was very large, accounting for 36% of the group. In this paper, the peak cooperation rate of the two groups appeared at 0.4 and 0.5, which made the overall cooperation rate lower than the literature data.

From the perspective of cultural differences between China and the west, traditional Chinese culture pays attention to reconciliation and compromise, emphasizing avoiding two extremes in treating people and seeking balance in contradictions, so there were more people with a cooperation rate of 0.4 to 0.6; while the western way of thinking is rational, divisive and extreme to a certain extent, so many people chose to cooperate completely or not at all.

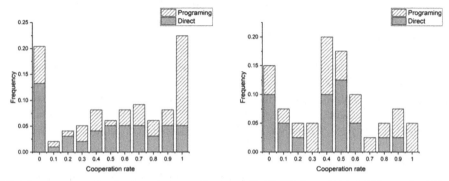

Fig. 6. Frequency distribution of cooperation rate: (Left) US data, (Right) Chinese data. The abscissa was the cooperation rate, and the ordinate was the proportion of participants with different cooperation rates in the total number of participants.

In the literature experiment, there were 39 individualists and 59 prosocial people in 98 participants. The average cooperation rate of the individualists was 0.364 ($SD = 0.333$), and that of the prosocial participants was 0.671 ($SD = 0.349$). One-way ANOVA showed a significant difference ($p < 0.001$).

In this study, the average cooperation rate of individualists is 0.413 ($SD = 0.295$), and that of the prosocial participants is 0.448 ($SD = 0.30$). There is no significant difference between the two value orientations ($p = 0.724$).

In the literature data, the interaction between the decision-making method and social value orientation is not significant ($F(1,94) = 1.636$ and $p = 0.202$), which can not show that prosocial drivers can make AVs more cooperative. In this paper, the interaction between the decision-making method and social value orientation is not significant, either ($p = 0.252$).

Under different cultural backgrounds and thinking modes between China and the West, people's cooperative behavior shows different rules. In Chinese culture, the balanced and harmonious thinking mode made more participants keep the cooperation rate at about 0.5, while the rational and extreme thinking mode of the west made many participants chose to cooperate completely or not at all, which was the main difference brought by different cultures. In terms of gender, the cooperation rate of men was lower than that of women in both Chinese culture and western culture.

8 Discussion

The following conclusions can be drawn from the experiments. Compared with manual direct decision making, setting the auto-driving program in advance had a more cooperative trend, that was, the cooperation rate is higher. When the system automation level was raised, the initial cooperation rate of the system is higher, and the final cooperation rate of the participants was also higher. From manual direct decision-making, early setting of an autopilot vehicle program, to the initial cooperation rate of 0.5, and to the initial cooperation rate of 0.7, the final cooperation rate of the participants showed an increasing trend. The above data shows that:

1. When the decision-making time is advanced, people will be more cooperative as they are able to think from a broader perspective;
2. When the automation degree of the system is improved, the system can automatically make some decisions, which will affect people's choices. When the system has a higher tendency of cooperation, it can promote people's cooperative behavior.

With regard to gender, in addition to manual real-time decision-making, the cooperation rate of women is always higher than that of men in the other three decision-making modes, and this proves that:

3. Women are more cooperative than men when making decisions from a macro perspective;
4. On the whole, women tend to cooperate more than men, while men show more competitive tendencies.

In terms of social value orientation, there is no clear evidence that prosocial people are more inclined to cooperate than individualists. In the third chapter, in the experiment of programming automatic driving in advance, the rate of cooperation among individualists was higher than that of prosocial people. However, in the other three decision-making methods, the cooperative rate of individualistic participants was low, while the rate of prosocial orientation was high.

In terms of cultural background, the experimental data provided by this study and the literature showed that in Chinese culture, with a balanced and harmonious thinking mode, people's cooperation rate mainly maintained at about 0.5, while in western culture, people tended to make more extreme choices of complete cooperation or complete noncooperation with a rational and accurate thinking mode.

In general, this article makes an initial study on how system default values interfere with people's cooperative behavior, and explores the influence of different cultural backgrounds on human cooperative behavior. The number of samples in this study is not enough, and the experiment was conducted online, so it was not easy to control unrelated variables, which may lead to some contingency in the results. In future research, we can further increase the number of samples to make the results more valid. There are few research on whether the intelligent system with high automation can promote human's cooperative behavior. Therefore, more researches are supposed to be carried out in this field. Besides, this paper only sets 0.5 and 0.7 two levels of initial cooperation rate, which did not show significant difference under this situation, in which case, different levels of cooperation rate could be established so as to further study the impact of automation system on human cooperative behavior, and explore the optimal value of system defaults in human-computer interaction.

It should be noted that this study hopes to explore the human decision-making style and the influence of intelligent machine cooperation tendency on human cooperation behavior in a human-machine collaboration context at the theoretical level, so the experimental scenarios were designed in an abstract manner, and subsequent experiments could be conducted in more realistic scenarios to verify the conclusions of this paper.

Acknowledgments. This study was supported by the National Natural Science Foundation of China (NSFC, 72171015 and 72021001) and the Fundamental Research Funds for the Central Universities (YWF-21-BJ-J-314).

References

1. Dewitte, S., Cremer, D.D.: Self-control and cooperation: different concepts, similar decisions? A question of the right perspective. J. Psychol. **135**(2), 133–153 (2001)
2. Mannix, E.A.: Resource dilemmas and discount rates in decision making groups. J. Exp. Soc. Psychol. **27**(4), 379–391 (1991)
3. Ariely, D., Wertenbroch, K.: Procrastination, deadlines, and performance: self-control by precommitment. Psychol. Sci. **13**(3), 219–224 (2002)
4. Kollock, P.: Social dilemmas: the anatomy of cooperation. Ann. Rev. Sociol. **24**(1), 183–214 (1998)
5. Kortenkamp, K.V., Moore, C.F.: Time, uncertainty, and individual differences in decisions to cooperate in resource dilemmas. Pers. Soc. Psychol. Bull. **32**(5), 603–615 (2006)
6. Trope, Y., Liberman, N.: Construal-level theory of psychological distance. Psychol. Rev. **117**(2), 440 (2010)
7. Oosterbeek, H., Sloof, R., Van De Kuilen, G.: Cultural differences in ultimatum game experiments: evidence from a meta-analysis. Exp. Econ. **7**(2), 171–188 (2004)
8. Güth, W., Tietz, R.: Ultimatum bargaining behavior: a survey and comparison of experimental results. J. Econ. Psychol. **11**, 417–449 (1990)
9. Rauhut, H., Winter, F.: A sociological perspective on measuring social norms by means of strategy method experiments. Soc. Sci. Res. **39**(6), 1181–1194 (2010)
10. Giacomantonio, M., De Dreu, C.K., Shalvi, S., Sligte, D., Leder, S.: Psychological distance boosts value-behavior correspondence in ultimatum bargaining and integrative negotiation. J. Exp. Soc. Psychol. **46**(5), 824–829 (2010)
11. Agerström, J., Björklund, F.: Temporal distance and moral concerns: future morally questionable behavior is perceived as more wrong and evokes stronger prosocial intentions. Basic Appl. Soc. Psychol. **31**(1), 49–59 (2009)
12. Agerström, J., Björklund, F.: Moral concerns are greater for temporally distant events and are moderated by value strength. Soc. Cogn. **27**(2), 261–282 (2009)
13. Soderberg, C.K., Callahan, S.P., Kochersberger, A.O., Amit, E., Ledgerwood, A.: The effects of psychological distance on abstraction: two meta-analyses. Psychol. Bull. **141**(3), 525 (2015)
14. de Melo, C.M., Marsella, S., Gratch, J.: Social decisions and fairness change when people's interests are represented by autonomous agents. Auton. Agent. Multi Agent Syst. **32**(1), 163–187 (2017). https://doi.org/10.1007/s10458-017-9376-6

15. de Melo, C.M., Marsella, S., Gratch, J.: Human cooperation when acting through autonomous machines. Proc. Natl. Acad. Sci. **116**(9), 3482–3487 (2019)
16. Joireman, J.: Environmental problems as social dilemmas: the temporal dimension. In: Understanding Behavior in the Context of Time, pp. 289–304 (2005)
17. Kuhlman, D.M., Marshello, A.F.: Individual differences in game motivation as moderators of preprogrammed strategy effects in prisoner's dilemma. J. Pers. Soc. Psychol. **32**(5), 922 (1975)
18. Eagly, A.H., Crowley, M.: Gender and helping behavior: a meta-analytic review of the social psychological literature. Psychol. Bull. **100**(3), 283 (1986)
19. Eckel, C.C., Grossman, P.J.: Are women less selfish than men? Evidence from dictator experiments. Econ. J. **108**(448), 726–735 (1998)
20. Eckel, C.C., Grossman, P.J.: Differences in the economic decisions of men and women: experimental evidence. In: Handbook of Experimental Economics Results, vol. 1, pp. 509–519 (2008)
21. Andreoni, J., Vesterlund, L.: Which is the fair sex? Gender differences in altruism. Q. J. Econ. **116**(1), 293–312 (2001)
22. Simpson, B.: Sex, fear, and greed: a social dilemma analysis of gender and cooperation. Soc. Forces **82**(1), 35–52 (2003)
23. Balliet, D., Parks, C., Joireman, J.: Social value orientation and cooperation in social dilemmas: a meta-analysis. Group Process. Intergroup Relat. **12**(4), 533–547 (2009)
24. Bogaert, S., Boone, C., Declerck, C.: Social value orientation and cooperation in social dilemmas: a review and conceptual model. Br. J. Soc. Psychol. **47**(3), 453–480 (2008)
25. Gächter, S., Herrmann, B., Thöni, C.: Culture and cooperation. Philos. Transa. Roy. Soc. B Biol. Sci. **365**(1553), 2651–2661 (2010)
26. Hofstede, G., Hofstede, G.H.: Culture's Consequences: International Differences in Work-Related Values, vol. 5. Sage (1984)
27. Lee, Y.T.: What is missing in Chinese-Western dialectical reasoning? Am. Psychol. **55**, 1065–1067 (2000)
28. Ho, D.Y.F., Chiu, C.Y.: Component ideas of individualism, collectivism, and social organization: an application in the study of Chinese culture (1994)
29. Roto, V., Palanque, P., Karvonen, H.: Engaging automation at work – a literature review. In: Barricelli, B.R., et al. (eds.) HWID 2018. IAICT, vol. 544, pp. 158–172. Springer, Cham (2019). https://doi.org/10.1007/978-3-030-05297-3_11
30. Sheridan, T.B., Verplank, W.L.: Human and computer control of undersea teleoperators. Massachusetts Institute of Technology Cambridge Man-Machine Systems Lab (1978)
31. Siegel, M.S.: Persuasive robotics: how robots change our minds. Doctoral dissertation, Massachusetts Institute of Technology (2008)
32. Murphy, R.O., Ackermann, K.A., Handgraaf, M.: Measuring social value orientation. Judgm. Decis. Mak. **6**(8), 771–781 (2011)

A Socio-technical Framework for Addressing the Influence of Work Time and Income on Work Well Being

Xiangang Qin[1,2(✉)] 🆔 and Xinchen Wang[1,2]

[1] School of Digital Media and Design Arts, Beijing University of Posts and
Telecommunications, Beijing, China
qinxiangang@bupt.edu.cn
[2] Beijing Key Laboratory of Network Systems and Network Culture, Beijing University of
Posts and Telecommunications, Beijing, China

Abstract. In contrast to the striking discussion of working overtime in the media,
it remains unclear in academic research whether longer work time leads to
job burnout and procrastination. Informed by job demands-resources model and
challenges-hinderance model, this study examined the role of work hour, time perspective, and income in predicting job burnout and procrastination at work. The
results of this survey study, conducted with 223 Chinese employees located in 30
provincial areas, show that work hour only predicted emotional exhaustion. Neither emotional exhaustion nor procrastination at work was predicted by income.
Screen time on mobile phone predicted procrastination. By contrast, time perspective predicted both. The findings suggest that work hour can work as resources
when it is appraised as supporting personal growth and development, whereas
income was not necessarily appraised as supportive of personal development.
Additionally, a theoretical perspective of imbalance between effort and reward
explained job burnout and procrastination better than their independent effects.
Theoretical framework for promoting off-task activities based on context-aware
persuasion was proposed. Finally, informed by the philosophy of socio-technical
design, this study called for a holistic and collective-oriented perspective to design
technical systems for employee.

Keywords: Job burnout · Procrastination at work · Work hour · Time
perspective · Income · Job demands-resources model · Context-aware persuasion

1 Introduction

Ever since Kenichi Ohmae coined the term "low desire society" to describe the phenomenon of worrying about an uncertain future and unwillingness of possession or
consumption in Japanese youth (Ohmae 2018), as a society shares similar cultural and
geographical background with Japan, there has been debate about whether China is
slipping into a similar state of low desire society (Shaojie 2020).

© IFIP International Federation for Information Processing 2022
Published by Springer Nature Switzerland AG 2022
G. Bhutkar et al. (Eds.): HWID 2021, IFIP AICT 609, pp. 141–157, 2022.
https://doi.org/10.1007/978-3-031-02904-2_7

Despite the disagreement over whether China is marching toward a low desire society, the topic of nine-nine-six work schedule (996) and overtime working went viral on social media of China and became an emerging challenge for employers and government to address (Howsitlike 2020). 996 work culture was believed to have helped China increase the economy at a rapid speed and will continue to help China make "outstanding achievements like it did in the last four decades" (Howsitlike 2020). On the other hand, 996 work culture faced the backlash from employees. Chinese tech workers set up a popping-up GitHub project named 996.ICU (refers to 'Work by 996, sick in ICU') to protest 996 schedule (*996.ICU* 2019). "996" work schedule means working for at least 60 h a week and violates the stipulations of labor law of China that the labors shall work for no more than 8 h a day and no more than 44 h a week (*996.ICU* 2019). CGTN (China Global Television Network) expressed opinion on '996' schedule that "Work to a better life, not ICU", which to some extent reflected the official position on this issue (Ran 2019). The media believed that working overtime may result in mental, emotional and physical health, high levels of sleep deprivation, increased anxiety, extreme fatigue, and stress (Howsitlike 2020). The sudden death of a young female employee at Chinese tech giant Pinduoduo (拼多多) after working long hours past midnight renews the controversy over working overtime. However, as far as we know, there is scant literature in the fields of Human-computer Interaction (HCI) and HWID (Human-Work Interaction Design) that investigated the association of work hours with the phenomenon of low desire, technology use, and how the interaction system in workplace should be designed to address the related challenges. This paper first pioneered this area by examining the impact of work hour and psychological time of a personality on work-related well-being, namely job burnout, and work-related behavior, namely procrastination and time spend on mobile phone. Secondly, this paper challenged both the necessity of 996 schedule and the traditional socio-technical perspective emphasizing that "socio-technical practices create boundaries" since the booming digital economy, technology advances and popularity of staff home (职工之家) are potentially helpful in dissolving the boundary between work and life, ease the conflicts of bounded entities (e.g. employee-employer, workplace-home, work-entertainment-leisure), and enable people to better balance work and non-work responsibilities (Cox et al. 2014). Finally, inspired by the existing staffs' home that were aimed to improve the work well-being by setting up a sense of being at home, and built on both the findings of this study and socio-technical systems design (STSD) methods (Baxter and Sommerville 2011), a new pragmatic framework of socio-technical system was proposed to make the work environment more acceptable to employee and deliver better value to employers.

2   Literature Review

In this section, we reviewed the literature about the core concepts and theories upon which the present study based, four predictors (i.e., work hour, income, screen time on mobile phone and time perspective), three dependent variables (i.e., job burnout, procrastination) and their interplay and socio-technical systems design (STSD) methods.

2.1   Job Burnout (JBO)

JBO can was defined as "a syndrome of emotional exhaustion, depersonalization, and reduced personal accomplishment that can occur among individuals who do 'people work' of some kind" (Maslach and Jackson 1981). As the definition of JBO implies, the construct of JBO consists of three dimensions including emotional exhaustion (EE), depersonalization (DP) and low personal accomplishment (LPA). EE refers to feelings of being emotionally overextended and exhausted by one's work (e.g. "I feel emotionally drained from my work") (Maslach and Jackson 1981); DP describes an "unfeeling and impersonal response towards recipients of one's care or service" (e.g., "I feel I treat some recipients as if they were impersonal 'objects'"); LPA describes "feelings of competence and successful achievement in one's work with people" (e.g., "I can easily understand how my recipients feel about things"). As far as we know, no existing literature has measured "low desire" at work with valid psychometric scale. However, Ohmae (2018) indicated in his book that low desire was characterized by lack of motivation for marriage, giving birth, owning real-estate, and even working. Blocking progress has been thought to be the behavioral sign of burnout when it was first coined by Freudenberger (1974). In the literature based on empirical evidence, extinction of motivation or incentive has been found to be correlated with JBO (Margaretha 2019; Tajeri Moghadam et al. 2020) and hence job burnout was selected as the psychological indicator of "low desire" in present study.

As implied by Ohmae (2018), the young Japanese faced higher risk of low desire than their parents. This study posited that younger Chinese suffered more from JOB than older Chinese (Hypothesis 1–1).

2.2   Procrastination at Work (PAW)

Procrastination at work refers to the phenomenon of "putting off work related action by engaging in nonwork-related actions during work hours." (Metin et al. 2016). Although procrastination has been studied enormously, large proportion of research in related field has been conducted to investigate the issue of academic procrastination (Hong et al. 2021; Li et al. 2020; Metin et al. 2016). By contrast, studies about procrastination in the workplace were only at the beginning.

Procrastination was found to be composed of two subdimensions, namely soldiering and cyberslacking. Soldiering refers to offline off-task activity, such as taking long coffee breaks, gossiping or daydreaming. Cyberslacking describes online off-task activity, such as using work-unrelated applications on mobile phone. Cyberslacking was considered a phenomenon emerged with the prevalence of using computers and mobile technology with Internet at work. The development of technology provided employee with more chances of cyberslacking (Metin et al. 2016).

PAW was proved to have relevance for a number of consequential negative outcomes such as lower-salaries, shorter employment duration, likelihood of unemployment, labor productivity, and work performance (Metin et al. 2016; Zabelina et al. 2018). As a result, procrastination might impair employee well-being (Metin et al. 2016). However, brief procrastination may also have positive effects on productivity and employ well-being (Vitak et al. 2011). Additionally, the factors that may shape and impact procrastination in the workplace remains unconclusive (Hen et al. 2021; Vitak et al. 2011). People in a culture of collectivism and high level of power distance (e.g., Turkey and China) are supposed to be more inclined to have procrastination at work due to being unable to take decisions lack of autonomy to their supervisor (Metin et al. 2016). This study thus posited that procrastination may exist in Chinese employees as behavioral phenomenon of low desire. However, given the age differences of low desire, younger Chinese may have more procrastination activities (Hypothesis 1–2).

2.3 Job Demands and Resources Model (JD-R), Work Hour and Income

The job demands-resources (JD-R) model has been adopted widely as an influential theoretical framework in understanding how job characteristics impact job well-being. According to JD-R, job burnout may develop by following two processes. The first process was determined by job demands (JD) and the second process was determined by job resources (JR) (Demerouti et al. 2001). JD describes "those physical, psychological, social, or organizational aspects of the job that require sustained physical and/or psychological effort". Job resources, on the other hand, refer to those 'physical, psychological, social, or organizational aspects of the job' that "be functional in achieving work goals", "reduce job demands and the associated physiological and psychological costs", and "stimulate personal growth and development" (Demerouti et al. 2001, p. 501).

   According to existing literature, while JD may lead to exhaustion, JR is probably responsible for withdraw behavior and disengagement from work in the long run (Demerouti et al. p. 2001). Among the wide range of job demands, fatigues resulting from time pressure/urgency was thought to be responsible for the relationship between JD and exhaustion (Demerouti et al. p. 2001). In the context of 996 schedule wherein working for long hours was considered as organizational aspect of the job that require sustained physical and psychological effort, this study posited that longer work hours may act as JD and increase job burnout, EE in particular (Hypothesis 2–1). On the other hand, as proved by existing literature (Crawford et al. 2010), the income and welfare may act as JR to decrease procrastination (Hypothesis 2–2).

   Mobile phone use during working hours has become prevalent for both work-related and unrelated purposes, this study supposed that mobile phone was also considered as job resources in achieving work goals and reduce job pressure. Therefore, screen time on mobile phone may also predict JBO and PRO (Hypothesis 2–3).

2.4 Challenge and Hinderance Demands Model (CHD) and Time Perspective (TP)

In addition to work hours, some researchers argue that the impact of job demands on work well-being (e.g., exhaustion) may be moderated by how JD was appraised (Crawford et al. 2010). JD-R was later on updated and extended with CHD theory regarding appraisal of stressors to explain the inconsistencies in relationships between demands and engagement in literature. According to CHD, job aspects that were considered as hinderance job demands (HJD) may lead to emotional exhaustion due to being appraised as impediment to personal learning, development, and growth. By contrast, job aspects that were considered as challenging job demands (CJD) may also play a motivational role and "good" stressors, and hence were appraised as supporting employees' growth and development. Different with the prediction of JD-R, CJD thus implied that the prediction of work hour to work well-being varies depending on how work hour was appraised. When long work hour was appraised as impediment to personal development, it will increase exhaustion. On the other hand, when long work hour was considered as CJD, it may decrease exhaustion.

In present study, the appraisal of work hour was examined using time perspective (TP). TP originally refers to "the totality of the individual's views of his psychological future and psychological past existing at a given time" (p. 75). TP reflects individuals' "dispositional tendencies to use and overuse particular temporal perspectives, developing trait-like temporal biases" (Stolarski et al. 2020). Five dimensions of TP was defined by Zimbardo and Boyd (1999): Past-Positive (PP) refers to warm and sentimental view of the past, Past-Negative (PN) reflects negative and aversive view of the past, Present-Hedonistic (PH) refers to orientation on immediate pleasure and little consideration of future consequences, Present-Fatalistic (PF) refers to the feeling of little control over one's life, an attitude of helplessness, and Future refers to striving for future rewards and goals.

TP has been proved to be associated with burnout and procrastination. Young people with high level of procrastination were more pessimistic and negative about past events, felt hopeless and helpless, and were less focused on future plans than their counterparts with low and medium level of procrastination (Zabelina et al. 2018). In sum, this study hypothesized that subdimensions of TP can predict JOB and PRO (Hypothesis 3–1). By contrast, balanced time perspective buffers against the burnout and increases job satisfaction (Akirmak and Ayla 2019) (Hypothesis 3–2).

According to CHD, challenges tend to be appraised as stressful demands that have the potential to promote mastery, personal growth, or future gains. Examples of challenges include demands such as a high workload, time pressure, and high levels of job responsibility. Employees tend to perceive long work hour as opportunities to learn, achieve, and demonstrate the type of competence that tends to get rewarded. The mechanism underpinning challenging job demands (CJD) was supported by effort–reward imbalance model (ERI) (Siegrist et al. 1997; Van Vegchel et al. 2005). Working overtime and time pressure are two of the six sub-dimensions of effort scale in ERI Questionnaire. Reward consists of three underlying sub-dimensions, including money, esteem and security/career opportunities. According to ERIM, JBO was determined by the imbalance between efforts and rewards. As extrinsic ERI hypothesizes, health is a function of imbalance between extrinsic effort and reward. High extrinsic effort and low reward increase the risk of poor health (Van Vegchel et al. 2005). An review study showed that 5 out of 6 studies about the relationship between ERI and burnout found an association between ERI and job-related well-being, wherein risk for exhaustion increased with high effort and low reward (Van Vegchel et al. 2005). In present study, informed by extrinsic ERI hypothesis, we posited that JBO and PAW was the results of longer worktime and low family income (Hypothesis 3–3).

2.5   Socio-technical Systems Design (STSD) Methods

In this study, socio-technical system design (STSD) method refers to an design approach that take into account both individual, family, organizational and social factors(Baxter and Sommerville 2011). In line with the idea of social design, STSD aims to develop and design artifact for the public good and interests rather than merely for individual interests (Dell and Venkatesh 2012). Given the emphasis on family in tradition of China, this study posited that the success of STSD also depends on the extent to which the families of employee were considered. It is important for solving the problems related to low desire society since the problems uncovered in this study were rooted in China, which was normally seen as a collectivism-oriented society and recently highlighted its' outlook for "common prosperity" (Insights, n.d.). As a result, compared with the traditional user-centered method (UCD), the STSD in this study was grounded on a "holistic design" perspective arguing that "all aspects that influence the future use situation should be developed in parallel" and "one person or team should have the overall responsibility for the integration of all aspects" (Gulliksen et al. 2003). Additionally, the traditional HCI methods have focused on the individual interests from requirement analysis to evaluation of system. By contrast, this study strives for a collective-oriented methodology focusing on the stakeholders within the organization and society. We posited that if 996 harms the experience of employee, it will not only have detrimental effect on employee, but also on the organization, family, community and the whole society.

3   Materials and Methods

3.1   Data Collection and Sampling

Participants (N = 223; age mean [M] = 30.2, standard deviation [SD] = 4.7, Max = 57, Min = 22; male = 106, female = 117) were recruited from Wenjuanxing (问卷星) online survey service platform. They were located in 30 different provincial areas. Eighty-seven worked in Tier 1 cities (i.e., Beijing, Shanghai, Guangzhou, Shenzhen) in the past one year, 92 worked in Tier 2 cities (Capital cities of provinces or autonomy areas), 34 worked in Tier 3 cities, and the rest worked in counties or countryside. As showed in Table 1, the majority of participants were employed by private enterprises (111), followed by state-owned enterprises (46), government or public institutions (38), foreign enterprises (27) and self-employed (1).

Table 1.   Distribution of participants by employers

Employed by	Number
Private enterprises	111
State-owned enterprises	46
Government or public institutions	38
Foreign enterprises	27
Self-employed	1

3.2 Measures of Independent Variables

Work hour per week (WHPW) were calculated based on responses of two self-report questions about their normal work days and work hours per day in the past one year.

Household income (HI) was collected by one self-report item, "How much was the combined gross income of all members living together of your household". Effort–reward imbalance index (ERI_I) was calculated by the ratio of WHPW to HI.

In effort to examine the impact of use of technology on job well-being and the construct validity of cyberslacking as one dimension of procrastination, the screen time on mobile phone (STMP) was collected with one self-report item (i.e., "How much time did you use your mobile phone on average in the past one year").

TP was measured using 25 items from the Chinese version of Time Perspective (Chen 2016), which is adapted from the English version of TP by Zimbardo and Boyd (1999). It included five sub-components of TP: past-positive (6 items; e.g., 'Familiar childhood sights, sounds, smells often bring back a flood of wonderful memories', Cronbach's $\alpha = .75$), past-negative (7 items; e.g., 'Painful past experiences keep being replayed in my mind', Cronbach's $\alpha = .81$), present-hedonic (4 items; e.g. 'I do things impulsively', Cronbach's $\alpha = .81$), present-fatalistic (3 items; e.g. 'It doesn't make sense to worry about the future, since there is nothing that I can do about it anyway', Cronbach's $\alpha = .64$), future (5 items; e.g. 'I keep working at difficult, uninteresting tasks if they will help me get ahead', Cronbach's $\alpha = .56$). Cronbach's alpha values for the subscales were .57–.77 in Chen (2016). Participants responded to each item on a five-point Likert scale ranging from 1 = 'very uncharacteristic' to 5 = 'very characteristic'.

$$DBTP = \sqrt{(oPN - ePN)^2 + (oPP - ePP)^2 + (oPF - ePF)^2 + (oPH - ePF)^2 + (oF - eF)^2}$$

Finally, balanced TP was measured using Derivation from the Balance Time Perspective (DBTP), which was introduced by Stolarski et al. (2011). "o" refers to the 'optimal' points on each of these subdimensions of TP, and "e" means 'empirical' scores on each of these subdimensions of TP. "e" points were derived from P. Zimbardo and Boyd (2008). The 'e' point is 4.6 for Past-Positive (90th percentile), 3.9 for Present-Hedonistic (80th percentile), 4.0 for Future (80th percentile), 1.95 for Past-Negative (10th percentile), and 1.5 for Present-Fatalistic (10th percentile).

3.3 Measures of Dependent Variables

JBO was measured using 9 items ('I feel burned out from my work'.) from the Emotional Exhaustion subscale JBO by (Maslach and Jackson 1981). Cronbach's alpha values was .85 in the sampling of this study. Participants responded to each item on a five-point Likert scale ranging from 1 = 'very uncharacteristic' to 5 = 'very characteristic'.

PAW was measured using 12 items from the Procrastination at Work Scale (Metin et al. 2016). It included two sub-components of PAW: soldiering (8 items; e.g. 'When I work, even after I make decision, I delay acting upon it', Cronbach's $\alpha = .88$), cyberslacking (4 items; e.g. 'I spend more than half an hour on social network sites', Cronbach's $\alpha = .82$). The scale was translated into Chinese by the researcher of present study and Chinese version was presented to participants in combination with the original English version. Participants responded to each item on a five-point Likert scale ranging from 1 = 'very uncharacteristic' to 5 = 'very characteristic'.

4 Results

4.1 Descriptive Data

Table 2. The descriptiveness of independent and dependent variables

	M	SD	Min	Max
WHPW	47.6	9.1	30	91
HI	228	157	0	100[a]
ERI_I	10.1	9.3	1.0	72.0
STMP	342.9	142	30	810
TP_PAN	2.8	0.7	1.3	4.7
TP_PAP	4.1	0.6	1.7	5.0
TP_PRF	2.7	0.9	1.3	4.7
TP_PRH	2.4	0.8	1.0	4.3
TP_F	4.1	0.4	2.4	5.0
DBTP	2.55	.70	.6	4.7
JBO_EH	2.4	0.7	1.1	4.4
PRO_SO	2.2	0.8	1.0	4.6
PRO_SL	2.6	1.0	1.0	5.0

[a]In thousand.
Notes: WHPW refers to Work hour per week; HI refers to Household income; ERI_I refers to Effort–reward imbalance index; STMP refers to screen time on mobile phone; TP_PAN refers to past-negative of time perspective; TP_PAP refers to past-positive of time perspective; TP_PRF refers to present-fatalistic of time perspective; TP_PRH refers to present-hedonic of time perspective; TP_F refers to future of time perspective; JBO_EH refers to exhaustion of job burnout; PAW_SO refers to soldiering of procrastination at work; PAW_SL refers to slacking of procrastination at work.

As showed in Table 2, the average WHPW was 47.6 h and significantly higher than the stipulations of labor law of China (t(222) = 5.98, p < .01); The average HI was 228 thousand RMB; The average STMP was 342.9. Among the five subdimensions of TP, TP_PAP and TP_P were significantly than other three subdimensions ($t_{TP\_PAP-TP\_PAN}$

$(222) = 19.4, p < .01; t_{TP\_PAP-TP\_PRH} (222) = 25.3, p < .01; t_{TP\_PAP-TP\_PRF} (222) = 18.9, p < .01; t_{TP\_P-TP\_PAN} (222) = 20.2, p < .01; t_{TP\_P//TP\_PRH} (222) = 24.3, p < .01; t_{TP\_P//TP\_PRF} (222) = 19.0, p < .01)$. The differences between subdimensions of TP and rating scores of TP_PAP alongside TP_P indicated that the participants experienced more positively in the past and were future-oriented. The average rating score of JBO_EH was significantly lower than the neutral level value of 3 (t (222) = 12.9, p < .01), which indicated that did not suffer from serious problem of emotional exhaustion and extinction of motivation. Finally, the average rating scores of PRO_SO (M = 2.2) and PRO_SL (M = 2.6) also indicated that the participants did not have serious phenomenon of putting off work related action.

4.2 Difference Tests

Independent samples T tests were conducted to examine the differences of variables between younger (younger than 30 years old, N = 106) and elder employee (N = 117). The results showed that young employee had significantly longer STMP (t(221) = 2.7, p < .05), higher level of TP_PAN (t(221) = 2.6, p < .05), higher level of TP_PRH (t(221) = 2.3, p < .05), higher level of JBO_EH (t(221) = 3.8, p < .01), higher level of PRO_SO (t(221) = 3.7, p < .01), and PRO_SL (t(221) = 22, p < .05), and lower level of TP_F (see Table 3). Hypothesis 1–1, 1–2 were supported.

Table 3. The differences of variables between younger and elder employees

	<30 years	>= 30 years	t values
WTPW	48.14	47.46	0.54
HI	21.21	23.95	−1.3
ERI_I	10.88	9.34	1.2
STMP	370	318	2.7**
TP_PAN	2.93	2.67	2.6**
TP_PAP	4.03	4.15	−1.7
TP_PRF	2.82	2.61	1.7
TP_PRH	2.56	2.32	2.3*
TP_F	3.98	4.13	−2.5*
DBTP	2.61	2.50	0.76
JBO_EH	2.58	2.22	3.8**
PRO_SO	2.39	2.01	3.7**
PRO_SL	2.78	2.50	2.2*

Notes: WHPW refers to Work hour per week; HI refers to Household income; ERI_I refers to Effort–reward imbalance index; STMP refers to screen time on mobile phone; TP_PAN refers to past-negative of time perspective; TP_PAP refers to past-positive of time perspective; TP_PRF refers to present-fatalistic of time perspective; TP_PRH refers to present-hedonic of time perspective; TP_F refers to future of time perspective; JBO_EH refers to exhaustion of job burnout; PAW_SO refers to soldiering of procrastination at work; PAW_SL refers to slacking of procrastination at work.

4.3   The Prediction of JBO and PRO by WHPW, HI, ERI_I, STMP and TP

Table 4. The linear regression analysis of JBO and PRO by WHPW, HI, ERI_I, STMP and TP

JBO_EH				PRO_SO			PRO_SL		
Predictors	Beta	R^2	t	Beta	R^2	t	Beta	R^2	t
WHPW	.14	.02	2.1*	.05	.002	.69	.09	.008	1.3
HI	−.12	.01	−1.8	−.11	.013	−1.7	.02	.00	.25
ERI_I	.16	.03	2.4*	.13	.02	1.9	.07	.004	.97
STMP	.11	.01	1.7	.15	.02	2.3*	.29	.08	4.4**
TP_PAN	.62	.38	11.7**	.50	.25	8.6**	.42	.18	6.8**
TP_PAP	−.13	.02	−2.0**	−.18	.03	−2.7*	−.27	.07	−4.2**
TP_PRF	.54	.29	9.5**	.44	.19	7.2**	.41	.17	6.6**
TP_PRH	.55	.30	9.7**	.54	.29	9.5**	.44	.19	7.2**
TP_F	−.37	.14	−5.9**	−.44	.19	−7.2**	−.35	.12	−5.5**
DBTP	.30	.09	4.7**	.24	.06	3.6**	.26	.07	4.1**

Notes: WHPW refers to Work hour per week; HI refers to Household income; ERI_I refers to Effort–reward imbalance index; STMP refers to screen time on mobile phone; TP_PAN refers to past-negative of time perspective; TP_PAP refers to past-positive of time perspective; TP_PRF refers to present-fatalistic of time perspective; TP_PRH refers to present-hedonic of time perspective; TP_F refers to future of time perspective; JBO_EH refers to exhaustion of job burnout; PAW_SO refers to soldiering of procrastination at work; PAW_SL refers to slacking of procrastination at work.

Linear regression analysis was conducted to examine the predictors of JBO and PRO. The results showed that WHPW significantly predicted emotional exhaustion of JBO ($\beta = .14, t = 2.1, p < .05$), whereas it failed to predict soldiering and slacking of PRO ($\beta = .05, t = .69, p > .05$; $\beta = .09, t = 1.3, p < .05$). Hypothesis 2–1 was partly supported. HI did not predict JBO and PROs ($\beta = -.12, t = -1.8, p > .05$; $\beta = -.11, t = -1.7, p > .05$; $\beta = .02, t = .25, p > .05$). Hypothesis 2–2 was not supported. STMP did not predict JBO_EH ($\beta = .11, t = 1.7, p < .05$), whereas it significantly predicted PRO_SO and PRO_SL ($\beta = .15, t = 2.3, p < .05$; $\beta = .29, t = 4.4, p < .01$) Hypothesis 2–3 was partly supported. ERI_I significantly predicted emotional exhaustion ($\beta = .16, t = 2.4, p < .05$) but failed to predict PRO_SO and PRO_SL ($\beta = .13, t = 1.9, p > .05$; $\beta = .07, t = .97, p > .05$). Hypothesis 3 was partly supported. JBO, PRO_SO and PRO_SL were significantly predicted by the five subdimensions of TP. While past positive (TP_PAP) and future (TP_F) decreased the risk of JBO, PRO_SO and PRO_SL, past negative, present hedonic and present fatalistic increased the risk of them. DBTP significantly increased the risk of JBO, PRO_SO and PRO_SL (Table 4).

5   Discussion

While the discussion about phenomenon of working overtime and its impact on work well-being, health and life quality went viral in the media of China, there is a scant academic literature on this topic to provide empirical evidence for the related controversies and remedies. Additionally, whether the widely used theories of JD-R and CHD also apply to explaining the phenomenon of JOB and PRO remains inconclusive. Based on the survey data of 223 Chinese employee located in 30 provincial areas and aged from 22–57, this study contributed to the line of research on the related topics by answering four major research questions: 1) Whether Chinese employees, younger ones in particular, are facing the challenges of low desire society as their Japanese counterparts (Hypothesis 1–1, 1–2); 2) Whether JD-R is correct in positing that the work hours positively correlate with job burnout and procrastination (Hypothesis 2–1), and income decrease the job burnout and procrastination (Hypothesis 2–2); 3) Whether the use of technology (i.e. STMP) was considered as job resources and contribute to the job burnout and procrastination (Hypothesis 2–3). 4) Whether CHD is correct in suggesting that the appraisal of time (i.e. TP), balanced TP and phone use may predict the job burnout and procrastination (Hypothesis 3–1, 3–2, 3–3). While most of the hypotheses of this study were supported by the results, some failed to get supporting evidence. In the sections below, the results and implications of the findings were discussed.

5.1   Low Desire in Chinese Youth

While the participants in this study did not face high risk of JOB and PRO on average, the younger participants were more inclined to have problems related to low desire. Although this result supported the hypothesis informed by Ohmae (2018), it was unexpected given the staggering economy of Japan in which the theory of low desired society is rooted. China reaped one of the fastest economic development in the past four decades and the success of economy was reflected on the low level of emotional exhaustion and off-work activities in this study. However, differences between ages indicated that the young Chinese may not harvest the achievement of society as their parents. Chinese under 30 witnessed the booming economy of China and hence were supposed to be more positive on past than their parents who suffered from the shortage of material and poverty to some extent. However, the results of this study indicated that the Chinese society needs to divert some attention from the issue of economy development to the issue of declining positiveness of experience. The higher level of present hedonic and lower level of future among young Chinese echoed the phenomenon of 'little but certain happiness' (小确幸, xiao que xing in Pinyin). Problems including the surging price of real-estate, cost of raising kids, unevenly distributed educational resources, hopelessness of living better than their parents and disparity of income may help explain their higher level of emotional exhaustion, soldiering and slacking at work.

5.2   Income as Job Resource and Reward

JD-R implied that income and welfare may act as job resources to motive employee to achieve hard goals and decrease procrastination (Demerouti et al. 2001). However, the result of present study failed to support the argument of JD-R. The positive prediction of emotional exhaustion by ERI_I, instead partly echoed the argument of ERI that high effort and low reward increases JBO (Van Vegchel et al. 2005). Although JD-R proposed that work well-being (i.e., JBO in this study) relies on two factors, namely demands and resources, an interactive theoretical framework highlighting the role of imbalance between effort and reward fit the results of this study. Despite the finding that decreasing work hour and increasing income did help reducing emotional exhaustion at work, what really needed from the stand point of employer is to find a golden ratio of ERI_I, the hard line of income and ceiling of work hours. Additionally, the failure of ERI_I in predicting procrastination suggested that the subjective emotional exhaustion can be addressed to some extent by adjusting the ratio of work hour to income or simply decreasing the work time, whereas such attempt will not work for reducing the off-work activities during working hours. Frequent and long-during off-work activities are undoubtedly harmful for work productivity. Chinese employers are facing the challenges of how to reduce the off-work activities in the context that decreasing work time and increasing income helped little.

5.3 Work Hour and Appraisal of Time

One interesting finding of this study is that TP explained bigger variance in both JBO and PRO than the self-report work hours, supporting the correlation between TP and PRO (Gupta et al. 2012; Zabelina et al. 2018). However, this study was in line with the finding of Zabelina et al. (2018), instead of Gupta et al. (2012), that past negative increase the risk of PRO. This result indicated that the investment of return on improving appraisal of work time may reap more benefits than simply decreasing the work hours. Measures to help decrease experiences of past negative experience, present fatalistic, present hedonic, imbalance between dimensions of TP and increase past positive experience alongside future experience will work for reducing emotional exhaustion and off-work activities. According to CJD, reasonably appraisal of work time also plays a motivational role and "good" stressors. When worktime was appraised as supporting employees' growth and development, it helps reducing JBO and PRO. It would be helpful to spare some worktime to support employee's growth and development by extending lunch hour, offering training program, organizing activities for fun, developing expertise, increasing mental and physiological health. Power nap after lunch was not unusual in many Chinese enterprises, which may be appraised as supporting employees' growth and development.

5.4 Implications for Designing Interventions

A review study distinguished four types of procrastination interventions, including self-regulation, cognitive behavioral therapy, other therapeutic approaches, and new developments in the realm of concentrating on individuals' strengths and resources (van Eerde and Klingsieck 2018). Among the various interventional methods, time management was designed in the form of setting goals and monitoring time in effort to organize work to accomplish tasks effectively and efficiently. Despite the failure of screen time on mobile phone in predicting emotional exhaustion, it was found to be effective in predicting the two components of procrastination in this study. This finding hence supported the construct of procrastination with cyberslacking as one component. This finding also paved an avenue for future interventional practices to use mobile phone as the platform of implementing context-aware interventions. Time management was adopted widely as an intervening method in existing literature to tackle the problem of procrastination. Screen time limits were designed to reduce the overuse problem and regulate time spent on mobile phone. However, it's an open question over the negative versus positive effect of using mobile phone in the workplace (Vitak et al. 2011). One possible solution is following the idea of setting limits for screen time with time limits during work hours. For instance, changing the screen color to grey scale to reduce the engagement to contents on mobile phone implicitly when screen time exceeds the limit. On the other hand, this study showed that emotional exhaustion was significantly associated with procrastination. Interventions aiming at managing time may work better in combination with emotional designs and activities. Off-work activities with fun for short time may function as a cheap perk that makes employee "feel like valued professionals who are paid for their output rather than harried wage-earners who must account for every minute of their time" (Beyerstein 2015). Chinese tech companies have actually realized the significance of allowing for "off-work activities" with workplace amenities like free afternoon tea and snacks, napping room, treadmill, showering room, Yoga room, table tennis, and eye exercise (认识百度 2021). Despite being considered as cut-rate bribery to "induce workers to put in more hours with cheap incentives, instead of paying them better wages" (Beyerstein 2015), the results of present study suggested that effort in designing off-task activities may make employee to appraise work time as opportunities for personal development more than just for company development. With the increased capacity of artificial intelligence, providing personalized off-task activities based on detecting the mental and physiological status was potential for overcoming or mitigating the negative effect of JBO and PRO on work well-being and eventually on work productivity.

5.5   A Framework for Context-Aware Persuasion

The prediction of procrastination by screen time on mobile phone and time perspective suggests that screen time on mobile phone and time perspective can be potentially used as contextual factors to predict and manage procrastination in the workplace. Besides, this paper thus proposed an architecture for designing context-aware persuasion based on mobile device with three layers of context-aware components including context acquisition, procrastination inference, and persuasion dialogue. Figure 1 illustrated the proposed architecture.

At the layer of context acquisition, the data of time personality and screen time on mobile phone are acquired via self-report questionnaire manually and usage logging tool automatically. Both iOS and Android offered APIs of screen time. For instance, the screen time of all applications and individual applications can be acquired with UsageStats in Android system.

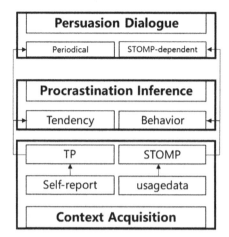

Fig. 1. The architecture for context-aware persuasion of procrastination. TP means time perspective, STMP means screen time on mobile phone

At the layer of procrastination inference, the tendency of procrastination is predicted based on the results of self-report questionnaire of time personality. The initial threshold value of risking procrastination can be determined by the "e" points (P. Zimbardo and Boyd 2008). By contrast, the behavior indicator of procrastination is based on the screen time in everyday life. The initial threshold value of risking procrastination can be inferred based on the average screen time over the past one week.

At the layer of persuasion dialogue, risk of procrastination tendency is notified periodically at the beginning and adjusted according to users' feedback on the frequency of notification (e.g., shorten the period of notification when one user indicated that the notification is too frequent). Risk of procrastination behavior is notified depending on the real screen time which is acquired via usage-related APIs. An alert dialogue will pop up to remind user that he/she will delay work when the screen time exceed the threshold value.

5.6   A Framework for Socio-technical System

The failure of work hour and income in predicting individuals' JOB and PRO suggested that there are probably other impacting factors. Informed by the perspectives of STSD and socio-technical approach (Abdelnour-Nocera and Clemmensen 2018), this study proposed a social-technical framework for addressing the issue of low desire (STDLD). In general, STDLD is a holistic and collective-oriented design method echoing the "need for more research papers is the development of the holistic framework itself" (Campos et al. 2015).

At empathy phase, not only the employees' needs should be investigated, the needs of colleagues, employers, families, community should also be taken into account. As a result, persona, a popular way of describing requirements of user is not valid anymore since it focuses only on the needs of individual user. This study proposed a new way of describing target user: people. People is a group of humans that may be impacted by the wellbeing of employee. For example, the pain points can be co-shaped by other people in the physical and social environment surrounding the individuals.

At definition phase, the problems to be solved should not merely of the employee. Instead, the organisation, family, living community should be taken into account. For example, the goal of designing HCI system should consider how other people may contribute to the solution and may be influenced by a solution.

At creation phase, a group of people should participate in the design. However, the participants and their way of participating in the process of creation is different from the traditional participatory design method. In STDLD, the stakeholders should include a group of "persona" who will design the technical system with the goal of improving their experience as a group of people and reducing the negative experience by solving the problems caused by inappropriate interactivity among them.

At the phase of prototype and evaluation, the people should design the system for all not only for themselves and how their positive experience may impact others' experience should be evaluated. STDLD thus call for a new way of evaluating the experience of design. For example, the feeling of other employee and families should be considered when one employee feel comfortable with the system and are willing to work long hour.

6   Conclusion

Despite witnessing the booming economy of China, this study found that young Chinese faced higher risk of low desire than elder Chinese due to longer work time, negative experience of past, hedonic experience of present, fatalistic experience of present, lack of future goal. The results extended JD-R and CHD theories with highlights on designing off-work activities to make work time appraised as opportunities for personal development and growth.

References

996. ICU (2019). https://996.icu/

认识百度 (2021). https://talent.baidu.com/component1000/corp/baidu/weixin/environment.html

Abdelnour-Nocera, J., Clemmensen, T.: Theorizing about socio-technical approaches to HCI. In: Barricelli, B.R., et al. (eds.), Human Work Interaction Design. Designing Engaging Automation, HWID 2018, IFIP Advances in Information and Communication Technology, pp. 242–262. Springer, Cham (2018). https://doi.org/10.1007/978-3-030-05297-3_17

Cox, A.L., Dray, S., Bird, J., Peters, A., Mauthner, N., Collins, E.: Socio-technical practices and work-home boundaries. In: MobileHCI 2014 - Proceedings of the 16th ACM International Conference on Human-Computer Interaction with Mobile Devices and Services, pp. 581–584 (2014). https://doi.org/10.1145/2628363.2634259

Ran, B.: Behind "996" schedule: work to a better life, not ICU (2019). https://news.cgtn.com/news/3d3d774d336b544f33457a6333566d54/index.html

Maslach, C., Jackson, S.E.: The measurement of experienced burnout. J. Organ. Behav. 2(2), 99–113 (1981). https://doi.org/10.1002/job.4030020205

Gonçalves, F., Campos, P., Clemmensen, T.: Human work interaction design: an overview. In: Abdelnour Nocera, J., Barricelli, B.R., Lopes, A., Campos, P., Clemmensen, T. (eds.) HWID 2015. IAICT, vol. 468, pp. 3–19. Springer, Cham (2015). https://doi.org/10.1007/978-3-319-27048-7_1

Dell, D.A., Venkatesh, M.: Social design's implications for the IS field. In: iConference 2012: Proceedings of the 2012 iConference, Toronto, pp. 346–353 (2012). https://doi.org/10.1145/2132176.2132221

Zabelina, E., Chestyunina, Y., Trushina, I., Vedeneyeva, E.: Time perspective as a predictor of procrastination. Procedia Soc. Behav. Sci. **238**(2018), 87–93 (2018). https://doi.org/10.1016/j.sbspro.2018.03.011

Crawford, E.R., LePine, J.A., Rich, B.L.: Linking job demands and resources to employee engagement and burnout: a theoretical extension and meta-analytic test. J. Appl. Psychol. **95**(5), 834–848 (2010). https://doi.org/10.1037/a0019364

Demerouti, E., Nachreiner, F., Bakker, A.B., Schaufeli, W.B.: The job demands-resources model of burnout. J. Appl. Psychol. **86**(3), 499–512 (2001). https://doi.org/10.1037/0021-9010.86.3.499

Baxter, G., Sommerville, I.: Socio-technical systems: from design methods to systems engineering. Interact. Comput. **23**(1), 4–17 (2011). https://doi.org/10.1016/j.intcom.2010.07.003

Freudenberger, H.J.: Staff burnout. J. Soc. Issues **30**(1974), 159–165 (1974). https://doi.org/10.1111/j.1540-4560.1974.tb00706.x

Hofstede Insights. Country Comparison. https://www.hofstede-insights.com/product/compare-countries/

Howsitlike. What is China's 996 Work Culture (2020). https://www.howsitlike.com/blog/What-is-China%27s-996-Work-Culture#:~:text=Definition of 996 Culture 996 is a work, have adopted this culture as their official schedule. Accessed 2 March 2020

Shaojie, H.: Low Desire? No, It's Risk Aversion. NewsChina Magazine (2020). http://www.newschinamag.com/newschina/articleDetail.do?article_id=5898&section_id=25&magazine_id=. Accessed 21 Feb 2021

Siegrist, J., Klein, D., Voigt, K.H.: Linking sociological with physiological data: the model of effort- reward imbalance at work. Acta Physiologica Scandinavica **640**, 112–116 (1997)

Gulliksen, J., Göransson, B., Boivie, I., Blomkvist, S., Persson, J., Cajander, Å.: Key principles for user-centred systems design. Behav. Inf. Technol. **22**(6), 397–409 (2003). https://doi.org/10.1080/01449290310001624329

Vitak, J., Crouse, J., LaRose, R.: personal internet use at work: understanding cyberslacking. Comput. Hum. Behav. **27**(5), 1751–1759 (2011). https://doi.org/10.1016/j.chb.2011.03.002

Hong, J.C., Lee, Y.F., Ye, J.H.: Procrastination predicts online self-regulated learning and online learning ineffectiveness during the coronavirus lockdown. Pers. Individ. Dif. **174**(2021), 110673 (2021). https://doi.org/10.1016/j.paid.2021.110673

Ohmae, K.: How to ignite the low desire society (Chinese) (1st ed.). Shanghai Translation Publishing House, Shanghai (2018)

Beyerstein, L.: Slacking Workers of the World Unite (2015). https://inthesetimes.com/article/slacking-workers-of-the-world. Accessed 2 Mar 2020

Li, L., Gao, H., Xu, Y.: The mediating and buffering effect of academic self-efficacy on the relationship between smartphone addiction and academic procrastination. Comput. Educ. **159**, 104001 (2020). https://doi.org/10.1016/j.compedu.2020.104001

Stolarski, M., Bitner, J., Zimbardo, P.G.: Time perspective, emotional intelligence and discounting of delayed awards. Time Soc. **20**(3), 346–363 (2011). https://doi.org/10.1177/0961463X11414296

Stolarski, M., Zajenkowski, M., Jankowski, K.S., Szymaniak, K.: Deviation from the balanced time perspective: a systematic review of empirical relationships with psychological variables. Pers. Individ. Dif. **156**, 109772 (2020). https://doi.org/10.1016/j.paid.2019.109772

Moghadam, M.T., Abbasi, E., Khoshnodifar, Z.: Students' academic burnout in Iranian agricultural higher education system: the mediating role of achievement motivation. Heliyon **6**(9), e04960 (2020). https://doi.org/10.1016/j.heliyon.2020.e04960

Margaretha, M.: Motivation and job burnout: the mediating role of organizational citizenship behavior. Int. J. Manag. Sci. Bus. Adm. **5**(4), 27–33 (2019). https://doi.org/10.18775/ijmsba.1849-5664-5419.2014.54.1004

Hen, M., Goroshit, M., Viengarten, S.: How decisional and general procrastination relate to procrastination at work: an investigation of office and non-office workers. Pers. Individ. Dif. **172**, 110581 (2021). https://doi.org/10.1016/j.paid.2020.110581

Van Vegchel, N., De Jonge, J., Bosma, H., Schaufeli, W.: Reviewing the effort-reward imbalance model: drawing up the balance of 45 empirical studies. Soc. Sci. Med. **60**(5), 1117–1131 (2005). https://doi.org/10.1016/j.socscimed.2004.06.043

Zimbardo, P.G., Boyd, J.N.: Putting time in perspective: a valid, reliable individual-differences metric. J. Pers. Soc. Psychol. **77**(6), 1271–1288 (1999). https://doi.org/10.1037/0022-3514.77.6.1271

Zimbardo, P., Boyd, J.: The Time Paradox: The New Psychology of Time That Will Change Your Life, Free Press, New York (2008)

Gupta, R., Hershey, D.A., Gaur, J.: Time perspective and procrastination in the workplace: an empirical investigation. Curr. Psychol. **31**(2), 195–211 (2012). https://doi.org/10.1007/s12144-012-9136-3

Baran Metin, U., Taris, T.W., Peeters, M.C.W.: Measuring procrastination at work and its associated workplace aspects. PAID **101**(2016), 254–263 (2016). https://doi.org/10.1016/j.paid.2016.06.006

Akirmak, U., Ayla, P.: How is time perspective related to burnout and job satisfaction? A conservation of resources perspective. Pers. Individ. Dif. (2019). https://doi.org/10.1016/j.paid.2019.109667

Chen, W.: Time Perspective: the revision of the inventory and the influence on Risky Driving Behavior. Southwest University (2016)

van Eerde, W., Klingsieck, K.B.: Overcoming procrastination? A meta-analysis of intervention studies. Educ. Res. Rev. **25**(2018), 73–85 (2018). https://doi.org/10.1016/j.edurev.2018.09.002

Co-designing Prototypes for User Experience and Engagement in Automation
Case Study of London-based Airport Future Workplace

Parisa Saadati[1]([⊠]) [iD], José Abdelnour-Nocera[1,2] [iD], and Torkil Clemmensen[3] [iD]

[1] University of West London, London, UK
{parisa.saadati,abdejos}@uwl.ac.uk
[2] ITI/LARSyS Portugal, Funchal, Portugal
[3] Copenhagen Business School, Frederiksberg, Denmark
tc.digi@cbs.dk

Abstract. Here we present a case study to explore the implications of the co-design of future autonomous technologies for user experience (UX) and engagement. Given the high demand for automation in daily life and workplaces, there is a need to assess the value of co-design with the end-users to evaluate users' experiences and engagements in multiple contexts such as work, health, entertainment, and learning. The term automation in this paper also covers some of the so-called AI or more sophisticated automation. This case is driven by a member of the innovation department of the airport and UX researchers. Our main objective was to employ participatory design and work domain analysis (WDA) as a means for co-designing future automated systems for smart work in airport terminal operations. Over two weeks in two workshops in a London-based airport, we used participatory design and scenario-based design methods to explore how and where we should draw a line between end-user agency and automation to improve the work experience supported by automation in the future workplace. Users' experiences such as sense of control, welfare, and social sustainability were assessed. Our findings will be used for creating prototypes and demos for the airport of the future. We also came with a framework for designing prototypes and selecting new systems for redesigning the workplaces.

Keywords: HCI · Participatory design · Automation · Personas · User experience · Interaction Design · HWID

1 Introduction

Automation and the introduction of Industry 4.0 interactive technologies in industrial work systems have brought new ambiguities in the challenges and burdens on interactive systems designers [25]. The term automation in this paper also covers some of the so-called Artificial Intelligence (AI) or more sophisticated automation. Socio-Technical System Design (STSD) has identified and addressed several problems in understanding and developing complex autonomous systems [1, 4, 10, 13]. Despite many positive

© IFIP International Federation for Information Processing 2022
Published by Springer Nature Switzerland AG 2022
G. Bhutkar et al. (Eds.): HWID 2021, IFIP AICT 609, pp. 158–177, 2022.
https://doi.org/10.1007/978-3-031-02904-2_8

outcomes, these methods have not materially changed industrial software engineering practices [40]. Two of the main reasons behind this are not knowing the users well and involving them only in the testing stage of any new system development instead of the design process [3, 5]. The challenges of designing systems are increasing with changing demographics, which impact and pressure the limited resources to meet complex systems' needs. Therefore, service design and co-design processes are utilised to facilitate collaboration in new ways [34]. Human beings are the multiple stakeholders (i.e., customers, operators, decision-makers) who collaborate and interact with the different systems [38]. Designing future technologies needs more cross-organisational collaborations to produce innovative and creative outcomes.

Researchers have studied various user experience (UX) aspects to implement advanced interactive technologies employing automation in different platforms [1, 4, 13, 37]. These technologies support and improve end users' work but not necessarily and automatically guarantee a positive response from them in relation to aspects of their experience, such as a sense of control or transparency on machine decisions [1]. More studies on UX and innovation are needed in light of advances in AI and the growing use of more sophisticated automation technologies [13].

There is a significant value in developing and refining design guidelines for human-AI interaction [2, 28]. Simultaneously, there is a need for cooperation and better communication in human teams and individuals and AI systems to achieve better UX goals for future automation scenarios, namely AI/UX goals. Hence, future autonomous systems need to be carefully co-designed to achieve expected service quality goals for end-users. This is especially the case in safety and operationally critical work domains such as airports. Thus, understanding the relation between human work and interaction design is crucial and part of the agenda of the sub-field of Human-Work Interaction Design (HWID) [12]. Human Work Interaction Design (HWID) is a comprehensive framework that establishes relationships between extensive empirical work-domain studies and HCI designs. It builds on the foundation of Cognitive Work Analysis (CWA) [12]. HWID is currently positioned as a modern, lightweight version of CWA.

In this paper, we report on a case study that employs participatory design and work domain analysis (WDA) [8] as a means for co-designing future automated systems considering AI/UX goals in the context of airport terminal operations. HCI studies [28, 39, 42] suggest that using co-design can bring more success when some participant users are not professional developers. However, the latter's input towards designing interaction significantly impacts design and user engagement [36, 44, 45]. Despite disputes and differences between stakeholders' internal cultures or communication [43], a common understanding and a shared vision to develop a new design can be facilitated to an efficient outcome.

The presented case study is driven by a member of the innovation department of a London- based airport and two UX researchers. This paper describes the process of a team of UX researchers and operational decision-makers of an airport in co-designing two scenarios supporting smart work in the terminal. Recruitment of the participant was based on interest, role, and familiarity with the topic. Workshop sessions resulted in two future work scenarios leading to automated systems' prototyping using Abstraction Hierarchies for each scenario. The objective is to explore and illustrate how a

London-based airport uses participatory design, interaction design, and WDA methods to decide future autonomous Industry 4.0 systems. The paper concludes with lessons we learned in three themes, operational environment, organisational environment, and co-designing workshop settings. These themes presented the findings clustered mainly in design approaches, social sustainability, and user sense of control.

2 Related Work

2.1 The Smart Workplaces

'Smart Workplaces' is a vision where the organisation is fully connected with all stakeholders via proactive adaptation to the organisation's real-time needs, including operational necessities and customer requests. Besides many technical factors, national, cultural, geographic, social, and organisational factors will have an important role in designing optimal socio-technical systems as they impact users' interaction (i.e. both operators and employees) and the smart systems in their work and lives [1, 12]. For example, security concerns in airports necessitate more investigations prior to boarding, resulting in long queues and waiting times for passengers. Hence, airports need to be more innovative in their operations and stakeholders' handling (passengers and workers) and their real-time needs [27].

Industry 4.0 has enabled innovation in design and manufacturing [21] and led to more "smart workplaces" in industrial settings. There are, however, blurring gaps, challenges, and concerns in the design of industry 4.0 future technologies. Moreover, and specific to the case of airports, there are more challenges such as data privacy, immigration, and security, or reduced workforce employment, which impose legal and public policy pressures on implementing "Airport 4.0" [27, 28]. In a complex organisation employees are generally not considered in the design process nor satisfied with the new technologies and systems involved in the smart workplaces. Therefore, we will argue that using specific approaches similar to the co-design workshops we suggested for designing future smart workplaces can lead to positive work experiences. Specifically, such workshops with specific design tools or templates can increase the human counterpart's (employees/end-user) engagement with the final product in the future smart workplace [31].

Industry4.0 means organisations should prepare for new forms of work, and novel interactions between humans and machines, which implies redesigning the job and the workplace for more cooperation between human and machine workers. In such workplaces, the shared tasks between the two counterparts are expected to be flexible and allocated fairly to ensure the human counterpart's well-being. Therefore, industrial tasks are expected to become more knowledge-intensive to change employees' roles [28]. Operators of the future may transition to makers who work alongside digitalised and automated production systems with essential creativity to solve unexpected and unforeseen challenges rather than assist or monitor non-discretionary workflow steps or processes [46].

New smart workplace systems change and directly impact the operational workers, their well-being, system performance, and the work's nature [25]. Due to AI implementation in such systems, there is also significant value in developing and refining design guidelines for human-AI interaction in future systems [2, 28]. There is a need for cooperation and better UX goals for human teams and individuals interacting with AI systems, namely AI/UX goals [2]. Hence, future autonomous systems need to be carefully co-designed to achieve expected service quality goals for end-users.

2.2 Participatory Design, Persona, and UX

Co-design, or participatory design, is a dominant design technique. Approaches that have emerged to promote user engagement in system development have been implemented in different industries, such as aviation [36, 44, 45]. The co-design approach has gained interest in developing commercial and business applications [11] as both a system development approach and philosophy; participatory design advocates the direct participation of stakeholders, especially users or their representatives. The participatory design process emphasises mutual learning, as none of the participants, either ´designer' or 'user' knows everything. Designers are expected to have technical knowledge on the issue, the process, and future users. This knowledge may be applied from an academic perspective to create new knowledge or an industrial point of view to innovate systems and product designs. Also, designers may include users who intimately know the domain and the use context, i.e. the activity and practices into which the new technology will be introduced [44]. Users in co-design approaches may often have a strong sense of ownership and commitment to the created software products [11]. A persona is a communicational tool typically used within User-Centered Design [35], which was introduced for mass-market software development. Personas in co-design projects have begun to include users and others in either persona inceptions or assemblies or its deployment. Personas in co-design are usually used as objects of conversation in design, validation of designs via designer-created personas, and user-created personas [28].

A study for future automation work in Finland shows that UX design needs to balance its brand and image and its values to its customer [28]. This study nominated several AI/UX goals regarding the future automated systems: Sense of control, Trust in human-automation cooperation, Sense of freedom, Ownership of the process, Relatedness to the work community, Meaningfulness to the work community, and Success and achievement [28]. We embedded the same AI/UX goals in our study.

2.3 Human Work Interaction Design

HWID studies how to understand, conceptualise, and design for the complex and emergent contexts in which information and communication technologies (ICT) and work are entangled [12]. HWID models are based on the characteristics of humans and work domain contents and the interactions during their tasks and decision-making activities. HWID focuses on integrating work analysis (i.e. WDA methods) and interaction design methods (e.g. goal-oriented design and HCI usability) for smart workplaces. The ultimate goal of HWID is to empower users by designing smarter workplaces in various work domains.

Applying the HWID framework to specific workplaces considering several independent and entangled factors is essential [12]; numerous theories, concepts, techniques, and methods developed for other work environments. Environmental contexts such as national, cultural, geographic, social and organisational factors will have an important role in designing optimal HWID framework, as they impact the interaction between users and smart systems in their work and life. More work-related factors include the users' knowledge/skills, application domain, work contents and goals, and the nature of tasks or newly introduced technologies to be considered in the interaction performance. Developing the HWID framework requires establishing design goals, evaluation of usability and user experience, engagement of all stakeholders, and transparent design processes.

2.4   Work Domain Analysis and Abstraction Hierarchies

WDA is part of the broader CWA framework that supports and structures the analysis needed when designing a flexible and adaptive system [48]. WDA, as part of that framework, focuses on analysing the limitations and constraints of a work domain and workers' behaviour; and mapping these constraints in the design of the system that will support the workers. Using WDA has two distinct advantages. First, WDA is a multi-dimensional analysis that incorporates the physical and the social environment to provide a detailed description. Secondly, WDA can be paired with interface design [18] to generate new information system designs. WDA has shown success in the design of analytic information displays in power plant displays [9], social systems [19], healthcare decision support [8], community building [14], and smart universities [1].

Abstraction Hierarchy (AH): we decided to use the Abstraction Hierarchy (AH) from the Work Domain Analysis (WDA) design method toolset, as it is one of the main analysis techniques providing a discreet and complete description of a work domain at different abstraction levels. Furthermore, AHs are suitable to use by stakeholders from different backgrounds with little or no experience of WDA [3, 6]. AH is a cognitive engineering approach to human-machine systems design supported by empirical studies of operators' fault-finding strategies. In this case study, AH developed concepts and methods for modeling the conceptual design of industrial automation systems [29].

AH describes a system, product, or experience at five levels of abstraction: (1) functional purpose, (2) abstract function, (3) generalised function, (4) physical functions, and (5) physical forms. The concepts and elements define the system's goal and purpose at the highest level (1–2), and the lowest levels of the model (3–5) describe the physical components of the system [41]. Using the model from top to bottom answers how the solution and experience are achieved, whereas moving from the bottom towards the top of the model reveals why particular elements or components of the solution and experience exist [8]. Despite its origins in the analysis of safety-critical domains, AHs are used as design tools for innovation in other domains that demand less rigor and regulation [22].

2.5   Future Scenario

Researchers predict future industries' development or services based on grounded foundations to answer whether technological developments in future workplaces are realistic or desirable for the wider public [23]. Decision-makers can use the resulted knowledge to avoid the negative consequences of using such future technologies [23]. 'Scenarios' are common tools used in many future studies [23, 28] with different approaches to increase creativity. It is popular to use simple stories based on trends and events to capture future possibilities. This can generate ideas by facilitating brainstorming sessions for more realistic scenarios or adopting 'blue sky thinking' to turn current trends and signals into the future experience [23].

Johnson introduced the Science Fiction Prototyping method as a practical guide for intelligent environment research. He believes that using fiction is a way to imagine our future in a whole new way [24]. One popular study [28] used science fiction prototyping as a practical design tool that works based on stories grounded in current science and engineering research to act as prototypes for people to explore a wide variety of futures.

3   Case Study Questions and Setting

Aviation is one of those sectors where brand, value, and organisational image have a significant role in their offerings. Customer and, more recently, worker satisfaction are among the main drivers for this sector to select more sustainable competitive advantages strategies and the latest technologies [52]. Our reported case study is not an exception to such practices. This study focused on understanding people, directly and indirectly, working towards selecting the new technologies or dealing with such systems' UX goals. We offer insights based on our empirical studies that can be used to analyse and evaluate the lesson learned in co-designing for future scenarios. We co-created scenarios, personas, and AH as design methods to answer several questions: How co-designing with stakeholders can help bring UX and work to the center of automation? How to improve work engagement through automation design? How can using personas lead to optimal task allocation between workers and autonomous future technologies?

3.1   Field Observations and Workshops Proposal

Case studies are considered adequate and necessary research tasks in social sciences [15]. We collected qualitative data from our case studies and used that as an efficient method to develop theories inductively. The case studies' primary focus area understood the overall approaches for selecting and introducing the new automated technologies and developing new digital solutions in complex companies. We analyse the case studies using qualitative data collected through two trial observations, interviews, and the Attrakdiff survey on active trials. However, we do not aim to discuss the field observation data in this paper.

Our observations on the trials and the shortfalls seen regarding the use, usability, and UX of these tested technologies helped us suggest the airport user-centered design tools and methods for introducing new automated systems. We suggested that using co-design workshops with employees can help the organisations select an efficient automated system for emergent future in a complex organisation - a system with better user engagement and interaction than their trials. This suggestion then triggered two co-design workshops with 14 researchers, industry decision-makers, and employees. We suggested the following framework for their future scenarios in the workshops (Fig. 1).

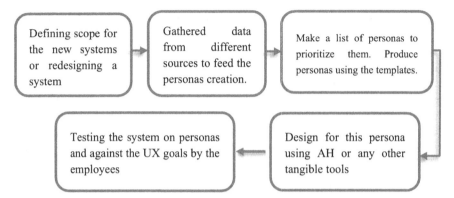

Fig. 1. Co-designing workshop for new automated systems

3.2 Workshops 1 and 2

After running several observations on the aforementioned trials, we noticed that the airport selects their future technologies mainly by running trials and observing how the trials proceed. However, customer and employee satisfaction and UX in the trials were not easily assessed and articulated.

We invited a number of employees from operational, tactical, and strategic organisational layers to be involved in a co-design workshop with two university design researchers. The workshop used design tools to facilitate knowledge exchange and understanding between diverse stakeholders. Participants were selected from different departments: automation manager and two of his team members, procurement manager, HR talent recruiter, an employee from service design, a baggage data scientist, an operational data scientist, a business change/IT infrastructure specialist, a business analyst and personal assistant with background and interest in design and one intern with a computing background (Table 1).

Table 1. The number of participants from academia and industry at each workshop.

Workshop	Design researchers	Design practitioners			Total
		Decision maker	Worker	Consultant	
1	2	4	7	1	14
2	2	4	4	1	11

The design researchers introduced topics and design techniques such as focused groups, brainstorming and mind mapping, trending technologies and innovation, automation requirements, design thinking, and the concept framework to workshop 1. Participants engaged in prototyping system concepts for autonomous systems needed in their departments. They considered the customer demands and value proposition of such systems in their design. All participants had enough experience with autonomous technologies and leading Industry 4.0 implementation either by researching the field or working in the case company implementing industry 4.0 new digital technologies.

The first workshop aimed to map and identify current trends and developments within the aviation industry and construct a corpus of ideas about future technologies for their smart workplace. Each group produced two future technologies concepts in the first round after refining the categories into the future's short and concrete experiences. We had a sharing and voting session to discuss and converge on the most appealing alternative future scenarios. From a list of suggested scenarios (automated helpers, autonomous tugs, context-aware guest invites system, baggage tracing, and the smart asset management.), the participant selected two:

- Autonomous Tug and Pushback Taxi (ATPT)
- Automated Asset Management and Maintenance (AAMM)

In workshop 2 we used customer job (part of value proposition canvas), persona's template, AI/UX goals [28] and AI guidelines [2], sketching, and AH [9] to prototype the short-listed future scenarios voted in the workshop 1. Researchers fulfilled a facilitator role supporting participants unfamiliar with the design tools and were active designers while engaging in creative tasks. In the last stage of workshop 2, each group, walk-through their concept [51] using their low fidelity prototype and received feedback from other colleagues and decision-makers on how likely the idea is feasible. Finally, group members evaluated their design with UX goal templates [2, 28].

3.3   Workshop Outcome

Scenario 1 - Autonomous Tug and Pushback Taxi (ATPT)
Participants in team one were asked to assess the current pains and future gains of airplanes' Tug and Pushback Taxies services. The result presented in the customer job tabular format is part of the new proposed system's value proposition (Table 2).

Table 2. Participant result on the customer jobs, users, pains, and gains on scenario 1

Main users	Pain	Gains
NATS (National air traffic services)	Not sustainable	Less human involvement in the dangerous job (Ground handlers)
Ground handlers	Resource dependency	
	Increased CO2 footprint	Engine CO2 reduction
Airlines	Increased noise pollution	Noise reduction
Pilots	Increased fuel waste	Optimise roots (currently pilots
AOM/APOC	Increased traffic congestion	selects the routs)
Data scientist	Time-consuming	Fuel safe, customer service

Participants considered different stakeholders and end-users from a pilot, ground handlers, NATS (National Air Traffic Services)- ground movement, APOC (Airport Operation Centre), AOM (Airport Operation Management) to Data Scientist, TUG manufacturer, and Autonomous Technologies. After prioritising the stakeholders, they have selected three stakeholders based on their importance and influence for creating assumption-based personas. They used their own or other participants' experience and data from the field and workplace in their discussion to select the final stakeholders for creating personas. Figure 2 is an example of a ground handler persona designed by the scenario1 participants.

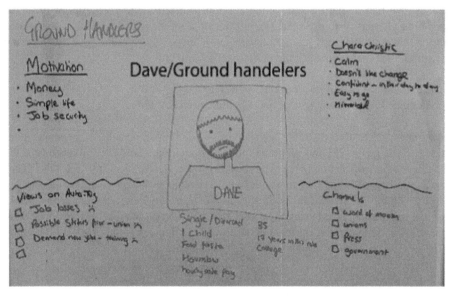

Fig. 2. Scenario 1-ATPT- ground handler persona

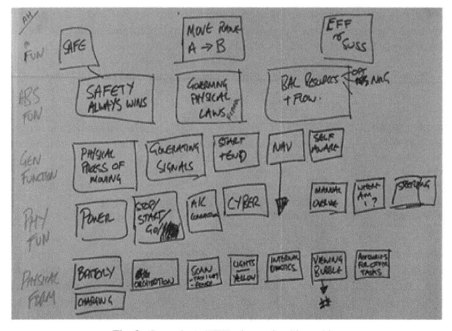

Fig. 3. Scenario 1-ATPT- abstraction hierarchies

Scenario 1 - Prototype
The team proposes self-driving taxies navigated by AI between the allocated lanes. For refueling, the taxies communicate this to the central system and can automatically find their nest. Currently, airports use tugs that are partially automated and need to work with human counterparts. These systems are not initially fully autonomous and may need to be orchestrated with a central brain initially, and after enough learning for AI, they can become autonomous. The tug can take or get to a certain point. Therefore, the possibility of plane crashing is unlikely to happen. There are many difficult crossings over taxiways, and the team believed AI could help find the route more efficiently. Other participants are concerned that this system should either have a process to monitor the system or a human overseer who monitors the system. The team believed ATPT systems would have a different level of automation at the start (e.g., AI advising and the human approve it) till both can build sufficient trust, then the human role will gradually step back, and AI takes over. The team has concerns when an accident happens, who should blame, human or the system. After going through the AH result (Fig. 3) and testing the UX goals with their personas, the team concluded that ATPT should be more flexible. Currently, this system may not be economically beneficial for the airport.

Scenario 2 - Asset Management and Maintenance (AAMM)
Like the other team, this group used their field data and experience to assess the customer pains in the current system and proposed future gains. Then they have listed the stakeholders and the potential end-users (Table 3).

Table 3. Participant result on the customer jobs, users, pains, and gains on scenario 2

Main users	Pain	Gains
Managers Ground handlers Analysts Other relevant departments	Lack of information on the status of equipment Poor quality of information Health and safety concerns in current systems Insufficient deployment (e.g., staff needed) Required number of unnecessary visits (including Repeat Inspection or Preventative Maintenance)	Real-time information using RFIDs More reliable, valid information using analytics Safer workplace Less human is required Reduce the number of unnecessary trips

Participants prioritised a list of the stakeholders who may work with AAMM, from the systems resource allocator, planning manager, remote engineer to Jarvis (AI engine) and the apprentice engineer. Their role and impact were covered in the prototype of the system. Figure 4 is a sample of Jarvis AI Engineer persona created by the team.

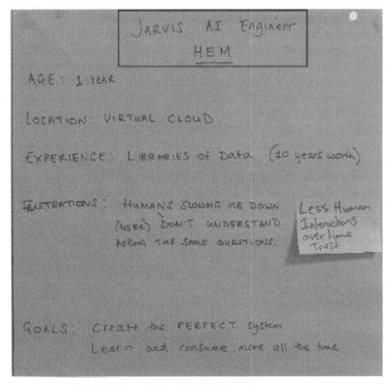

Fig. 4. Scenario 2 - AAMM - AI engineer persona

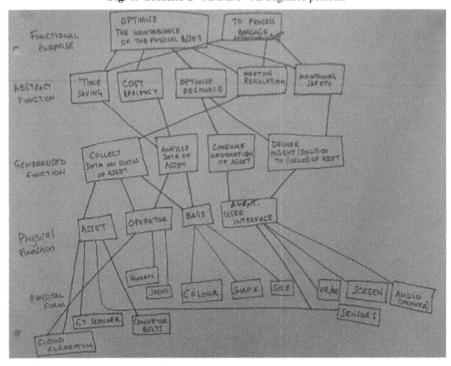

Fig. 5. Scenario 2 - AAMM - abstraction hierarchies

Scenario 2 - Prototype

Team 2 used Fig. 5 for the AAMM concept walkthrough. This system works with sensors, IoT, standard digital twin working with AI engineer (Jarvis) digging the data for more insight continuously. Jarvis interface works with voice commands and has visualised results to share with the human counterpart. A twin system works with video analytics and AI engineer with remote access while using mixed reality and sensors. The system has an interface with a screen divided into one for the real videos (streaming the baggage systems) and one for the digital twin. Jarvis (AI Engineer) can send information about the failure to the resource allocator. Apprentice can learn more efficiently using the digital twin and apply changes to the twin instead of watching the simulation. Therefore, learning through mixed reality can enable new workers to learn step by step without damaging the existing system.

As well as having an AI engineer helping the engineering by using augmented reality, AAMM also has a real remote engineer (or a team of engineers) on the airport side. When the problem is identified, the remote engineer can step in and sort the issue. This system can increase the efficient use of high valued experienced engineers and specialists. The workforce can change to a much more significant percentage of less experienced human counterparts and a core of remote engineers' experienced engineers.

4   What We Learned

This case study's main contribution is helping the airport co-design automation scenarios incorporating workers' UX and their work. The primary learning insights are based on the interactions and outputs from the field observations, focus group, brainstorming session, co-design workshops transcripts, and researchers' notes. We also considered the group discussions during both concept walkthroughs to find valuable insights. We coded all the data and clustered our findings into the initial headings resulting from the literature review. We added one new heading based on the most alluded insight about the workshop settings. We removed the repeated comments and summarised our findings into three themes: operational environment, organisational environment, and co-designing workshop settings. The section closes with a short recommendation for co-designing for sustainable work in future automation.

4.1   Operational Environment

Humanistic Elements of Interactive Systems

Analysis of the functions' allocation is necessary to identify the optimal distribution of functions and tasks between a partly autonomous system and the user [12]. The role of AI and systems and the task allocation were clear for the participants in their design. Both teams show interest in providing physical support of human workers by robots or machines as an essential aspect of the new technologies, precisely, for tasks with a range of unpleasant, repetitive, too exhausting, or unsafe nature [26, 50].

For an effective, successful, and safe support of users in physical tasks, robots or machines should interact smoothly and intuitively with their human counterparts [50], and that humans should be adequately trained [20]. All participants agreed that working with the machine could increase their performance in both scenarios. They trust in the power of the machine and AI in a busy complex environment like an airport. In both scenarios, they wanted the machine to be replaced for more unpleasant, dangerous jobs or jobs with a task allocation nature, which can quickly turn to algorithms and codes. They all want to improve the interaction for all users and change the systems to communicate with more visualisation, gestural interface, and voice commands.

Sense of Control: Although a sense of control for higher valued jobs was important for participants in both scenarios, lower-skilled jobs were believed to be more efficient by machines making the decisions. In ATPT scenario, it was a concern that human decision-makers should have more power to approve the system's decisions to be fully trusted. Currently, systems with these features are used in airports, and this system cannot bring a unique value proposition.

Training and Skill Development: In scenario 2, one persona was described as an apprentice who was not happy with the airport's old operating system and was keen to implement the modern system. Understanding the new generation who are "Technology Savvy" is a critical well-being factor. It is crucial to study resilience and ability to keep roles multi-skilled and avoid de-skilling the workforce by Industry 4.0 in airports. Labour capacity can be doubled by dual-trained staff who are flexible and multi-tasked [16]. The London-based airport can use digital technologies as a more accessible, appealing, flexible, and faster training platform (e.g. eUniversity, virtual classrooms, augmented reality, digital twins, mobile learning). This was an exciting finding for the workshop's decision-maker as it can take some burden from human trainers and leave that to digital twins with mixed reality for job training.

Agile Working: Cross-functional "purpose teams" in the same fashion as semi-autonomous working teams are described at the core of socio-technical theory [47]. Experts from entirely different disciplines –engineering, marketing, and logistics – can work together in smaller units. This is not just about collaboration within teams, but it will transform the entire organisational unit. Scenario 2 suggested the "Scaled Agile Framework" in various divisions to achieve better performance using Jarvis, "AI engineer" to make the best use of remote engineers in various airport sites. Creating agile organisations and eliminating hierarchical and functional boundaries will bring new demands on human resource management, development paths to leadership, and project career tracks.

The Value of Information
The value of information is now more recognised in collaborations between humans and machines, given the machine's high power in decision-making in highly automated systems. For instance, informing users about the decision in scenario 1 and asking for professional human approval can significantly increase the trust in the system [20]. However, other studies show that the number of information items or tasks users

receives in an automated process should be personalised and up to the point of their desire/tolerance [13].

Not enough functions allocated to a user will lead to underload and boredom and thus decreased performance. Too many allocated functions will lead to cognitive, perceptive, or motoric overload and increase negative emotions (e.g., stress, anxiety) [45] and user's error [4, 49]. Meanwhile, users can cope with emotions after spending some time with autonomous technology and developing some routines [12]. Considering the design progress, the more time participants spent in the design and engaging themselves with the design, the more interest they developed in using the airport system.

Providing an abundance of information and transparency is a critical necessity in interactive technologies. Trust, transparency, and acceptance of losing control (i.e., shared authority between the user and system) can improve the user's interaction by revealing ambiguous feelings toward the automation. Other psychological factors under study include worries about practical challenges and security of the technology (e.g., hacking a system) and reliability of the process itself (e.g., flat mobile phone battery for systems that rely on applications). Users may lose their trust in the decision-making of an automated system when other humans who will not follow the same process are involved and can impact the outcome. For example, if self-driving tugs use a specific system, than drivers who do not use the system and won't follow the same rules [13]. Both groups considered this not only for the psychological factors discussed but also the culture of associating AI systems with high risks in the airports as the system takes control from the human counterpart.

Blame Culture: Another critical situation is when responsibilities are shared between users and the system. Ability to identify responsible parties related to a bad outcome (i.e. user error versus system failure) can impact users' performance [33]. Team members of scenario 1 have concerns that having a blame culture in the aviation sector will be an issue for task allocation in their proposed system. They want to ensure the tug manufacturer takes responsibility when the blame goes on the system.

Data Volume and its Influences on Technology Acceptance: Due to the high volume of data in an airport, all personas and participants show interest and need to use AI systems to increase their efficiency. However, in our field observation, we noticed that low-skilled jobs have a different perspective and are scared of losing their jobs regarding AI systems. (e.g., the Receptionist serving her notice period left the airport for a less technologically advanced firm after she had a new robot colleague. She believed in the first-mover airport; her job would die quicker than other institutions). Considering we did not have any representatives from the low-skilled groups, the result may be biased.

Trust and Safety Consideration: Controllable designed interface and work environment, and feeling safe while using new technologies are among other factors that can increase users' performance. Scenario 1 can impact human life, and trusting a system like this reminded the participants of the Air France accident due to autopilot failure in 2009 [7].

Aviation insurance policies are considered in the designs as a limit by our team 1. AI is associated with risk as it takes control from human for insurance in aviation.

Involving Users in the Design Process
It will be of great importance to ensure that the future's autonomous systems will be designed to fit into everyday life. Motivating the users to engage with the new technologies is still a challenge due to a lack of understanding of the end-users individual experience and interaction with such technologies. Users can have different roles or backgrounds that can affect their discovery, collaboration, and learning of the interactive systems [30]. At the end of this workshop, through increased awareness of the work domain, most participants understood how a future automation prototype could better fit their work environment. They have agreed that there is a relation between modes of discovery, design improvements, interaction, and socio-spatial aspects. At the end of the session, one of the participants with a senior manager position referred to co-designing and WDA methods to select and design future automation scenarios and prototypes for the airport.

Automation Level to Match Workers' Needs: Using automation in interactive systems requires considering potential changes in human activity and the new coordination demands on the human operators. These experiences depend highly on the automation type and level [37] and the extent to which the developer has allowed the machine to make decisions. In both scenarios, participants required different decision-making levels, which also reflected well in the system prototype.

4.2   Organisational Environment

Industry 4.0 success in any organisation will be the result of countless trials and restructurings. The London-based airport is not an exception to this. One trial case study failed as the existing surveyors did not find a proper location in the terminal for an automated kiosk. The innovation team believed such jobs had never existed in their structure before.

The restructuring of the workforces can include several aspects such as employment and worker qualifications, change in the future trends for occupations, qualification types and levels, and new organisational structures, which are at the core of traditional principles of socio-technical systems design [47]. All participants believed that these changes are undergoing in the airport. Moreover, scenario 2 shows how the proposed system can change the workforce into a more significant percentage of less experienced human counterparts and a core of experienced remote engineers. Therefore, while scenario 2 considered using more low-skilled staff and experts more efficiently, scenario 1 may reduce low-skilled jobs.

Creating persona for the AI engine and the autonomous systems in both scenarios shows that machines may be considered an important part of the organisational structure in future structures. Despite this, machine counterparts are important assets for future organisations and significantly impact the system's performance. Creating personas for AI in scenario 2 is a must in the airport's domain (as AI systems are associated with a risk level) and helps understand machines' motivation and goals to work easier with humans. They believed AI behaves differently in various domains. For example, the same robot in one airport trial will have different behaviour in a supermarket domain.

Co-designing for Sustainable Work in Future Automation
In both scenarios, there was a concern that there would be a change in using new systems to use expert and low-skilled workers. Frey and Osborne's study estimated that 47% of US jobs are at risk [17], mainly low-skilled jobs. Similar to the result of scenario one for cutting jobs among ground handlers by replacing ATAP. From a societal perspective, the rise in automation means replacing workers with robots and machines across a vast range of airports, from drivers to ground handlers or expert engineers to NAT workers. Decision-makers in the workshops felt responsible for redesigning the business models considering the principles and requirements of Industry 4.0 while bringing new systems into this sector. To discover the proper training and disruptive R&D investments, organisations must rethink their strategies [32]. They are also responsible for "Social Sustainability" (i.e. for employees) as part of their Cooperate Social Responsibility. This implies that organisations need to adapt their culture, prepare their employees for the changes in their job descriptions, and set up training for relevant skills to avoid human resource replacements or, eventually, job cuts for the current employees.

The future automation design process should determine the content and format of information to be shared with users to create an experience of certainty and trust.

4.3 Co-designing Workshop Settings

We noticed that using such workshops for better employees' engagement in the emergent future system design or even selecting the trials is beneficial for complex organisations. For a better result in the ideation process, providing a context, scenario, and better facilitation is required. Previous studies cover how the ideation process can be more comfortable and quicker for the participants [21, 39]. We observed that selecting the right design tool can provide a better reflection of the participants' knowledge. For example, participants found AH complicated to use without the design researchers' help. Adding more tangible elements [39], such as pre-structured cards and easy-to-use collaborative tools, can always be beneficial.

Moreover, there is a need to use data-driven design tools for the co-design workshops for future scenarios. Accessibility to relevant data in the templates, collaborative platforms or any other forms can provide better context and understanding for the participants before using these tools. Preparing the environment to ideate is another important factor; participants should sufficiently understand the scenario, products, and the future system's domain and environment. In these workshops, the participants were employees from various departments and familiar with the work domain. However, we initially prepared them with brainstorming, group discussion, etc. They were also feeding each other with the relevant data; for example, the innovation team and the HR employee actively responded to the question raised by other employees. The whole process provided them with an exemplary scenario to generate and manage their ideas. Otherwise, we must provide sufficient (internal/external) data for the context and persona creation. In line with the environment preparation and facilitator's instructions, planning for a scenario in advance for every co-design workshop for future systems is essential. This can help the participant access context and a road map to look forward and share more relevant information.

5   Conclusion

5.1   Limitations

We had planned to interview the practitioner and the decision-makers on our workshop's validity in their natural environment for the second phase of this study, which was cancelled due to the COVID-19 outbreak and the sudden impact on aviation human resource availability and layoffs. We also believed a link between the AH physical layers (involves contextual analysis) to structure data collection for creating personas. We observed that participants' engagement with AH as a design tool was not straightforward. Using examples and more tangible tools can help participants to use AH more efficiently. Further research aims to explore AH's possibility and its relation to personas as a design tool.

5.2   Conclusion

The presented case study's main aim is to explore and illustrate how a London-based airport uses participatory design, interaction design, and WDA methods to make decisions on future autonomous Industry 4.0 systems that incorporate workers' experiences. The paper presented two scenarios, ATPT and AAMM, in an airport domain based on customer profiles, personas, scenarios, AH, and a rough prototype to achieve this goal. The eight nominated AI/UX goals [28] were tested in the context of these two scenarios. After the workshop, it was highlighted in participants' responses that using this method helps them better understand workers and the aviation sector's needs and perspectives for selecting the new autonomous systems, which was not part of their practices before. This method gave participants a platform for sharing the experience and understanding of these systems. Remarkably, creating an AI engine persona shows how future workers are willing to share responsibilities in decision-making with their machine counterparts. Participants see their future workplace supported by more technology, more mobility, remote working, using digital twins, drones, wearables, and mixed reality (virtual reality and augmented reality). They believe new technologies will benefit from gestural interaction, more screens, and wearable, voice commanded systems that can communicate easily, remotely, and real-time access information via sensors. They believe these systems can increase the interaction and well-being of the workplaces.

This case study proves that designing with a socio-technical lens at the intersection of UX and Automation can work in real-world industrial applications. Participatory design activities were used as a powerful tool for envisioning future automation technologies and workers' well-being. The fact that UX researchers and airport employees jointly did WDA in these two scenarios shows how workers may be the best consultant to draw the line between automation and human activities for their well-being.

References

1. Abdelnour-Nocera, J., Oussena, S., Burns, C.: Human work interaction design of the smart university. In: Abdelnour Nocera, J., Barricelli, B.R., Lopes, A., Campos, P., Clemmensen, T. (eds.) HWID 2015. IAICT, vol. 468, pp. 127–140. Springer, Cham (2015). https://doi.org/10.1007/978-3-319-27048-7_9

2. Amershi, S., et al.: Guidelines for human-AI interaction. In: Proceedings of the 2019 CHI Conference on Human Factors in Computing Systems, pp. 1–13 ACM, Glasgow Scotland UK (2019). https://doi.org/10.1145/3290605.3300233

3. Barcellini, F., et al.: Designers' and users' roles in participatory design: what is actually co-designed by participants? Appl. Ergon. **50**, 31–40 (2015). https://doi.org/10.1016/j.apergo.2015.02.005

4. Barricelli, B.R., Roto, V., Clemmensen, T., Campos, P., Lopes, A., Gonçalves, F., Abdelnour-Nocera, J. (eds.): HWID 2018. IAICT, vol. 544. Springer, Cham (2019). https://doi.org/10.1007/978-3-030-05297-3

5. Baxter, G., Sommerville, I.: Socio-technical systems: from design methods to systems engineering. Interact. Comput. **23**(1), 4–17 (2011). https://doi.org/10.1016/j.intcom.2010.07.003

6. Bodin, I., et al.: Work domain analysis of an intensive care unit: an abstraction Hierarchy based on a bed-side approach. In: Proceedings of the Human Factors and Ergonomics Society Europe Annual Conference,. pp. 109–118 (2016)

7. Bureau d'Enquêtes et d'Analyses: Final Report on the accident on 1st June 2009 to the Airbus A330–203 registered F-GZCP operated by Air France flight AF 447 Rio de Janeiro. https://www.bea.aero/docspa/2009/f-cp090601.en/pdf/f-cp090601.en.pdf. Accessed 04 Mar 2021

8. Burns, C.: Cognitive work analysis: new dimensions. In: Campos, P., Clemmensen, T., Nocera, J.A., Katre, D., Lopes, A., Ørngreen, R. (eds.) HWID 2012. IAICT, vol. 407, pp. 1–11. Springer, Heidelberg (2013). https://doi.org/10.1007/978-3-642-41145-8_1

9. Burns, C.M., et al.: Evaluation of ecological interface design for nuclear process control: situation awareness effects. Hum Factors. **50**(4), 663–679 (2008). https://doi.org/10.1518/001872008X312305

10. Cabrero, D.G., et al.: A hermeneutic inquiry into user-created personas in different Namibian locales. In: Proceedings of the 14th Participatory Design Conference, vol. 1, pp. 101–110. ACM (2016)

11. Chin, G., Rosson, M.: A case study in the participatory design of a collaborative science-based learning environment (2004)

12. Clemmensen, T.: A human work interaction design (HWID) case study in e-government and public information systems. Int. J. Pub. Inf. **7**(3), 105–113 (2011)

13. Dikmen, M., Burns, C.: Trust in autonomous vehicles: the case of tesla autopilot and summon. In: 2017 IEEE International Conference on Systems, Man, and Cybernetics (SMC), pp. 1093–1098 (2017). https://doi.org/10.1109/SMC.2017.8122757

14. Euerby, A., Burns, C.M.: Improving social connection through a communities-of-practice-inspired cognitive work analysis approach. Hum Factors. **56**(2), 361–383 (2014). https://doi.org/10.1177/0018720813494410

15. Flyvbjerg, B.: Five misunderstandings about case-study research. Qual. Inq. **12**(2), 219–245 (2006). https://doi.org/10.1177/1077800405284363

16. Fox, W.M.: Sociotechnical system principles and guidelines: past and present. J. Appl. Behav. Sci. **31**(1), 91–105 (1995). https://doi.org/10.1177/0021886395311009

17. Frey, C.B., Osborne, M.A.: The future of employment: how susceptible are jobs to computerisation? Technol. Forecast. Soc. Chang. **114**, 254–280 (2017). https://doi.org/10.1016/j.techfore.2016.08.019

18. Hajdukiewicz, J., Burns, C.: Strategies for bridging the gap between analysis and design for ecological interface design. Proc. Hum. Factors Ergon. Soc. Ann. Meet. **48**(3), 479–483 (2004). https://doi.org/10.1177/154193120404800344

19. Hajdukiewicz, J.R., et al.: Work domain analysis for intentional systems. Proc. Hum. Factors Ergon. Soc. Ann. Meet. **43**(3), 333–337 (1999). https://doi.org/10.1177/154193129904300343

20. Hermann, M., et al.: Design principles for industrie 4.0 scenarios. In: 2016 49th Hawaii International Conference on System Sciences (HICSS), pp. 3928–3937 (2016). https://doi.org/10.1109/HICSS.2016.488

21. Inie, N., Dalsgaard, P.: How interaction designers use tools to manage ideas. ACM Trans. Comput.-Hum. Interact. **27**(2), 7:1–7:26 (2020). https://doi.org/10.1145/3365104

22. Jenkins, D.P.: Using the abstraction hierarchy to create more innovative specifications. In: Neville, A.S., Paul, M.S., Guy, H.W., Daniel, P.J. (eds.) Cognitive Work Analysis: Applications, Extensions and Future Directions, pp. 103–114. CRC Press (2017)

23. Jenkins, T., et al.: The future supermarket: a case study of ethnographic experiential futures. In: Proceedings of the 11th Nordic Conference on Human-Computer Interaction: Shaping Experiences, Shaping Society, pp. 1–13 ACM, Tallinn Estonia (2020). https://doi.org/10.1145/3419249.3420130

24. Johnson, B.D.: Science fiction prototyping: designing the future with science fiction. Synth. Lect. Comput. Sci. **3**(1), 1–190 (2011). https://doi.org/10.2200/S00336ED1V01Y201102CSL003

25. Kadir, B.A., Broberg, O.: Human-centered design of work systems in the transition to industry 4.0. Appl. Ergon. **92**, 103334 (2021). https://doi.org/10.1016/j.apergo.2020.103334

26. Kirk, A.K., Brown, D.F.: Employee assistance programs: a review of the management of stress and wellbeing through workplace counselling and consulting. Aust. Psychol. **38**(2), 138–143 (2003). https://doi.org/10.1080/00050060310001707137

27. Koenig, F., Found, P.A., Kumar, M.: Condition monitoring for airport baggage handling in the era of industry 4.0. J. Qual. Maintenance Eng. **25**(3), 435–451 (2019). https://doi.org/10.1108/JQME-03-2018-0014

28. Kymalainen, T., et al.: Evaluating future automation work in process plants with an experience-driven science fiction prototype. In: 2016 12th International Conference on Intelligent Environments (IE), pp. 54–61 IEEE, London, United Kingdom (2016). https://doi.org/10.1109/IE.2016.17

29. Lind, M.: Making sense of the abstraction hierarchy. In: Proc. Proceedings of the seventh European Conference on Cognitive Science Approaches to Process Control, pp. 195–200 (1999)

30. Lindley, J., et al.: Anticipatory ethnography: design fiction as an input to design ethnography. Ethnographic Praxis Ind. Conf. Proc. **2014**(1), 237–253 (2014). https://doi.org/10.1111/1559-8918.01030

31. Lu, Y., Roto, V.: Evoking meaningful experiences at work–a positive design framework for work tools. J. Eng. Des. **26**(4–6), 99–120 (2015)

32. Marr, B.: Why everyone must get ready for the 4th industrial revolution. https://www.forbes.com/sites/bernardmarr/2016/04/05/why-everyone-must-get-ready-for-4th-industrial-revolution/. Accessed 04 Mar 2021

33. Mourtzis, D., et al.: Modelling and quantification of industry 4.0 manufacturing complexity based on information theory: a robotics case study. Int. J. Prod. Res. **57**(22), 6908–6921 (2019). https://doi.org/10.1080/00207543.2019.1571686

34. Mugglestone, M., et al.: Accelerating the improvement process. Clin. Gov. Intl J. **13**(1), 19–25 (2008). https://doi.org/10.1108/14777270810850599

35. Nielsen, L.: Personas - User Focused Design. Springer, London (2019). https://doi.org/10.1007/978-1-4471-7427-1

36. Oostveen, A.-M., Lehtonen, P.: The requirement of accessibility: European automated border control systems for persons with disabilities. Technol. Soc. **52**, 60–69 (2018). https://doi.org/10.1016/j.techsoc.2017.07.009
37. Parasuraman, R., et al.: A model for types and levels of human interaction with automation. IEEE Trans. Syst. Man Cybern. Part A Syst. Hum. **30**(3), 286–297 (2000)
38. Polaine, A., et al.: Service Design: from Insight to Implementation. Rosenfeld Media, New York (2013)
39. Rygh, K., Clatworthy, S.: The use of tangible tools as a means to support co-design during service design innovation projects in healthcare. In: Pfannstiel, M.A., Rasche, C. (eds.) Service Design and Service Thinking in Healthcare and Hospital Management, pp. 93–115. Springer, Cham (2019). https://doi.org/10.1007/978-3-030-00749-2_7
40. Saffer, D.: Designing for Interaction: Creating Innovative Applications and Devices. New Riders, Indianapolis (2010)
41. Salmon, P.M., et al.: Using the abstraction hierarchy to identify how the purpose and structure of road transport systems contributes to road trauma. Transp. Res. Interdisc. Perspect. **3**, 100067 (2019). https://doi.org/10.1016/j.trip.2019.100067
42. Sanders, E.B.-N., Stappers, P.J.: Co-creation and the new landscapes of design. CoDesign **4**(1), 5–18 (2008). https://doi.org/10.1080/15710880701875068
43. Sarin, S., O'Connor, G.C.: First among equals: the effect of team leader characteristics on the internal dynamics of cross-functional product development teams. J. Prod. Innov. Manag. **26**(2), 188–205 (2009). https://doi.org/10.1111/j.1540-5885.2009.00345.x
44. Simonsen, J., Robertson, T.: Routledge International Handbook of Participatory Design. Routledge, Milton Park (2012)
45. Tan, W., Boy, G.A.: Tablet-based information system for commercial aircraft: on board context-sensitive information system (OCSIS). In: Harris, D. (ed.) EPCE 2018. LNCS (LNAI), vol. 10906, pp. 701–712. Springer, Cham (2018). https://doi.org/10.1007/978-3-319-91122-9_55
46. Taylor, M.P., et al.: Operator 4.0 or maker 1.0? Exploring the implications of industrie 4.0 for innovation, safety and quality of work in small economies and enterprises. Comput. Ind. Eng. **139**, 105486 (2020). https://doi.org/10.1016/j.cie.2018.10.047
47. Trist, E.L., Bamforth, K.W.: Some social and psychological consequences of the longwall method of coal-getting: an examination of the psychological situation and defences of a work group in relation to the social structure and technological content of the work system. Hum. Relat. **4**(1), 3–38 (1951). https://doi.org/10.1177/001872675100400101
48. Vicente, K.J.: Cognitive Work Analysis: Toward Safe, Productive, and Healthy Computer-Based Work. CRC Press, Boca Raton (1999)
49. Wouters, N., et al.: Uncovering the honeypot effect: how audiences engage with public interactive systems. In: Proceedings of the 2016 ACM Conference on Designing Interactive Systems, pp. 5–16. ACM, Brisbane QLD Australia (2016). https://doi.org/10.1145/2901790.2901796
50. Yerkes, R.M., Dodson, J.D.: The relation of strength of stimulus to rapidity of habit-formation. Punishment: Issues and experiments, pp. 27--41 (1908)
51. Tools | Service Design Tools. https://servicedesigntools.org/tools.html. Accessed 27 Jan 2021
52. Why sustainability is now the key driver of innovation (2009). https://hbr.org/2009/09/why-sustainability-is-now-the-key-driver-of-innovation

Artificial Intelligence (AI) for Human Work

Mood-Based Song Recommendation System

Shashwati Tidke$^{(\boxtimes)}$, Ganesh Bhutkar⬤, Dnyanal Shelke, Shivani Takale,
and Shraddha Sadke

Centre of Excellence in HCI, Vishwakarma Institute of Technology, Pune, India
{shashwati.tidke18,ganesh.bhutkar}@vit.edu

Abstract. A study of existing music systems showed that many music applications fail to recommend songs based on emotion; instead, they use the user's history
to recommend songs. The objective of this research work is to extract emotions
from real-time input of the human face and suggest Bollywood songs based on the
detected emotion and other factors. According to the results of the survey taken for
this research work, users tend to listen to songs considering factors, genres, era,
singer, time of the day, and activity. The requirements for the proposed system
were the preparation of the dataset and finding relationships between different
factors considered for the research work. The proposed system includes identification of emotion from the human face and song filtration based on the algorithm
developed using the factors considered. Thus, the proposed system is an interactive
mood-based songs recommendation system that considers the current emotion of
the user along with vital factors related to songs and user preferences for these
factors while recommending songs. In future, this song recommendation system
can be improved by adding a bigger dataset of Bollywood and regional songs in
major Indian languages.

Keywords: Emotion detection · Songs categorization · Recommendation ·
Content-based filtering · Genres

1 Introduction

Music is an interesting part of life for being human, starting from the earliest stages
of life. For example, an infant's attention can be held easily by singing rather than by
speech. Moreover, the adults have reported listening to music for expressing emotions
and regulating their emotive state. It seems that music's prevalence is related to emotions
[22]. The psychological research supports the association between songs to listen and
mood of the user. Also, it can be used in various medical treatments as it is used to be
a stress reliever. In many workplaces music is used to keep employees motivated and
happy [10]. Music Therapy is used to treat the traumatic patients.

The music systems that exist today play songs, which are selected manually by users
or are recommended based on users' earlier preferences and, based on collaborative-
based filtering [2]. Some music applications provide playlists that are created for different
scenarios. For example, Spotify provides playlists for everyone, which are categorized

© IFIP International Federation for Information Processing 2022
Published by Springer Nature Switzerland AG 2022
G. Bhutkar et al. (Eds.): HWID 2021, IFIP AICT 609, pp. 181–200, 2022.
https://doi.org/10.1007/978-3-031-02904-2_9

based on genres and moods. Spotify and Saavn provide facilities to manually create their own playlists for users. But, segregating the playlists and annotating songs manually is quite time-consuming and laborious [8]. The system proposed in this research paper, is a recommendation system based on content-based filtering that seeks to predict the preference that the user would give to a song in an available playlist. For this prediction, the system utilizes vital factors related with music, along with user profile as well as user preferences. Some of these factors are collected through a user survey.

There are several recommendation systems which use factors like daily activity, time of the day and genre [1]. However, no such recommendation system has been developed which integrates the important metadata of songs and makes recommendations based on the integrated data. Also, recommendations based only on the context of songs are less effective. In addition to the context of songs, emotions of users should also be considered, to make recommendations more powerful. The novel approach is used to develop the proposed system which recommends songs based on integrated metadata of songs, important factors that influence selection of songs and emotions. Also, this system focuses on the basic needs of music enthusiasts as existing applications are troubling a lot for users: it uses technology to increase the interaction of the system with the user in many ways.

Music is a part of human life. Music is the language of the universe. Music can have considerable effects on cognition, emotion, and behavior. It also indicates that people use music to serve various functions, from emotion regulation and self-expression to social bonding. Therefore, the mood-based song recommendation system can be utilized as a virtual mood assistant that can help people feel better anytime [20]. Beyond just feeling good, having a better mood has other advantages. When users join their office in the morning, the system can recommend a list of Bollywood songs as background music, containing soothing melodies or recharge songs with happy or soul funk genre. This type of music in the morning or at start of weekday, can increase employee satisfaction, reduce anxiety at work, and contribute to their overall health. Also, it makes user mentally more creative. Depending on the pitch of the song, it can alter heart rate, breathing rate and blood pressure [14]. When people listen to high-pitched songs while exercising, their physical performance improves as music is said to be a good option to learn new things quickly and their consciousness of exertion decreases. Music is a powerful therapy that will make you calm down and in the moment of joy, it will make you cheerful. People who listen to low bass songs while studying, on the other hand, can boost their memory. Moreover, music develops the mind and boosts your self-confidence. They can also outperform students who study in silence or in a noisy environment. Not only happy songs lift up your mood, but also sad songs can heal wounds. When someone is in a bad mood, listening to sad songs can bring him pleasure and comfort. According to some doctors, music therapy has been a great source of help for them in the treatment of health issues like dementia, depression, anxiety or trauma. Music can be used to calm patients with mental illness or depression. People can cope with their pain by listening to music. People suffering through physical pain can experience less pain after listening to music. There are many children with a learning disability, who have responded positively to the music therapy [6]. Thus, music plays a more important role in our life than just being a source of entertainment. The mood-based song recommendation system can also be used in music therapy. The mood-based song recommendation system can have many positive effects on human body, mind, and overall health.

In this research paper, based on the results of the user survey taken, six factors which are emotion, singer, era, genre, time of the day and activity are considered for recommendation of songs. Users tend to listen to specific genres of songs in different emotions, activities and time of the day [21]. The proposed mood-based songs recommendation system is an interactive system made for entertainment of users. In interaction with users, the system takes user's information about his/her preferences for genres, era and singers at the time of registration into the system, which can be modified by the user anytime. Using this system, users can get recommendations based either on emotion or activity which he is performing. The emotion is extracted by capturing real time images [5]. Based on the preference decided by system and preference for genres in the user's profile, system selects two genres which can satisfy both system's and user's preferences simultaneously. The system filters out songs according to the selected genre and era in the user profile. The selected songs are then sorted such that songs of preferred singers will come at the top. These sorted songs are then recommended to the user.

2 Related Work

During the research work related to the song-recommendation system, following research papers and reports have been studied.

In 2013, the International Conference on Machine Learning (ICML) organized the competition – 'Challenges in Representation Learning' in which one of the challenges was 'The Facial Expression Recognition Challenge' to find the effective algorithm for emotion detection from the human face. A brief report on challenges and top submissions of this competition is available now [11]. For this challenge, the dataset 'FER-2013' containing 35887 images, was created by Carrier P. and Courville A. Out of 56 submissions, top 3 submissions used Convolutional Neural Network (CNN) and the winner used Support Vector Machine (SVM) as a loss function to train the model. The results showed the importance of SVM-loss function in facial emotion detection. Using the similar method for recognizing emotions from human faces, Akhtar R. created the facial-emotion-recognition package in Python which creates a bounding box around the face of the person present in the picture and puts a text at the top of the bounding box representing the recognized emotion [9]. This package is indeed highly accurate to use for detection of emotions.

In the next study titled 'A Survey of Affect Recognition Methods: Audio, Visual, and Spontaneous Expressions', the existing emotion detection systems use only intentionally displayed and overemphasized expressions of first emotion [25]. But human behavior can differ in visual look, audio profile, and timing from naturally occurring behavior. This research describes various factors in human emotion detection. On the bases of this paper the user survey questionnaire is designed. The paper surveys the different factors to analyze human mood. Similar user survey has been conducted to understand factors that differ from person to person while regulating emotions.

In addition to earlier systems Mortensen M. et al. [16] gathered mood ratings of both music and users explicitly. So, this recommender system is positively evaluated using real-world data in a live implementation, with live users interacting with the system using collaborative-filtering.

The system proposed by Bansal D. et al. [3] was developed to capture physiological signals from the user via a wearable computing device. By using these signals, it enhanced the accuracy of the recommendations made by the recommender system by tracking the user's emotional state through these signals. Using this device, the proposed system can be enhanced. In this proposed system, Emotional effects of the past recommendations on the user are stored in the system's database and used in future recommendations, as the same musical track's effects can be varied between different users. In the paper by Kabini H. et al. [13], they have discussed the fact that visual appearance and audio profile affect human behavior. They have discussed human emotion perception from a psychological perspective. This perspective is taken in count while creating the algorithm of this system.

To develop emotion-based music recommendation system, Bhutada S. et al. [5], assigned an emotion to every song and filtered songs according to the detected emotion. Whereas Dureha A. [7] used an audio emotion recognition algorithm and generated playlists of songs for different emotions. Songs are then filtered based on the current emotion of human and emotions of songs. Filtered songs are recommended to the user. Combining these two approaches in the proposed system, genre is assigned to every song in the dataset. Songs are then categorized according to labelled genres to create playlists.

A lot of work has been done in the field of emotion detection and mood-based songs classification. The demand is for a better approach to recommend songs. Andjelkovic I. et al. [1] has developed the hybrid recommender system named Mood play, which makes recommendations based on both contexts of songs and mood of the user. This system uses an interactive interface to take real time input from the user. Based on input taken at the recommendation time and pre-existing data in the user profile, songs get recommended. The proposed system uses a similar approach of creating a user profile and taking input at real time to make the system interactive. The system which has been proposed, not only concentrated on User experience but also on accuracy.

To improve the accuracy of Facial Emotion Detection (FER), Gala P. et al. [10] propose a system work which makes use of Viola-Jones (VJ) algorithm with Principal Component Analysis approach to extract essential facial features. The accuracy of the FER system only depends upon the extracted features during processing. The final out-come of this system attains an accuracy level of about 86.67%. This algorithm can be used for FER.

In 2017, Cook T. et al. [7], conducted the user survey of 794 university students to study their music preferences while regulating emotions. This study provides a quantitative analysis of the relationship between different genres and three categories of emotions. Related results are used to develop the algorithm for the proposed system.

To develop a mood-based songs recommendation system, existing techniques [7, 11, 25] in the field of emotion detection, emotion regulation and songs recommendation are studied. Results and analysis of relationships between different genres and emotions are studied to develop the algorithm for the proposed system. During the literature survey, drawbacks in the existing music applications and different approaches for the development of the mood-based songs recommendation system are analyzed.

3   Research Methodology

This section discusses several research activities that have been conducted during design of the proposed Mood-Based Song Recommendation System. These activities involve user survey, dataset preparation, emotion detection and design of the proposed system.

3.1   User Survey

To analyze the weight of various factors in recommending songs, a collection of rich opinions of potential end users was required. A user survey has been conducted for this research work, to know factors that users consider while selecting songs in different moods. This survey collected the users' experiences and their expectations from the music applications. The relationships and dependency among factors from the results of the user survey has been observed and listed down [4]. These relationships are used at the time of developing the algorithm for filtration of songs.

3.2   Dataset Preparation

The dataset containing all the factors gathered during the user survey was not available anywhere. So, a dataset of songs has been prepared by performing web-scraping and extracting the required information from the web. Since the extracted data was in raw format, some data cleaning techniques have been applied.

3.3   Emotion Detection

With the help of results of the user survey, the sequence of factors based on which filtration occurs, the contents of the user profile, inputs to be taken from the relevant user during the registration process and inputs to be taken during the use of the system by the user has decided. And finally the algorithm for the filtration of songs based on the current mood of the user and activity performed by the user, has been designed.

4   User Survey

This section describes the purpose of taking the user survey and results acquired through it about factors influencing mood, their sequences and priorities while recommending songs.

4.1   Purpose

User survey was an important part when designing the mood-based song recommendation system to understand the user's experience as well as perception about the current music applications and song selection. The purpose of this survey was to gain knowledge about factors that users consider while selecting songs, sequence of those factors, to know the most listened genres and the other features that they expect from the music applications.

4.2 User Profile

The survey of 100 users has been taken for this research work, where users were given the questionnaire designed with Zoho Survey [26] to fill in the first few questions asked for the personal information like user age and gender. Then, next few questions were to know the user interest and knowledge level of music. Further questions were asking for personal preferences from users about their choices in era, genres and pitch of songs. At the end, the questions were asked to understand user preferences regarding the factors affecting the selection of the songs.

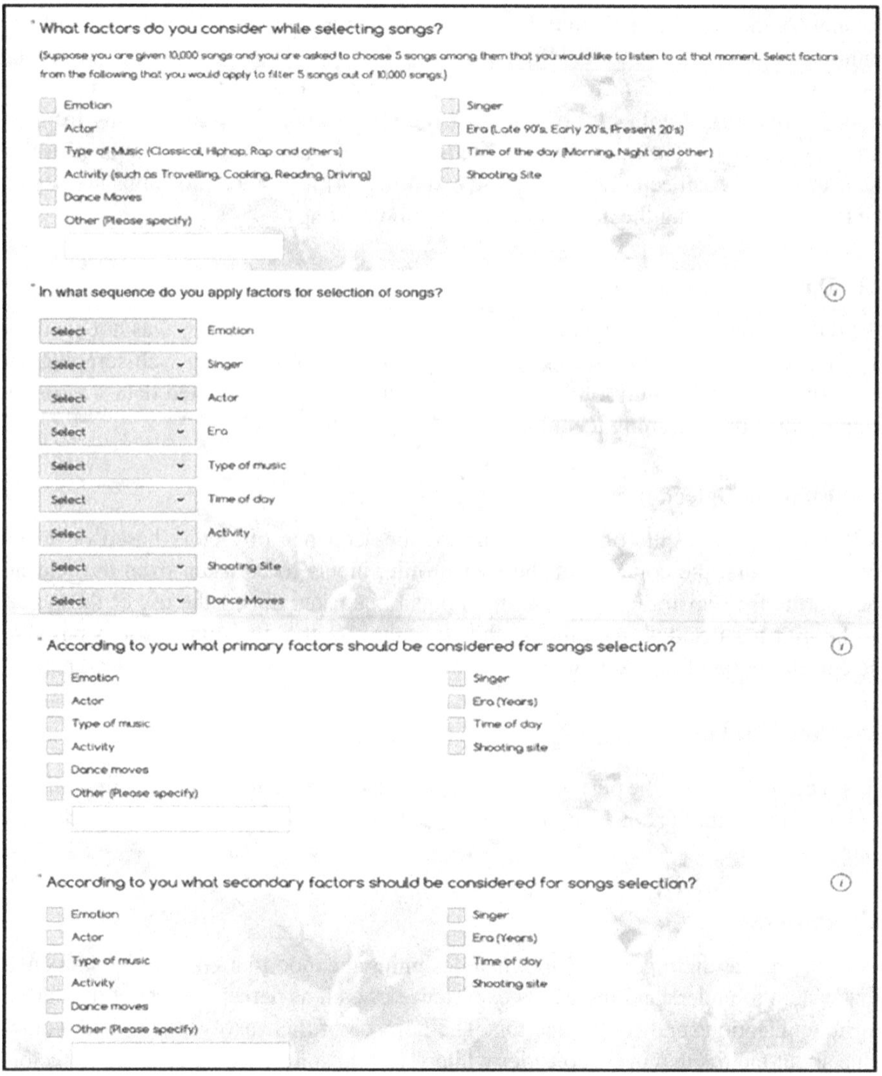

* What factors do you consider while selecting songs?

(Suppose you are given 10,000 songs and you are asked to choose 5 songs among them that you would like to listen to at that moment. Select factors from the following that you would apply to filter 5 songs out of 10,000 songs.)

- Emotion
- Actor
- Type of Music (Classical, Hiphop, Rap and others)
- Activity (such as Travelling, Cooking, Reading, Driving)
- Dance Moves
- Other (Please specify)
- Singer
- Era (Late 90's, Early 20's, Present 20's)
- Time of the day (Morning, Night and other)
- Shooting Site

* In what sequence do you apply factors for selection of songs?

- Select Emotion
- Select Singer
- Select Actor
- Select Era
- Select Type of music
- Select Time of day
- Select Activity
- Select Shooting Site
- Select Dance Moves

* According to you what primary factors should be considered for songs selection?

- Emotion
- Actor
- Type of music
- Activity
- Dance moves
- Other (Please specify)
- Singer
- Era (Years)
- Time of day
- Shooting site

* According to you what secondary factors should be considered for songs selection?

- Emotion
- Actor
- Type of music
- Activity
- Dance moves
- Other (Please specify)
- Singer
- Era (Years)
- Time of day
- Shooting site

Fig. 1. Section of questionnaire related with factors used in selection of songs

Figure 1 shows some questions asked in survey regarding preference about factors and whose responses were highly important for the development of the proposed system. In the user survey, user profiles and comprehensive participation is an important aspect [20]. In the survey, 51% users were in the age group of 0–20 years, 38% users were in 20–40 years and remaining 11% users were above 40 years. About 55% male and 45% females participated in the user survey. The results of this survey are drawn by mainly focusing on the responses of those users, who spend more time listening to music than normal crowd. We got 21% users listening to songs for less than 2 h, 77% users listening for 2–5 h and 2% users listening for more than 5 h. Responses of 33% users having skills in music were compared with that of 67% users not having skills in music. These profiles played an important role in the analysis of the user survey.

4.3 Survey Result

Among the different factors - emotion, singer, genre, activity, era and/or time of day are the most preferred factors for selecting songs, as seen in Fig. 3. This is reflected in higher user preference in terms of a greater number of users selecting a specific factor. Users were also given freedom to select as many factors as per their aspiration (Fig. 2).

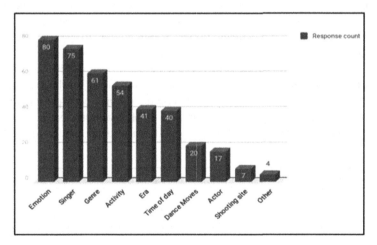

Fig. 2. Factor preferences (in selection of songs) given by users during the survey

Users have given preference to genres such as Soul/Funk, Dance, Classical, Rap/Hip-hop, Pop and Jazz. This is reflected in higher user preference in terms of a greater number of users opting for a specific genre. The bar graph in Fig. 3 shows that users hardly listen to other genres.

From the results, six factors have been considered which are emotion, singer, genre, era, activity and time of day to recommend songs. Also, the six genres selected, include - Soul/Funk, Dance, Classical, Rap/Hip-hop, Pop and Jazz.

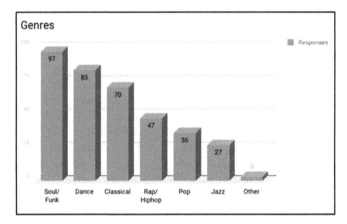

Fig. 3. Genre preferences (in selection of songs) given by users during the survey

5 Dataset Preparation

Results of experimentation gain accuracy if the dataset is relevant and larger. With a smaller dataset, filtration considering six factors would have become too difficult and non-effective as there was a need for the dataset containing sufficient number of songs.

According to the survey conducted for this research work, most of the users participated in the survey prefer to listen to Bollywood songs – famous in India. There was a need for a dataset of Bollywood songs with a variety of features like its era, singers, genres and other parameters. Off-the-self dataset consisting of all these features, was not readily available. So, this own updated song dataset has been prepared with due consideration of selected factors as seen in Fig. 4. This section describes the dataset schema, data collection through web-scraping and related data cleaning methods.

song_name	year	singers	lyricist	Composer	movie_name	movie_director	actors	genre
Rakshassi	2018	Blaaze| Kailash Kher| Nakash Aziz	Abbas Tyrewala	A.R. Rahman	2	S. Shankar	Rajinikanth| Aks	Dance
Mechanical Sundariye	2018	Armaan Malik| Shashaa Tirupati	Abbas Tyrewala	A.R. Rahman	2	S. Shankar	Rajinikanth| Aks	Pop
Wo Pehli Mulaaqaat	1946	Surendra	Shewan Rizvi	Sajjad Hussain	1857	Mohan Sinha	Nigar Sultana| S	Dance
Jhamak Jhamak Liye Teg Tamak	1946	Shamshad Begum	Yashodanandan Joshi	Sajjad Hussain	1857	Mohan Sinha	Nigar Sultana| S	Classical
Dilli Tere Qile Par Honge	1946	Chorus	Shewan Rizvi	Sajjad Hussain	1857	Mohan Sinha	Nigar Sultana| S	Classical
Chupke Hi Chupke Na Jaane	1946	Khan Mastana| Rajkumari Dubey	Anjum Pilibhitt	Sajjad Hussain	1857	Mohan Sinha	Nigar Sultana| S	Pop
Meri Ho Gayi Unse Baat	1946	Suraiya Jamaal Sheikh (Suraiya)	Shewan Rizvi	Sajjad Hussain	1857	Mohan Sinha	Nigar Sultana| S	Classical
Umeedon Ka Tara	1946	Suraiya Jamaal Sheikh (Suraiya)	Anjum Pilibhiti	Sajjad Hussain	1857	Mohan Sinha	Nigar Sultana| S	Classical
Gham E Aashiyana Satayega Kab	1946	Suraiya Jamaal Sheikh (Suraiya)	Mohan Singh	Sajjad Hussain	1857	Mohan Sinha	Nigar Sultana| S	Classical
Teri Nazar Mein Main Rahu	1946	Suraiya Jamaal Sheikh (Suraiya)| Surendra	Shewan Rizvi	Sajjad Hussain	1857	Mohan Sinha	Nigar Sultana| S	Pop
Vaada Tumse Hain Vaada	2008	Pandit Jasraj	Sameer	Adnan Sami	1920	Vikram Bhatt	Rajneesh Duggal	Rap/HipHop
Tujhe Main Pyar Karu	2008	Kailash Kher	Sameer	Adnan Sami	1920	Vikram Bhatt	Rajneesh Duggal	Rap/HipHop
Bichua	2008	Shubha Mudgal	Sameer	Adnan Sami	1920	Vikram Bhatt	Rajneesh Duggal	Dance
Aise Jalta Hai Jiya	2008	Asha Bhosle	Sameer	Adnan Sami	1920	Vikram Bhatt	Rajneesh Duggal	Pop
Aanewale Kal	2018	Rahul Jain	Shakeel Azmi	Harish Sagane	1921	Vikram Bhatt	Zarine Khan| Ka	Soul/Funk
Kuch Iss Tarah	2018	Arnab Dutta	Shakeel Azmi	Harish Sagane	1921	Vikram Bhatt	Zarine Khan| Ka	Soul/Funk
Yaara	2018	Arnab Dutta	Shakeel Azmi	Harish Sagane	1921	Vikram Bhatt	Zarine Khan| Ka	Soul/Funk
Tere Bina	2018	Aakanksha Sharma| Arijit Singh	Raqueeb Alam	Asad Khan	1921	Vikram Bhatt	Zarine Khan| Ka	Soul/Funk
Sunn Le Zara	2018	Arnab Dutta	Shakeel Azmi	Harish Sagane	1921	Vikram Bhatt	Zarine Khan| Ka	Pop
Kaal Ke Antim Palon Tak	2007	Various Artists	Dr. Devendra Kafir	Akash Sagar	1971	Amrit Sagar	Manoj Bajpai| R	Classical
Sehlenge Hum	2007	Shibani Kashyap	Zaheer Anwar	Akash Sagar	1971	Amrit Sagar	Manoj Bajpai| R	Soul/Funk
O Tere Saath Saath Meri	1956	Lata Mangeshkar	Rajendra Krishan	Ramchandra Narhar Chitalkar (	26 January	Ramesh Saigal	Ajit| Nalini Jayw	Pop
Phir Dharti Par Aa Jaa Re	1956	Asha Bhosle| Prabodh Chandra Dey (Manna Dey)	Rajendra Krishan	Ramchandra Narhar Chitalkar (	26 January	Ramesh Saigal	Ajit| Nalini Jayw	Soul/Funk
Ro Ro Ke Dil Pukare	1956	Lata Mangeshkar	Rajendra Krishan	Ramchandra Narhar Chitalkar (	26 January	Ramesh Saigal	Ajit| Nalini Jayw	Soul/Funk
Aankh Royi Magar	1956	Lata Mangeshkar	Rajendra Krishan	Ramchandra Narhar Chitalkar (	26 January	Ramesh Saigal	Ajit| Nalini Jayw	Soul/Funk
Sone Ki Jahan	1956	Lata Mangeshkar	Rajendra Krishan	Ramchandra Narhar Chitalkar (	26 January	Ramesh Saigal	Ajit| Nalini Jayw	Soul/Funk

Fig. 4. Song dataset prepared with relevant fields

5.1 Schema of Dataset

The dataset was prepared for its reusability in future, even if additional filtering features may be added or extracted as per system requirements in the future the dataset consisted of total 9 columns as depicted in Fig. 4. These columns are related with fields such as song name, era, singer(s), genre, lyricists, music composer(s), movie name, movie director and actor(s). The information of songs will be displayed on the screen while playing particular songs or in future filtration based on these fields. This information includes the fields - lyricists, music composer, movie name, movie director and related actors. Therefore, it was necessary to include these fields in the dataset prepared.

5.2 Data Collection through Web-Scraping

The technique of web-scraping was used to collect sufficient amounts of song data for the preparation of dataset. A ParseHub tool was used for web-scraping to collect information from any dynamic website into Spreadsheets files which later converted into Comma Separated Value (CSV) files [19]. The content for the dataset was collected from a site named Lyrics Bogie [15]. A total of about 4200 Bollywood songs have been collected using web-scraping. Figure 4 shows the schema of dataset and format of data collected.

5.3 Data Cleaning Process

As the data collected through web-scraping was in raw format, data cleaning process was applied on the data. The data cleaning processes included removing extra white spaces and removing Uniform Resource Locator (URLs) of all the songs. The additional commas in the column - 'singers', could have caused problems, while converting dataset files in CSV format. Thus, commas were replaced by | (or) sign. Genres obtained by web-scraping were not so useful and accurate. Therefore, the genres were entered manually during preparation of a dataset.

6 Machine Learning Aspects

A recommendation system is a system which recommends relevant choice or decision based on factors chosen by the user. This system will recommend the most likely songs to the user, based on the factors - emotion, singer, genre, era, activity and time of day. Most of the applications like Saavn, Ganna and Spotify, use the recommendation system to predict the most likely song, based on the user's history [17].

This recommendation system is based on content-based filtering. It processes a huge amount of data considering the user's preference and interest. This system, initially, detects the human face from the captured image. It locates the face, and binds it within a box to crop it. Then, it converts the cropped image into grayscale. On the grayscale image, facial key-points get located. According to positions of the located facial key-points, SVM classifiers detect the emotion. The system uses the detected emotion for song filtration. Filtration of songs considering emotion and other six factors is implemented using the relationships and dependency among the factors. Next part of this section discusses the relationships among six factors and their usefulness while developing algorithms for the proposed system.

6.1   Relationship among Factors Considered for Recommendation of Songs

From the results of the user survey, the major factors contributing in selection of songs are selected. These factors include - genre, singer, era, emotion, activity, time of day. Among these factors, an emotion and activity are poorly related to each other. Users either choose activity-based songs or emotion-based songs at a time. Genre is a factor which has relation with the most of the other factors. A particular singer always sings songs of some specific genres. In different emotions, genres of different bass get preferred. Preferences for genres get changed according to time of the day and the activity. Users listen to genres that they like and rarely listen to other genres.

6.1.1   Priorities for Genres According to Emotions

There are three types of emotions. These three categories include - positive emotions, energy-driven emotions (which can lead to arousal) and negative emotions [7]. Table 1 shows a short list of emotions, along with their category.

Table 1. List of emotions, along with their category

No	Name of emotion	Category of emotion
1	Happy	Positive
2	Surprise	Positive
3	Anger	Energy-driven/Arousal
4	Sad	Energy-driven/Arousal
5	Fear	Negative
6	Contempt	Negative
7	Disgust	Negative

According to the survey taken by Cook T. et al. [7], the preferences given by users to different genres during emotion management process are shown in Table 2.

Table 2. Genre precedents for regulation of emotions

Preference	Positive emotions	Energy-driven emotions	Negative emotions
High to low	Soul/Funk	Dance	Soul/Funk
	Jazz	Rap/Hip-hop	Classical
	Dance	Soul/Funk	Jazz
	Rock	Pop	Pop
	Rap/Hip-hop	Rock	Rap/Hip-hop
	Classical	Classical	Dance

6.1.2 Recommendation of Genres as Per the Phase of the Day

For the proposed song recommendation system, the songs have been classified into three types according to the pitch of songs, which includes - High bass songs, Medium bass songs and Low bass songs as suggested by Swaroop S. [23]. Genres comprising these types of songs are shown in Table 3.

Table 3. Breakdown of genres as per bass of songs

Energy-driven/High bass genres	Medium bass genres	Low bass genres
Dance	Soul/Funk	Jazz
Rap/Hip-hop	Pop	Classical

Table 4 shows the type of songs that should be recommended to users as per time of the day.

Table 4. List of types of songs recommended as per time of the day

Phase of the day	Time of the day	Type of songs
Early morning	4:00 am–6:59am	Low bass songs
Morning	7:00 am–11:59 am	Energy-driven/High bass songs
Afternoon	12:00 pm–3:59 pm	Low bass songs
Evening	4:00 pm–7:59 pm	Medium bass songs
Night	8:00 pm–3:59 am	Low bass songs

6.1.3 Interpretation for Genres as Per User Activities

During this research work, the classification of activities has been done into three types as suggested by Sloan J. [24]. The categorized user activities are shown in Table 5. Type 1 activities are those which need lots of energy like walking/running, exercising, partying and others. Since high bass genres lead to arousal, they are preferred for this type of activity. Type 2 activities are those which require concentration and focus like reading, studying and meditating. According to Elizabeth Hoyt [12], listening to low bass genres can make us calm and can increase our focus; whereas high bass genres can distract us from our work and decrease our productivity. Hence, low bass genres are preferred for Type 2 activities. Type 3 activities are those which require neither much energy nor much concentration like household chores, daily activities like brushing teeth, cooking, travelling and doing some hobby related activities. Medium bass genres are preferred for these activities.

Table 5. Trifurcation of activities

Type 1 (Energy)	Type 2 (Concentration)	Type 3 (Others)
Walking/Running	Study/Work	Household chores
Partying	Meditation	Cooking
Exercising		Travelling
		Hobby related activities

6.2 Proposed System

Mood-based song recommendation system provides interaction between users and the music system. The main aim of this system is to recommend songs concerning current emotion or activity. Whenever the user opens this system for the first time, user has to complete the profile by providing their own preferences for era, genres and singers of songs. Users can select multiple eras, genres and singers. System gives three eras to select that are Mid 90's, Early 20's and present 20's songs. Then, the system asks the user to select his preferred genres out of six genres (Soul/Funk, Dance, Classical, Jazz, Pop and Rap/Hip Hop). The system, then, successively filters out singers in the preferred era and singers singing genres preferred by the user. The filtered list will be given to the user, from which the user has to select his preferred singers. The information about era, genres and singers given by the user, will be saved to the user's profile. Figure 5 shows contents of user profile.

If the registration has completed already, the system asks the user whether one wants to listen to songs based on emotion or activity. If the user selects emotion, the system will extract emotion from the user's face image. Whereas on the selection of activity, the system provides a list of activities mentioned in the Table 5. Using Table 5, the system decides the type of activity that the user is doing while listening to the songs. Then, the system checks the current time and decides the phase of the day. The phases considered for the proposed system are morning, afternoon, evening, night. Based on the emotion/activity and time of the day system decides genres that are suitable for the current situation. Then, the system recommends songs by considering both the decided genres and the information in the user's profile. Figure 6 shows the entire architecture of the proposed system.

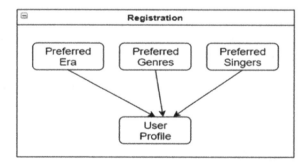

Fig. 5. Preferences accepted through user profile during registration

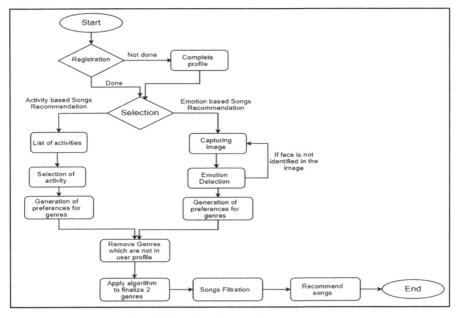

Fig. 6. Flowchart for song filtration process

6.3 Emotion Detection

The system first captures the image of the user's face by using the device's camera. Before starting the camera, it takes permission from the user to get access to the camera. The captured image acts as input for the emotion detection module. From the input image, the emotion of the user gets detected. To detect facial emotion from the image, facial-emotion-recognition package [9] is used in the proposed song recommendation system. It detects the face in the given image and creates a bounding box around the face of the person present in that image as seen in Fig. 7. At the top of the bounding box, it puts text representing the recognized emotion.

Fig. 7. Sample input image for emotion detection

6.4 Algorithm to Detect Genre for the Songs based on Activity or Emotion

This section provides a mathematical model to detect the specific genre. It considers six factors - emotion, genres, era, singer, time of the day, activity. Using these factors, the genre preferences have been set and are stated in Sect. 6.1. Each of the six genres is coded with a unique number as shown in Table 6.

Table 6. Code numbers given to different genres

Code number	Medium
1	Dance
2	Rap/Hip-hop
3	Soul/Funk
4	Pop
5	Jazz
6	Classical

After detecting emotion or taking activity input from the user, the system creates a list of preferences for a particular emotion or activity as stated in Table 2 (for emotions) and/or Table 5 (for activities). For simplification, let's say this list as list_1. In the next step, the system selects the phase of the day considering the time. And it creates another list of genre preferences considering the time of the day using Table 4. Let's say this is list_2. The user preferred genres are taken as the primary choice and remaining will be secondary choices. Those genres which are not present in the user's profile are removed from lists i.e. list_1 and list_2. The sequence of the lists will not be disturbed while removing the secondary genres. The average of code number of the first genre in list_1 and in list_2 is calculated. The float average is converted into integer using floor function. This integer average is treated again as a code number. The system takes the genre corresponding to the integer average using Table 6. This yielded genre does not ensure that it will be in primary choices. So, the genre is redirected to further steps. The system selects the type of bass of selected genre using Table 3. Preference list for the selected bass, taken from Table 1, is considered as the final preference list. Again from the final preference list, the genres not present in the user profile get removed. Finally, the top two genres of this final preference list are selected for the filtration process as described in the next section.

6.5 Filtration of Songs for Dynamic Preferences

Dynamic Preferences are those which are inputted by the user. Here, the era, genre and singer(s) are dynamic preferences. As shown in Fig. 8, a filtration of songs for recommendation starts from era. The system first filters songs according to eras stored in the user profile. Applying the algorithm, described in Sect. 6.4, two genres are selected. Then, the songs are filtered from the dataset in order with era and genres. This list is once more sorted to such an extent that the user preferred singers are given the highest priority. Here, the user preferred singer is considered a primary choice. Thus, the final list of songs considering the singers is ranked in order of user preferred singer and other singer.

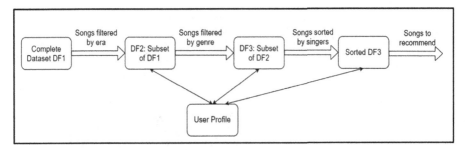

Fig. 8. Songs filtration process based on era, genre and singer

6.6 Results

The mood-based song recommendation system is designed in accordance with the results of the user survey. The distinctive feature of this system is that it recommends songs based on the factors such as singer, genre, era, activity, and time of the day. Content-based filtering is performed on these factors to suggest songs to users. The majority of the song recommendation system does not account for the activity and time of day while recommending songs to users. For this reason, other song recommendation systems are loosely linked to the emotions and preferences of the user. While the proposed system analyses the current status of users and feelings for recommending songs which makes it more interactive. The user search time can be reduced by recommending songs according to the actual emotional state of the user.

7 Web Application

An interactive and responsive web User Interface (UI) for the proposed system has been designed as depicted in Fig. 9, and it is compatible with device of any size. For the development of this UI, several web development tools such as Hypertext Mark-up language (HTML 5), Cascading Style Sheets (CSS), Bootstrap, Visual Studio Code, JavaScript (JS), node.js, Node Package Manage (npm) and ReactJS have been used and it makes the Mood-based Song Recommendation System more interactive.

Fig. 9. User interface of mood-based song recommendation system

7.1   Web UI Development Tools

This section discusses about web development tools used.

HTML5: HTML5 is a mark-up language used for structuring and presenting content on the World Wide Web. It is the fifth and last major HTML version, which is mentioned in World Wide Web Consortium (W3C) as recommendation for front-end. The current specification of HTML is known as the HTML Living Standard. In this web application, it is use for the formatting the text.

CSS: It is the language for describing the presentation of Web pages, including colours, layout, and fonts. It allows one to adapt the presentation to different types of devices, such as large screens, small screens or printers. CSS is independent of HTML and can be used with any eXtended Mark-up Language (XML) - based mark-up language. Most of the web application is developed using HTML and CSS. Here, it is used for styling the web pages.

Bootstrap: Bootstrap is an open and free HTML, CSS and JS toolkit. Using Bootstrap, a responsive website has been developed effectively. Here, it is used for making the web page responsive.

Visual Studio Code: Visual Studio Code is a streamlined code editor with support for development operations like debugging, task running, and version control. All of the source code has been written in Visual Studio Code.

Npm: It is the package manager for the Node JavaScript platform. It has been used to put modules in place, so that node can find them. It manages dependency conflicts intelligently.

React.js: React.js is an open-source JavaScript library. React.js is used for building user interfaces.

Node.js: Node.js is scalable, light and open language platform which makes building of an app easy even at enterprise level. So, it has played an important role in building our web UI.

Spotify Web API: This Application Programming Interface (API) can simply be used by registration on the web-site of Spotify. It prepares environment for application, and then project or app files and folders can be created.

7.2 Web UI Tabs

Functions of tabs present in the web UI of the Mood-based Song Recommendation System are as follows:

Try for Free: Users can use the Mood-based Song Recommendation System for free. In the free version of the system, users experience limited accuracy of the emotion detection algorithm.

Premium: For more accuracy and efficiency, users have to upgrade the system to the paid version through the premium button. In the paid version (which is not developed in the first phase), the system will use additional technologies in order to accurately detect emotion of the user. These technologies include- emotion recognition from speech and from heartbeats measured using sensors.

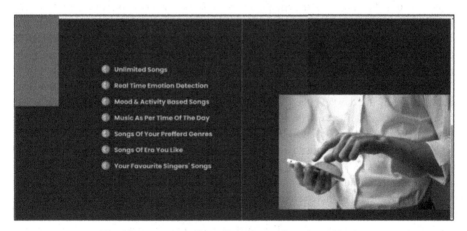

Fig. 10. Feature section of home page in web application

Home: The Home tab gives an overview about the system and its unique features as shown in Fig. 10. From the Home tab, users can start their free trials. In the free trial, the system prompts the user to take his picture and detects the emotion of the user in real time. The system then passes these parameters to the Spotify Web API for filtration. Filtered songs are then recommended to the user.

Music Player: A basic music player with a large number of songs from the Spotify database are available to users in this section. The users can search for specific songs and listen to them. Users can create their own playlists just like Spotify.

Recent: In the recent tab, users can see a list of recently played songs.

Contact: This section provides contact information about the authors and managers of this application.

8   Conclusion and Future Work

Songs are getting released and recreated every day, resulting in huge size datasets of songs. The task of maintaining songs, searching songs, creating playlists by processing large numbers of songs is tedious. To reduce time of searching, songs recommendation systems are needful in day-to-day life, to get songs played automatically depending on the emotional state of the user. The mood-based song recommendation system is made for entertainment by interacting with the user. Current music recommendation systems face the gap in personalization and sentiments while suggesting songs to the user. For this research work, a user survey is conducted. The factors that highly influence the selection of songs are evaluated through this user survey. In the proposed system, an algorithm is developed for the song recommendation. The system captures the image of the user and detects emotion from the facial expressions. According to the detected emotion or selected activity and five factors which include - singer, genre, era, activity and time of the day system recommend songs to the user. The system eases the work of the end-user by capturing the image using a camera, determining their emotion, and suggesting a customized play-list through a more advanced and interactive system.

Human work aspects - emotions and user preferences, as discussed in general HWID framework [7, 18] are considered in recommendation of songs. Few passionate users were involved, and their user experience has been considered in interaction design of this system. The environmental and contextual factor, as per general HWID framework such as time of the day has been vital factor in proposing a recommended song list to the users. Thus, the effect of HWID perspective [7, 18] can be observed prominently in system design of Mood-Based Song Recommendation System.

However, the database used for this research work contains a limited number of songs. So, with this system user do not get access to a large number of songs. The access to the large number of songs can be given by attaching a song library to this system. The dataset for this system consists of Bollywood songs only. This system can be extended for songs in various languages. It can be achieved by appending datasets of songs in various other languages. This system recommends songs using content-based filtering. Its recommendation can be improved by adding collaborative-based filtering. Hence, the system can recommend more appropriate songs using hybrid recommendation techniques.

Acknowledgement. The completion of this research work could not have been possible without participation and suggestions of several passionate users, who participated in related user survey. We thank all these users.

References

1. Andjelkovic I., Parra D., O'Donovan J.: Moodplay: interactive mood-based music discovery and recommendation. In: UMAP 2016: Proceedings of the 2016 Conference on User Modeling Adaptation and Personalization (2016)
2. Bali, V., Haval, S., Patil, S., Priyambiga, R.: Emotion based music player. J. Softw. Eng. Softw. Testing **2**, 2457–2516 (2019)
3. Bansal, D., Bhatt, P., Dusane, M., Saluja, A., Patel, K.: Emotion Based music playing device. Int. Res. J. Eng. Technol. **8**, 395–400 (2021)
4. Bhutkar, G., Raghvani, V., Juikar, S.: User survey about exposure of hate speech among Instagram users in India. Int. J. Comput. Appl. **183**(19), 24–32 (2021)
5. Bhutada, S., Sadhvika, C., Abigna, G., Reddy, S.: Emotion based music recommendation system. J. Emerg. Technol. Innov. Res. **7**, 2170–2175 (2020). ISSN 2349–5162
6. Ciubăncan, C.S., Ivanciu, LN., Șipoș, E.: Prototype music recommendation system – preliminary results in using music as therapy. In: Vlad, S., Roman, N.M. (eds.) 7th International Conference on Advancements of Medicine and Health Care through Technology. MEDITECH 2020. IFMBE Proceedings, vol. 88, pp. 267–273. Springer, Cham (2022). https://doi.org/10.1007/978-3-030-93564-1_30
7. Cook, T., Roy, A., Welker, K.: Music as an emotion regulation strategy: an examination of genres of music and their roles in emotion regulation. Soc. Educ. Music Psychol. Res. **47**, 144–154 (2019)
8. Dureha, A.: An accurate algorithm for generating a music playlist based on facial expressions. Int. J. Comput. Appl. **100**(9), 33–39 (2014)
9. Facial-emotion-recognition 0.3.4: Python Package. https://pypi.org/project/facial-emotion-recognition/. Accessed 2 Dec 2020
10. Gala, P., Shah, R., Shah, V., Shah, Y., Rane, S.: Moody player - a music player based on facial expression recognition. Int. Res. J. Eng. Technol. **5**(4), 3703–3707 (2018)
11. Goodfellow, I.J., et al.: Challenges in representation learning: a report on three machine learning contests. In: Lee, M., Hirose, A., Hou, ZG., Kil, R.M. (eds.) Neural Information Processing. ICONIP 2013. Lecture Notes in Computer Science, vol. 8228, pp. 117–124. Springer, Heidelberg (2013). https://doi.org/10.1007/978-3-642-42051-1_16
12. Hoyt, E.: The best study music: what to listen to while studying. https://www.fastweb.com/student-life/articles/the-best-study-music-what-to-listen-to-while-studying. Accessed 14 Jan 2021
13. Kabini, H., Khan, S., Khan, O., Tadvi, S.: Emotion based music player. Int. J. Eng. Res. Gen. Sci. **3**(1), 2091–2730 (2015)
14. Loviscach, J., Oswald, D.: In the mood: tagging music with affects. In: Peter, C., Beale, R. (eds.) Affect and Emotion in Human-Computer Interaction. LNCS, vol. 4868, pp. 220–228. Springer, Heidelberg (2008). https://doi.org/10.1007/978-3-540-85099-1_19
15. Lyrics Bogie. https://www.lyricsbogie.com/. Accessed 20 Oct 2020
16. Mortensen, M., Gurrin, C., Johansen, D.: Real-world mood-based music recommendation. In: Li, H., Liu, T., Ma, W.-Y., Sakai, T., Wong, K.-F., Zhou, G. (eds.) AIRS 2008. LNCS, vol. 4993, pp. 514–519. Springer, Heidelberg (2008). https://doi.org/10.1007/978-3-540-68636-1_57
17. Mrudula, K., Jain, H., Chandra, A., Bhansa, J.: Music recommendation based on facial expression. Int. J. Latest Technol. Eng. Manag. Appl. Sci. (2020). https://www.ijltemas.in/most-viewed-papers/music-recommendation-based-on-facial-expression/. ISSN No. 2278–2540. Accessed Jan 2020
18. Orngreen, R., Pejtersen, A.M., Clemmensen, T.: Themes in human work interaction design. In: Forbrig, P., Paternò, F., Pejtersen, A.M. (eds.) HCIS 2008. IIFIP, vol. 272, pp. 33–46. Springer, Boston (2008). https://doi.org/10.1007/978-0-387-09678-0_4

19. ParseHub: Web-scraping Software. https://help.parsehub.com/hc/en-us/categories/203678 627-Documentation. Accessed 14 Oct 2020

20. Patil, S., Bhutkar, G., Vaidya, P.: Psychological survey of color perceptions for Indian users. In: Rana, N.K., Shah, A.A., Iqbal, R., Khanzode, V. (eds.) Technology Enabled Ergonomic Design. Design Science and Innovation. Springer, Singapore (2022). https://doi.org/10.1007/978-981-16-6982-8_39

21. Rumiantcev, M., Khriyenko, O.: Emotion based music recommendation system. In: Proceedings of the 26th Conference of Open Innovations Association FRUCT, LNCS (2020). ISSN: 2305–7254

22. Swathi Swaminathan, E., Schellenberg, G.: Current emotion research in music psychology. Emot. Rev. **7**(2), 189–197 (2015). https://doi.org/10.1177/1754073914558282

23. Swaroop S.: Listening to music - a journey of understanding frequencies. https://www.headph onezone.in/blogs/audiophile-guide/mid-range-high-range-frequencies. Accessed 3 Nov 2020

24. Sloan, J.: Science shows what music to listen to at every moment of the day. https://www.mic.com/articles/99508/science-shows-what-music-to-listen-to-at-every-moment-of-the-day. Accessed 3 Nov 2020

25. Zhihong Zeng, M., Pantic, G., Roisman, T.S.H.: A survey of affect recognition methods: audio, visual, and spontaneous expressions. IEEE Trans. Pattern Anal. Mach. Intell. **31**(1), 39–58 (2009). https://doi.org/10.1109/TPAMI.2008.52

26. Zoho Survey: survey creation tool. https://www.zoho.com/survey/templates/customer-satisf action/technical-documentation-satisfaction-survey.html. Accessed 15 Sep 2020

Currency Recognition App for Visually Impaired Users in India

Ganesh Bhutkar$^{(\boxtimes)}$ (iD), Mansi Patil, Deepak Patil, Shivani Mukunde, Rajdeep Shinde, and Anamika Rathod

Centre of Excellence in HCI, Vishwakarma Institute of Technology, Pune, India
ganesh.bhutkar@vit.edu

Abstract. A system for the recognition of currency notes is one kind of intelligent system which is a very important need for visually impaired and blind users in the modern world of today. In this paper, we present a currency recognition app applied to Indian currency notes. Our proposed system is based on interesting features and correlations between images. It uses the Convolutional Neural Network for classification. The method takes Indian rupee paper currencies as a model. The method is quite reasonable in terms of accuracy. The system deals with the images of all the currency note denominations, some of which are tilted to an angle less than 150. The rest of the currency images consist of mixed, noisy, and normal images. It uses the current series (1996–2020) of currency issued by the Reserve Bank of India (RBI) as a model currency under consideration. The system produces an accuracy of recognition of 94.38% and gives an audio output to the users. The proposed technique produces quite satisfactory results in terms of recognition and efficiency. In the future, this app can be improved by adding a dataset of other currency notes of the world.

Keywords: Intelligent system · Indian paper currency · Currency recognition · Currency model · Convolutional neural network · Visually impaired users · Audio output

1 Introduction

Modern automation systems in the real world may require a system for currency recognition. It has various potential applications including banknote counting machines, money exchange machines, electronic banking systems, currency monitoring systems, and/or assistance to visually impaired people. The recognition of currency notes is a vital need for visually impaired or blind people. They are not able to differentiate among currency notes correctly. It is very easy for them to be cheated by other fraudulent people. Therefore, there is a genuine need to design a system to recognize the value of currencies easily regardless of their orientation, wear and tear, illumination, scaling, and other factors that may reduce the quality of the currencies. The World Health Organization (WHO) has estimated the number of visually impaired people all over the world to be about 285 million. Out of which 39 million people are completely blind, and the rest have low vision

© IFIP International Federation for Information Processing 2022
Published by Springer Nature Switzerland AG 2022
G. Bhutkar et al. (Eds.): HWID 2021, IFIP AICT 609, pp. 201–216, 2022.
https://doi.org/10.1007/978-3-031-02904-2_10

[12]. Several studies have been conducted for them and a few techniques for currency recognition have been proposed. Indian currency notes contain several features which enable the visually impaired (color-blind, partially sighted, and entirely blind people) to identify them, viz. intaglio printing, tactile mark, variable currency note size, large numerals, variable color, monochromatic hues and patterns.

Fig. 1. Sample notes of Indian national rupees (INR) 20 and INR 100 with identification marks

There is a feature providing identifiable and differentiable shapes for various denominations i.e., INR 20 in Vertical Rectangle, INR 100 in Triangle, as depicted in Fig. 1, and INR 500 in Circle. But these identification marks may fade after some years. Other techniques have focused on textures, colors, and/or sizes of currency notes. They have some limitations like if the currency note is worn out by excessive usage or if the image is not clear, then it gives an unpredictable output. Most of these techniques are sensitive to illumination conditions and may rely on taking images at fixed environment settings with camera location and image background.

The computational power and camera availability of current mobile phones make them a suitable candidate for currency recognition. In this paper, a mobile system for currency recognition that can recognize the Indian currency notes is proposed. A mobile application is developed to identify currencies that are partially visible, folded, wrinkled, or even worn by usage. The proposed system can recognize the current Indian currency notes of all types and that includes currency notes with INR values of 5, 10, 20, 50, 100, 200, 500, and 2000. This system employs voice communication to inform users about the identified value of the currency through the mobile speaker. This research paper has mainly described the design and development process of a currency recognition app for visually impaired users in India.

This currency recognition application for visually impaired users has been developed based on the generalized Human Work Interaction Design (HWID) framework, proposed by Orngreen et al. [13], as seen in Fig. 2. Human work aspects such as cognitive abilities and limitations of visually-impaired users, along with orientation, wear and tear, and scaling of currency notes are considered in the design of currency recognition application. A couple of visually-impaired users were involved, and their user experience has been considered in interaction design of this system. The environmental as per general HWID frame-work such as environmental illumination has been a vital factor in recognition of Indian currency notes. The contextual factors such as note orientation, texture, size wear and tear are also required to be considered in HWID context. Thus, the effect of HWID perspective [13, 14] can be observed prominently in system design of proposed currency recognition app.

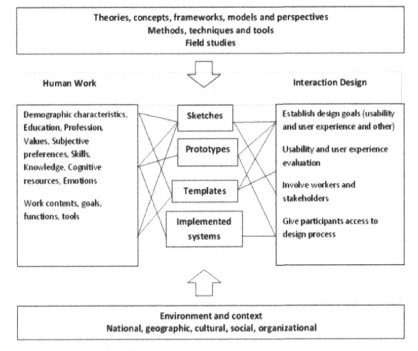

Fig. 2. Generalized HWID framework [13]

Visually impaired users have challenging life in developing countries like India. They have lesser education as well as employment opportunities. Only about 29% of visually impaired people go to school and are part of the education system. The employment rate among them is about 30% and they are getting jobs in customer care, hospitality and teaching fields [15]. These visually impaired users, including unemployed among them, have challenging socio-economic life and may face financial difficulties. Most of these users have to deal with money – the currency notes during their everyday life. The feature providing identifiable and differentiable shapes for various currency notes may not be useful as these shapes fade away after initial years of usage. The visually impaired users fail to differentiate among currency notes, even with tactile marks, variable note sizes, large numerals or variable colors, and it makes them easy targets for cheating by other dishonest people. Most of them use economical Android mobile phones. Therefore, there is a dire need for designing a mobile application, which will recognize the value of currency notes for these visually impaired users.

The real challenge for this currency recognition app is dealing with older currency notes, which are worn out or faded due to excessive usage. The illumination conditions and low-resolution cameras may lead to unclear images, making the currency detection even more challenging. The audio output, conveying note value to the visually impaired users, also face challenge of noisy surroundings. The proposed currency recognition app is an innovative and successful attempt to deal with these challenges and help visually impaired users to detect all currency notes in India.

2   Related Work

A related work of related research papers has been conducted to study image processing and image acquisition techniques. The research papers focusing on the recognition of Indian currency notes were studied. There are various techniques for currency recognition that involve currency texture, pattern, and/or color.

In the first paper, the authors - Vishnu et al. have proposed an interesting recognition method [11]. The currency images are normalized by using histogram equalization. They extracted five **features (Shape, Center, RBI Seal, Micro Letter, and Latent Image)** from images of currency notes by placing a rectangular box of specific dimensions, which discovers the Region of Interest (ROI). The extracted ROI can be used with **Pattern Recognition** and **Neural Networks Matching** techniques. First, they acquired the image using a simple flat scanner with fixed dpi, and with a particular size. A few filters were applied to extract the denomination values of currency notes. They used different pixel levels in different denomination notes. The Pattern Recognition and Neural Networks matcher techniques were used to match or find currency value/denomination of paper currency.

In another paper, the authors have chosen **Faster RCNN (Region-Based Convolutional Neural Network)** to train models and recognize Indian currency very well [1]. Faster RCNN has improved the running time of the network. They used Regions Proposal Network (RPN), which shared convolutional features of images with the network, and it simultaneously predicted the object and bounds with the score at each position. RCNN was trained to generate high-quality region proposals which were used by RCNN for faster detection.

In the next paper, six characteristic features were extracted [6]. The approach used includes several components such as **image processing, edge detection, image segmentation, features extraction, and comparing images**. The features extraction was performed on the image of the currency and it was compared with the features of the genuine currency. The Sobel operator with gradient magnitude was used for feature extraction. Paper currency recognition with good accuracy and high processing speed was of great importance for the banking system [4]. This study shows that by using the **Local Binary Pattern (LBP) algorithm,** 100% accuracy can be achieved in the case of good quality images and low computational cost is needed to meet the high-speed requirement in practical applications. The algorithm is highly used for texture analysis and feature extraction.

3 Peer App Review

A systematic review has been conducted for currently available Android apps related to Indian currency recognition. The selected apps include Mobile Aided Note Identifier (MANI) [7], IndicAI Vision [5], Roshni [8], Cash Reader [2], and Third Eye [10]. The app review is focused on five identified Android apps and aimed to provide interesting insights into functionalities and other design aspects. To examine such aspects of selected Android apps, an expert-based peer app review has been conducted by authors.

Initially, a review of five selected apps has been conducted based on app features and functionalities. These features/functionalities include App accuracy, Screen Reader, Voice- based User Interface (UI), Text-to-Speech, Voice-based Instructions, Easy Navigation, Fake Note Recognition, Active Feedback, and Multi-lingual Support. App Accuracy is calculated based on their accurate recognition of denomination of currencies for a certain number of currency scans for different denominations. Their comparative details are depicted in Table1.

The formula used for calculating accuracy (%) is given as –

$$\text{Accuracy} = \frac{\text{Number of True Positives} \times 100}{\text{Total Number of Currency Scans}}$$

Here, true positive denotes correct recognition of each denomination. The total number of currency notes scans includes 20 scans for each denomination.

Table 1. Comparison of selected currency recognition apps based on features and functionalities

Features and functionalities	Indian currency recognition apps				
	MANI	Roshni	Indic AI vision	Third eye	Cash reader
Accuracy (%)	80%	60%	55%	50%	50%
Screen reader support	Yes	Yes	Yes	No	No
Voice-based UI	Yes	Yes	Yes	No	No
Text to speech conversion	Yes	Yes	Yes	Yes	Yes
Voice-based instructions	Yes	Yes	No	No	No
Ease of navigation	Yes	Yes	No	No	No
Fake note recognition	Yes	No	No	No	No
Active feedback	Yes	Yes	No	No	No
Multi-lingual support	Yes	Yes	Yes	No	No

The following observations are made after carefully reviewing the selected apps as seen in Table 1, based on the app features and functionalities:

a. Only one App provides **Fake Note Recognition** functionality.
b. Few of the Apps (2/5) provide **Easy navigation** using Voice-based UI.
c. Most of the Apps (3/5) provide **Multilingual support.**
d. Few of the Apps (2/5) provide **Voice instructions** for first-timers or naive users.
e. In the current scenario, **MANI is** the most suitable app for visually-impaired users to recognize Indian currency with features like Active Feedback and Easy Navigation along with better accuracy.

4   Study of Indian Currency Notes

The government of India has introduced a currency note of INR 2000 in 2018. Its security features are depicted in Fig. 3. These features include watermark, micro- lettering, optical variable link, security thread, and latent image. Following are some common features which can be useful to blind users or visually impaired users in recognition of the currency notes.

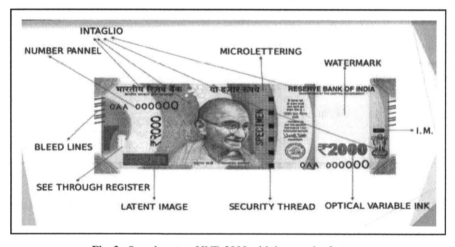

Fig. 3. Sample note of INR 2000 with its security features

Braille Marking or Bleed Lines: The Reserve bank of India launched braille-like markings on currency notes of INR 100, INR 500, and INR 2000. This is done to identify the currency value by visually impaired people. Depending on the number of lines printed on the note, the value of the note can be identified. The INR 100 notes have **four parallel angular lines** printed along the border, just beside the Mahatma Gandhi watermark. The INR 200 notes have **four angular bleed lines with two circles in between the lines**, whereas the INR 500 notes have **five parallel lines.** The INR 2000 notes have **seven parallel lines** as seen on the upper left side in Fig. 3.

Intaglio Printing: The Ashoka Pillar Emblem on the left, portrait of Mahatma Gandhi, the Reserve Bank seal, guarantee-promise clause, Reserve Bank of India (RBI), Governor's signature is printed in intaglio printing, i.e., in raised print which can be felt by soft touch, especially for blind users.

Identification Mark: The identification mark is on the left-hand side of each note on the front side. These marks have raised intaglio print and have different shapes for different denominations like a vertical rectangle for INR 20, square for INR 50, triangle for INR 100 and circle for INR 500. **A horizontal rectangle as an identification mark can be seen for a currency note of INR 2000, on the central right side in** Fig. 3.

5   Research Methodology

The research methodology is used for studying, evaluating, and analyzing the designs and design aspects of similar types of apps as well as related research work. Initially, related work and peer apps reviews have been conducted. The inferences gathered from related work and peer app review are further used in dataset preparation, model training and design of the proposed system.

5.1   Dataset Preparation

A dataset containing images of new Indian currency notes with INR values of 50, 100,200, 500, 2000 was not readily available. So, the dataset has been prepared by clicking the images of these notes and adding them into the Dataset. This dataset contains various Indian currency notes with INR of values 10, 20, 50, 100, 200,500, and 2000 with different backgrounds. This dataset had about 4000 images of notes. These images have variations in illumination, background, and rotation as seen in Fig. 4.

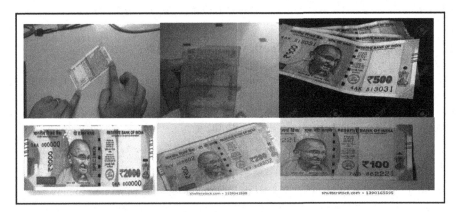

Fig. 4. Sample images of Indian currency notes

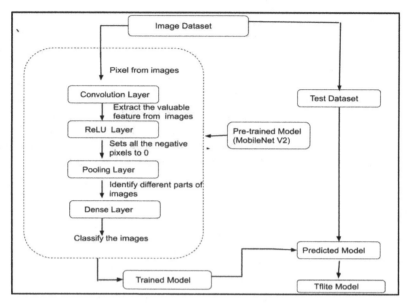

Fig. 5. Process of training proposed model

5.2 Currency Recognition Model Based on Machine Learning

A dataset containing images of new Indian currency notes with INR values of 50, 100,200, 500, 2000 was not readily available. So, the dataset has been prepared by clicking the images of these notes and adding them into the dataset. This dataset contains various Indian currency notes with INR of values 10, 20, 50, 100, 200,500, and 2000 with different backgrounds. This dataset had about 4000 images of notes. These images have variations in illumination, background, and rotation as seen in Fig. 4. The training process of proposed currency recognition model based on machine learning approach is represented in Fig. 5, along with related CNN layers and dataset.

6 Design of Proposed Currency Recognition System

According to Peer App Review, the Voice-Based UIs have been vital requirements for visually impaired users. Such users can't select a camera and take a picture of a currency note under consideration. Therefore, this Android app has been designed in such a way that the camera will automatically open with the app.

6.1 Model Training

Convolution Neural Network [3] is the most popular deep learning neural network that is used to detect and classify objects in images. The CNN has several layers as shown in Fig. 6, which carry out feature extraction by performing different calculations and manipulations. There are multiple hidden layers like the Convolution layer, ReLU layer, and Pooling layer that perform feature extraction from an image. Finally, the output of all hidden layers is passed as input to the output layer which identifies the object in the image.

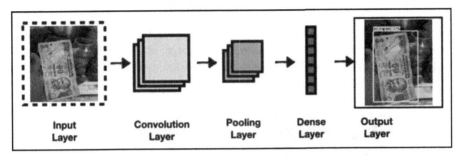

Fig. 6. Layers of convolution neural network (CNN)

The convolutional layer has several filters that perform the convolution operation. This layer considers every image as a matrix of pixel values. The dot product of this matrix and filter is computed to get the convolved feature matrix. Extracted features are moved to the ReLU layer which performs an element-wise operation and sets all the negative pixels to 0. It introduces non-linearity to the network, and a rectified feature map is generated. Pooling reduces the dimensionality of the feature map. Various filters are used by this layer to identify different parts of images like edges, corners, color in the image. The next flattening layer converts all resultant 2-D arrays from pooled features into single long continuous linear vectors which are fed as input to the fully connected layer to detect the image as shown in Fig. 7.

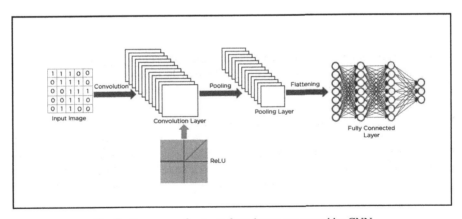

Fig. 7. Sequence of outputs from layers processed by CNN

6.2 Feature Extraction

To extract the features of the image, CNN uses a kernel over each image and adjusts the kernel as per the propagation in the network. A kernel is then convolved over the entire image to produce feature maps. This feature mapping of the input signifies the locations where a feature is present as shown in Fig. 8 for INR 100. As the layers become deeper and deeper, the network acquires the knowledge of larger and larger feature extraction. The initial layers take care of the smaller details of the image and deeper layers can identify the bigger picture.

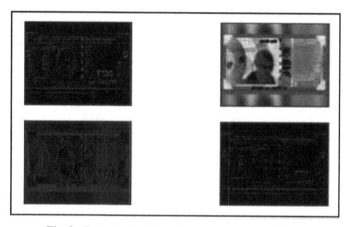

Fig. 8. Feature extraction of currency note of INR 100

6.3 Transfer Learning

The transfer learning technique was used to increase the accuracy of the model. Mobile Net V2 was used which could be directly used to train the dataset as it is already learned on a large dataset. The model was retrained to get better accuracy and to reduce the computational cost of the model. This learning approach is called Transfer Learning. MobileNetV2 is a convolutional neural network architecture that seeks to perform well on mobile devices. It is based on an inverted residual structure where the residual connections are between the bottleneck layers. The intermediate expansion layer uses lightweight depth-wise convolutions to filter features as a source of non-linearity. As a whole, the architecture of MobileNetV2 contains the initial fully convolution layer with 32 filters, followed by 19 residual bottleneck layers.

6.4 Model Deployment with TensorFlow Lite

TensorFlow Lite [9] is an open-source, product-ready, cross-platform Deep Learning framework that converts a pre-trained model in TensorFlow to a special format that can be optimized for speed or storage.

After the model was trained, it was converted to the TensorFlow Lite version. TensorFlow Lite model is a special format model that is efficient in terms of accuracy and is a light-weight version that will occupy less space. These features make TensorFlow Lite models the right fit to work on Mobile and Embedded Devices. TensorFlow Lite Converter converts a TensorFlow model to TensorFlow Lite flat buffer file (.tflite).

6.5 Model Testing

Once the model was trained, test images were fed to classify them into the correct classes. The results of the model are shown in Table 2. From the table, we can see that as the number of epochs increases, the accuracy and validation accuracy increase, and loss and validation loss decreases.

Table 2. Accuracy, loss, validation accuracy, and validation loss at each epoch

No of epochs	Accuracy	Loss	Val accuracy	Val loss
1	23.69	19.96	51.59	14.37
2	51.06	14.53	52.17	13.49
3	62.59	11.25	60.58	12.35
4	72.24	8.70	66.96	11.14
5	78.15	6.81	80.00	6.44
6	85.49	4.81	78.55	9.37
7	86.85	4.13	80.29	7.49
8	92.36	2.56	81.45	6.94
9	91.45	2.74	83.19	6.36
10	94.38	2.22	85.90	5.40

7 Mobile App

A mobile app was built using android studio. The user can directly open an application by using Google Assistant or users can use Talkback which is a built-in screen reader for visually impaired users. As shown in Fig. 9. the app consists of an instruction button at the top of the screen which on clicking will speak out the instruction. It also consists of the bottom sheet layout that shows the denomination of the note being predicted. When the app is opened, it will directly use the back camera of the phone to detect the note. Once the note is detected, it will tell the denomination of the note and show it on the bottom sheet layout as shown in Fig. 10.

An app can give an unpredicted output in case there is not enough light while detecting the currency note or if there is a continuous movement of the phone or the currency note that is to be detected.

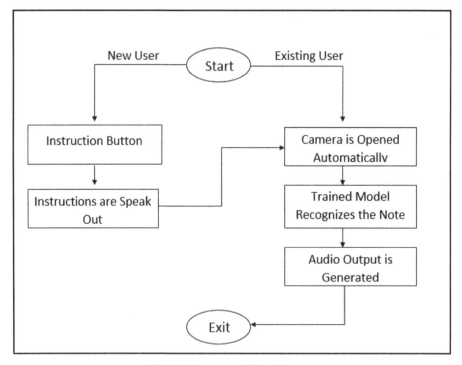

Fig. 9. System workflow diagram

Fig. 10. Layout of currency recognition app

7.1 Additional Features

Following are additional features incorporated in this mobile app:

Optical Character Reader (OCR): It is the electronic or mechanical conversion of images of typed, handwritten or printed text into machine-encoded text, whether from a scanned document or a photograph. It is used to detect text and numbers written on currency notes as shown in Fig. 11. It also shows the captured details of currency in light green color as seen in Fig. 11. In Settings Menu, there is an option of selecting OCR language from multiple languages as shown in Fig. 12.

Audio Help: It reads out related information or instructions for the user, in an audio format. As shown in Fig. 12, this information contains the use of various features of app like OCR and Currency Recognition.

Settings: It has different options such as flashlight, auto focus and multicolumn text as shown in Fig. 12. These options are discussed ahead.

Flashlight: If the flashlight option is enabled, the flash of the mobile will be used at the time of capturing currency. It helps to detect the currency notes under low or poor lighting conditions and provide result with better accuracy.

Auto Focus: This option helps to focus on the currency note for its accurate detection even though if currency is not stable while app is capturing currency for recognition. As

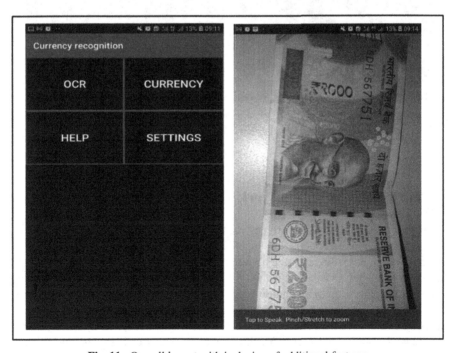

Fig. 11. Overall layout with inclusion of additional features

shown in Fig. 12. the Auto Focus option is automatically enabled for better accuracy by default.

Zoom: While using the OCR feature, the zoom feature helps to read the textual words more accurately.

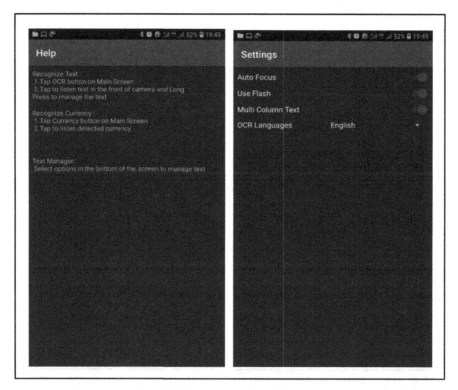

Fig. 12. Help screen and settings menu

8 Conclusion and Future Work

In this paper, a simple Indian currency recognition system has been proposed for the blind. Visually impaired people are unable to recognize the currency notes due to the similarity of paper texture and size between different categories. This Indian Currency Recognition app helps visually impaired people to recognize and detect Indian currency notes. The current currency recognition apps face the gap of providing audio instructions to the user and of accuracy while detecting the notes. The proposed system starts with capturing still images from the front camera. For currency recognition, this application uses TensorFlow lite and uses a Machine learning classification technique to detect currency based on images or paper using a mobile camera. This app has been designed using android studio. It also has an instruction button on the top that reads out the instructions for the user when clicked.

The Mobile Net V2 model was used to train our image dataset similar to this paper [1]. This author used Faster RCNN as a pre-trained model. As we built an android app, Mobile Net V2 is a more suitable model as compared to Faster RCNN as Mobile Net V2 reduces the complexity cost and model size which is suitable for devices with low computational power like mobile. TensorFlow model is converted into TensorFlow lite model to deploy it on the android app.

However, the dataset used for this app contains pictures of only Indian currency notes. So, with this system, the user cannot detect the denomination of other currencies. This can be done by including the dataset of other currency notes and training them, respectively. Thus, we expect our system to easily adapt to other currencies of the world while keeping at a similar level of accuracy and speed. This app also needs modification in terms of the user interface to be able to prompt the user in case the note has not been placed properly under the camera or is not detected.

In future, the proposed app will be added with several functionalities with initial focus on improving accuracy and other currencies recognition. App will also get the modification of prompting the user if currency is held too much close or out of camera reach to capture it properly in subsequent versions. There is also a plan of providing user with the guide through various functionalities of app using audio input and output so that it will be convenient for a blind user to go through all available functions. The recognition of fake currency is also one of the functionalities that will be incorporated in app.

References

1. Bhavsar, K., Jani, K., Vanzara, R.: Indian currency recognition from live video using deep learning. In: Chaubey, N., Parikh, S., Amin, K. (eds.) Computing Science, Communication and Security, COMS2 2020, Communications in Computer and Information Science, vol. 1235, pp. 70–81. Springer, Singapore (2020). https://doi.org/10.1007/978-981-15-6648-6_6
2. Cash Reader. https://play.google.com/store/apps/details?id=com.martindoudera.cashreader. Accessed 25 Jun 2021
3. Convolution Neural Network. https://www.simplilearn.com/tutorials/deep-learning-tutorial/convolutional-neural-network. Accessed 25 Jun 2021
4. Hassanpour, H., Farahabadi, P.: Using hidden Markov models for paper currency recognition. Expert Syst. Appl. **36**(6), 10105–10111 (2009)
5. IndicAI Vision. https://play.google.com/store/apps/details?id=com.hit.indicvision. Accessed 25 Jun 2021
6. Tanaka, M., Takeda, F., Ohkouchi, F., Michiyuk, Y.: Recognition of paper currencies by hybrid neural network. IEEE Trans. Neural Netw. **3**, 1748–1753 (1998). 0-7803-4859-1/98
7. MANI. https://play.google.com/store/apps/details?id=com.rbi.mani. Accessed 26 Jun 2021
8. Roshni. https://play.google.com/store/apps/details?id=com.%20Roshni.ipsa.myapplication&hl=en. Accessed 25 Jun 2021
9. TensorFlow. https://www.tensorflow.org/lite/guide/get_started#2_convert_the_model. Accessed 25 Jun 2021
10. Third Eye. https://play.google.com/store/apps/details?id=org.tensorflow.lite.examples.thirde. Accessed 25 Jun 2021

11. Vishnu, R., Omman, B.: Principal component analysis on Indian currency recognition. In: International Conference on Computer and Communication Technology (ICCCT), pp. 291–296 (2014)
12. WHO.   https://www.who.int/blindness/publications/globaldata/en/#:~:text=Globally%20the%20number%20of%20people,blindness%20is%20cataract%20(51%25).   Accessed 25 Jun 2021
13. Orngreen, R., Pejtersen, A.M., Clemmensen, T.: Themes in human work interaction design. In: Forbrig, P., Paternò, F., Pejtersen, A.M. (eds.) HCIS 2008. IIFIP, vol. 272, pp. 33–46. Springer, Boston, MA (2008). https://doi.org/10.1007/978-0-387-09678-0_4
14. Ham D., Wong W., Amaldi P.: Comparison of three methods for analyzing human work - in terms of design approaches. In: Workshop HWID: Describing Users in Context - Perspectives on Human Work Interaction Design, INTERACT, Madeira, Portugal (2005)
15. Agarwal, P.: How can Visually Impaired Persons Join the Workforce, Hindustan Times, 11 January 2022. https://www.hindustantimes.com/education/how-can-visually-impaired-persons-join-the-workforce/story-wcFDSob1CzlcVjy2yUOOuL.html

Correction to: Human Work Interaction Design

Artificial Intelligence and Designing for a Positive Work Experience in a Low Desire Society

Ganesh Bhutkar⊙, Barbara R. Barricelli⊙, Qin Xiangang⊙,
Torkil Clemmensen⊙, Frederica Gonçalves⊙,
José Abdelnour-Nocera⊙, Arminda Lopes⊙, Fei Lyu⊙,
Ronggang Zhou, and Wenjun Hou

Correction to:
G. Bhutkar et al. (Eds.): *Human Work Interaction Design,*
IFIP AICT 609, https://doi.org/10.1007/978-3-031-02904-2

Due to an oversight, the originally published front matter had the erroneous affiliation for a volume editor. This has been corrected in the revised version.

The updated version of the book can be found at
https://doi.org/10.1007/978-3-031-02904-2

Author Index

Printed in the United States
by Baker & Taylor Publisher Services